one

Laurent Garnier

David Brun-Lambert

1

i'll house you

Laurent Garnier
David Brun-Lambert

Electrochoc

First published in French by Flammarion in 2003, 2013

This edition first published in the United Kingdom in 2015 by Rocket 88, an imprint of Essential Works Limited, 29 Clerkenwell Green, London EC1R 0DU

All playlists are available on www.laurentgarnier.com

Translated from the French by Fish & Chips
www.zefishandchips.com
Cover and text design: Michael Gray
Editors: Julia Halford, Fiona Screen
Index: Diana LeCore

ISBN: 9781906615918

First edition
Printed in Malta by Gutenberg Press

laurentgarnierbook.com
rocket88books.com

Contents

side

So where should I start? What is my first memory? If I close my eyes, my ears start to pound. There was one night in particular, one that stands out from all the rest – one night, and, above all, one record that changed everything. And from the very next day it was as if a shockwave was sweeping across all Manchester.

First, the radios and clubs began to feel the tremors, and then the whole musical landscape started to break up at an unbelievable speed. It seeped into record shops, pubs and secret gatherings, late into the night when the rest of the city was fast asleep. The vibe touched everyone that came into contact with it.

That is how our story begins.

It was a typically rainy night in spring 1987. I found myself in a run-down area, walking along Whitworth Street, when I came across a red-brick building eroded by years of torrential rain and industrial smoke: the Haçienda. Bouncers stood on either side of the narrow entrance. Shadows lingered around the parked cars; dealers in waiting alongside groups of students out for a good time.

Once inside, I elbowed my way to the bar to order a drink. I paid my two pounds and turned to look at the crowd saturated in light. There were students, a few rough faces, but no signs of any trouble.

Mike Pickering, one of the pioneering DJs from Manchester, was playing that night. He mixed a selection of funk, Latino, hip-hop and some of the first electro tracks of that time. Then he put on a record that literally seemed to come out of nowhere, it was impossible to identify, it changed the whole atmosphere of the club: Farley Jackmaster Funk's Love Can't Turn Around. I felt like I had been punched in the gut. It sounded like the volume had doubled, the vocals were syncopated, the rhythm was heavy and the kick drum seemed to dominate everything. I watched how the people dancing reacted instinctively. It took them a few seconds to find their feet and then they just let go. The Haçienda's sound system pumped out huge bass sounds; I just couldn't believe it. What was this deep, hard sound? I finally got onto the dance floor and my cries joined those of the crowd. My arms were up in the air, my hair was standing on end, I had goose bumps, and my legs were all over the place – and the Haçienda's speakers kept on booming: LOVE CAN'T TURN AROUND.

All around me, the crowd was being whipped up into a frenzy. In spite of the air blasting out of the speakers, I reached out my hand and tried to touch them. My body kept on moving to the beat and then suddenly… that was it… it was over… the record ended. Pickering waited a few seconds to see the impact the record had had on the crowd. An icy silence

filled the Haçienda, still bathed in warm orange light. I was rooted to the spot in shock. I kept saying over and over, 'What was that? It was unbelievable!' Then I started shouting, 'I need that record!' However, Mike Pickering decided that we would not be hearing Love Can't Turn Around again that night.

The Haçienda must have scored an easy 6.5 on the Richter scale that night. And, while I staggered to the exit, my body crying out for the cool rain, a melody was going round and round inside my head. Something new had just come blazing into my life: house music.

So let's go back to what was I doing in England in the first place. I was never very good at school. It just wasn't my thing. However, in the Garnier family, if you weren't academic you were sent to catering school. Once I had finished my training, I was taken on as a footman at the French Embassy in London. The job had the advantage of being a few hundred miles away from my family in Bougival, which meant total freedom and a certain number of perks. I was 18 years old and had access to the heart of London's nightlife. I turned up at parties laden with bottles of Dom Pérignon that I'd 'borrowed' from the embassy's wine cellar. News like that travels fast. Within just a few weeks, my circle of friends had grown considerably and our group of ex-pats was soon being invited to all the private parties in London.

New friendships were made. I was hanging out with a group of people for whom music was of the utmost importance. Reputations were built around music, and if you knew about music you were expected to record mix tapes and hand them out. It took me ages to make these tapes, as I didn't have the right set-up. With two very basic record players and no pitch control, it could take me up to six hours to make one mix tape. I would record one track after the other, increasing in intensity, and if the difference in speed between two records became too obvious, I would slow one of them down or speed one of them up with my finger.

I had always been very passionate about music but, up until then, hadn't found the right environment. London's nightlife provided just that environment. My years at the embassy were marked by my discovery of nocturnal London, an underground world of music, parties, secrets and dirty dealings. Over the next two years, I went to dozens of fashionable and not-so-fashionable clubs and plenty of house parties that invariably ended in the walls, furniture and carpets being trashed. And I used to hang around some fairly dodgy sound systems set up in empty warehouses.

I began to establish my own night-time circuit. A nocturnal routine that each night led me to a series of venues that soon became home from home. In contrast, my days were spent in the luxury of the embassy where I took my job as footman very seriously. In the elegant surroundings of silk armchairs, Victorian paintings, gold-leaf ceilings and magnificent windows hung with heavy velvet curtains, I served the ambassador from the moment he awoke until he went to bed. I was also responsible for the service during embassy cocktail parties and receptions, where on several occasions I served Her Majesty the Queen, President Mitterrand and Princess Di.

Once the ambassador had gone to bed, I would call my friends, who were scattered right across London. We would arrange a place to meet, and after a couple of drinks would decide whether to go to Twist & Shout (60s rare groove) at the Camden Palace; Heaven, a club for thrill seekers; the Hippodrome, a massive club, amazing when Divine was performing there; Taboo, with parties organised by the very eccentric Leigh Bowery – where it was the utmost in cool to wear your shirt as a pair of trousers – or to Playground. Otherwise, there were always a number of last-minute parties held in dilapidated warehouses in the suburbs to choose from, where a heady cocktail of music, drugs and bumper cars was the norm.

Yet this continuous stream of parties only made sense because at the end of the week loomed Friday night, the most important night of the week. Every Friday night we bought a one-way ticket to the Mecca of English clubs: Philip Salon's Mud Club. During the week I consoled myself with the knowledge that Friday wasn't far off, and that it would bring its rewards. It was out of the question to even consider missing one Friday night at the Mud Club. So, even when I had to go back to France for family reasons, I would turn up at Bougival on Saturday morning completely wrecked from the night before. During my two years in London, nothing once stopped me from honouring my weekly rendezvous on the Tottenham Court Road.

It wasn't enough just to want to go to dance at the Mud Club; you had to earn your way inside. To get past the door you had to look eccentric, and that went for everyone. There were no exceptions. This approach had already made the reputations of many other legendary clubs. Those living in Paris in Fabrice Emaer's time at the Palace will remember the 'eccentric dress only' code on the door. At the Mud Club, like at the Palace, extravagance was the word. It was as much a part of the night as the decor, the music or the chosen theme. The reward was the sheer privilege of being dazzled by the magic of the club and the quality of the music.

Every Friday night my group of friends, a bunch of students, French expats and born-and-bred Londoners, met up in a flat at South Kensington. We sat around drinking until the alcohol began to take effect and then carefully chose our outfits for the night. Ridiculous skirts, three ruffled shirts worn one on top of the other, earrings for the guys and heavily gelled mohicans for the girls – anything was acceptable as long as it was decadent but not vulgar (or then again!) and eccentric without just being provocative.

Once through the doors of the Mud Club we were deep inside an old theatre. Where the orchestra had once played, there now stood a dance floor surrounded by four mirrored columns from which hung the huge sound system. A wide staircase led up to two balconies overlooking the people dancing below. Here you could sit and have a drink or carry on dancing. It was the ideal place to watch the Mud Club crowd come together. London types would dance happily alongside psychobillies (huge quiffs, checked shirts, dirty jeans; they wore the whole look as dictated by the band King Kurt). Pseudo punks (punk was long dead but wearing a black jacket with a 'No Future' badge and spiky hair was still happening) took the piss out of the trendy London set made up of photographers, models, starlets, hangers-on and the latest contemporary art hopefuls.

Our main reason for going down to the Mud was for the music, but it was also for the trashy extravagance and flippant attitudes, the drugs and wild abandonment, that gave this unique club such a powerful magnetism.

It was during these two years at the Mud Club that I followed a DJ with absolute loyalty for the first time ever. At the Mud, the DJ was one of the keys to the success of the night. He was expected to take risks but at the same time be subtle and have a solid knowledge of music. You couldn't just play any old music here, it wasn't simply entertainment. No way. The Mud had a certain vision of music and kept high standards, and the DJ had complete freedom to play what he wanted.

At that time, Mark Moore was an important figure on the London nightclub scene. Within a few months, his group S-Xpress shot to the top of the UK charts with their first single, Theme From S-Xpress, resulting in his name being known throughout Europe. His partner behind the decks was Jay Strongman. Together they were the heart and soul of Friday nights at the Mud. Their DJ sets covered go-go fresh from Washington DC as well as funk, soul and rockabilly. Go-go was the in thing at the time and, unlike hip-hop, which revolved around a DJ and a rapper, go-go was based on heavy percussive funk with a brass band feel. The message was positive, if slightly naïve, 'Put your hands up in the air, do it like you just don't care.'

It was at the Mud that I took speed for the very first time and danced for six hours non-stop, my body rushing with waves of euphoria.

I had never previously thought so much about the importance of the quality of the DJ's choice of music. I had never really understood the importance of his role, that he was not just a human jukebox but also a true communicator, at one with the people on the dance floor and a mentor leading the way. Every Friday I learnt a bit more, feeding on the musical risks being taken and the sheer emotion of every record played. I realised that the DJ was a storyteller, but that instead of words and sentences, he drew meaning from the long stream of intertwined rhythms and melodies. That was where I understood the importance of the DJ drawing in his public and establishing a relationship of trust.

I had always dreamed of working in a nightclub since I was a child. The hundreds of records that I had searched for, bought, listened to and catalogued over the years, piling up in my bedroom at home and then at the embassy, the hundreds of tapes that I had compiled and given away, were all a part of this goal. But it was at the Mud Club that my dreams really took shape. That was where I realised that I wanted to play for a crowd. To see dancing bodies bathed in light. To feel that change in the atmosphere slowly building up. To experience the incredible explosion of joy that only music can create.

In 1986, I resigned from my job at the French Embassy. I had spent two blissfully happy years there. The ambassador at the time was a fantastic man. I had benefited enormously from the freedom that I had. However, he was posted elsewhere and was replaced by a far duller and more austere man. I was with a girl at the time, and we decided to leave London and move up to Manchester together where there was a job waiting for me at her sister's restaurant. We loaded all our cheap old furniture, clothes and my record collection into a hired van and drove up the motorway, heading north.

Four hours later, we reached a sign saying: Welcome to Manchester. My first impressions of the city were not good, with its dirty walls, grey streets, even greyer sky and overbearing, hideous buildings. Manchester's industrial past had left its mark on the city. Everywhere I looked there was redbrick and vast wastelands, which seemed to stretch for miles. Everything looked cold, wet and grey. It all looked pretty dismal to me. But as soon as I met the people, my first impressions vanished. These people were far warmer and more caring than their proclaimed rivals, and had a natural talent for partying and making people feel at home.

Once I had settled my record collection into my new house (an ordinary terraced house), I went out to get to grips with Manchester's nightlife.

I soon realised that people in Manchester were far more into their bands than in London. Students wore t-shirts emblazoned with the names of local bands such as the Smiths, New Order and A Certain Ratio, all representatives of the Manchester scene. There was no star system here. Everyone was happy to go about their business anonymously, hanging out in the same places, taking the same drugs, getting drunk in the same pubs and having daft fights about football, then making it up over a drink before going out clubbing together. The Haçienda was at the heart of these nights out. It was an imposing brick building with no sign on the door. There was nothing special about it from the outside. It was stuck in the middle of nowhere.

Tony Wilson, a public and media personality in the UK who presented the local evening news on Granada TV and founded Factory (the record label that housed Joy Division, New Order and the Happy Mondays), opened the Haçienda on the May 21, 1982, alongside Rob Greeton, New Order's manager and Bernard Manning, a local comedian.

The people at Factory got the idea to open a club in Manchester after New Order, a band formed by the remaining members of Joy Division, had returned from New York where they had recorded their single, Confusion. They had experienced the big clubs over there and had come back inspired to create a huge club dedicated to dance-music culture in Manchester, the equivalent of New York's Sound Factory.

Tony Wilson and his partners found an old yacht exhibition building on the edge Manchester's city centre, in a no-go area, which the local population carefully avoided. At that time, Whitworth Street was one long stretch of dilapidated warehouses. Number 51 was a gigantic warehouse painted grey, a bit like a car park, with real potential to become a New York-style club in the UK.

Once they'd got their hands on the building, the owners commissioned designer Ben Kelly to get to work on designing the layout of the club. His very industrial designs for this project were the total opposite of everything else that could be seen in clubs in Europe at the time. Huge black-and-yellow striped metal posts delineated the venue space that could hold 1,500 people. A vast stage stretched the whole way down the right-hand side. The bar was at the back. Striped bollards were used to cordon off the dance floor overhung by a massive sound system. It was the first time I had seen such a well-designed balance between the lighting – hugely important for any good party – and the sound. A food bar stood near the entrance and, a little further, a narrow staircase led down to the Gay Traitor Bar, a small room that could hold about 40 people.

Inspired by the Situationist International, the owners of the Haçienda wanted their venue to function upon the same principles as a cooperative. It was an extension of the record label, Factory. The wall plaque next to the entrance read like a record label reference number: FAC 51 The Haçienda. Mike Pickering was hired as resident DJ. His job was also to oversee the music, including booking the bands and DJs, as well as the lighting people and the video artists. There was a 'No Dress Code' policy at the door and microphones were banned from the DJ booth.

However, since opening in 1982 the Haçienda had been losing money, despite Factory's efforts to ensure strategic promotional tactics. In one year there had been only three gigs that were sold out: two concerts by New Order (June 1982 and January 1983) and a concert by the Smiths (November 1983). By 1985, the Haçienda decided to diversify its events programme, giving more slots to alternative nights: Goth Night, No Funk Night, and Tuesday's Punk Night. Then, as the punk movement slowly began to fade, the Haçienda tried to develop new concepts to keep people interested. Thursday nights became a student night – the drinks were sold cheaply, and a mainly white crowd went wild to Dave Haslam's eclectic mix of dance music and rock. On Fridays, Mike Pickering started Nude Night (along with Martin Prendergast) playing black music that attracted people mostly from the Anglo-Jamaican community. They would come down from Moss Side and Hulme to listen to a wide range of music, including Eric B. and Rakim's Paid In Full, Dhar Braxton's Jump Back, salsa from El Gran Combo and Madonna's Into The Groove. There was no equivalent club to the Haçienda, whether in Manchester or in the north of England, and sooner or later every night bird ended up there. They came for the name of the night and not to listen to a specific DJ, whether it was Mike Pickering or Dave Haslam.

In accordance with Manchester City Council regulations, the Haçienda closed its doors every night at 2am. People in the know would carry on the party in somebody's flat, or at an illegal warehouse party on the outskirts of the city. The not-so-lucky ones would return quietly home to bed, while the pubs all around had closed for the night.

By the beginning of 1987, the Manchester music scene was experiencing a steady upsurge in house music. The movement started in Chicago and was a simple progression from disco and funk, but with a harder, more structured rhythm. While disco was structured upon a longer version of a song built around verse/chorus/verse/chorus/long break/verse/chorus, house music was essentially instrumental, stripped of the frills found in disco. There were no more soaring violins and backing singers, the only thing left was the driving rhythm.

From 1985, the earliest house music producers, Marshall Jefferson, Farley 'Jackmaster' Funk and Larry Heard, used vocal gimmicks and lyrics taken from popular disco themes like love, dance and sex. Soon the vocals began to lose their meaning and gave way to broken-up, syncopated voice samples. One of the distinctive elements of Chicago house is the way the voice becomes an instrument, using repetition and editing techniques. An even tougher, X-rated sub-genre began to emerge from the city's ghettoes, where the lyrics were reeled off in a series of pornographic rantings.

In Chicago itself, house music was very much a minority sound and was associated with the Warehouse, a black gay club, where DJ and producer Frankie Knuckles was resident. Although at the outset house music had been aired on all local Chicago radio stations, within a couple of years it was generally only played on local independent black music radio stations. What's more, distribution for this kind of music was almost non-existent. Record labels were run like small family businesses with no real promotional network. The artists had to take extra jobs to make a living, and most of them produced their music with the only hope that it would be played late one night at the Warehouse. It seemed that the odds were against this music finding its way out of the black neighbourhoods of Chicago. In Europe, young people's heads were still nodding to the sounds of rock guitars.

The story goes that a few records from prestigious labels like Trax and DJ International somehow made it to England into the hands of a couple of DJs from Manchester who decided to take a trip to Chicago. Mike Pickering was one of them. Once over there, he was invited to play at the Milk Bar in North Chicago, and played house music to a crowd of mainly white kids. They were used to dancing to UK electronic pop and ran up to the DJ booth saying, 'What's this music you're playing? It's awesome!' And Mike replied, 'But it's from here!' These young white kids from the north of Chicago had never come across this music before, even though it was being produced in the predominantly black neighbourhoods on the other side of their very own city.

In Manchester, as in Chicago, the black community was the first to adopt house music. For the first few months, the only person playing house music from Chicago was Mike Pickering at Nude on Friday nights at the Haçienda. Nude attracted a mostly Anglo-Jamaican crowd who came to 'jack'. Jackin' was a style of dance that can only be described as a latter-day answer to the Charleston. The dance was highly sexually charged, with fancy footwork and the torso doing repeated wave movements. Jackin' was serious stuff. Dancers came onto the floor to show off their technical prowess and, as with hip-hop, anyone who wasn't up to scratch was immediately sent out of the circle.

The first real event that the Haçienda dedicated entirely to house music took place in the autumn of 1987. It was a Trax Records night from Chicago. Trax was responsible for signing some of the most important dance records in the second part of the 80s. Adonis, Marshall Jefferson, Robert Owens and Liz Torres, four of the most prominent artists from Chicago, performed on stage for the first time in Europe in front of a crowd of people who had come down from the roughest areas of Manchester to see them. It was a far cry from any electronic music live p.a. you might see today. The musicians simply let a backing tape play while they sang or spoke over the top. That Friday, the Haçienda was packed full, and out of the hundreds of people crammed into the venue, only a handful was white. From then on, everybody was jackin'. I remember spending my whole night on the dance floor trying to dance like the others. The atmosphere was electric.

Soon after that, a DJ from Detroit came to play in Manchester. His name was Derrick May. He was one of the creators of a new sound called techno. This was a harder, darker and more futurist sound than house. Derrick had a reputation of being a bit of a magician behind the decks. His creativity and energy were a great inspiration to me. A few months later, he would become a driving force of the techno scene with his label Transmat, and would change everything with one classic track: Strings Of Life. Derrick May had come to DJ at Legends, a tiny club in Manchester. He danced and jumped about behind the decks while the crowd jacked on the dance floor.

Gradually, house music started to appeal to a wider audience. To satisfy an ever-growing demand, over 200 imports arrived each week at Spin Inn and Eastern Bloc, the first two record shops in Manchester to specialise in house music. DJs were playing Chicago house in the clubs. The radio stations soon caught on and began producing house music shows. Stu Allen, one of the top radio DJs in the city, even went as far as changing his hip-hop show to make space for house music.

The floodgates were open. Amidst some confusion, boxloads of records were being shipped over from Chicago on a regular basis. Some of these releases were already a few years old. No one back in Chicago had ever imagined that these records would one day sell in Europe. They had been lying around in some old storeroom until word got around, 'Man! In England, they say they like that house music thing!'

An important page of musical history was being written.

I became a regular at the Haçienda and was lucky enough to meet Dani Jacobs, the lighting engineer. We became friends and I gave him several mix tapes in the hope that he might pass them on to Paul Cons, who was in charge of booking the DJs and coming up with ideas for new club nights. Paul wasn't really a music buff but he knew a lot about clubs and how to draw in a crowd.

I had also stayed in contact with Bob, one of my London friends who was also mad about music. I was dead set on organising a night in Manchester and invited him up to stay for the weekend. We got a night at the Swinging Sporran, a small pub in the centre of town. They were pretty cool and gave us carte blanche for the night, as long as we pulled in a crowd. Our first attempt, called Repent, was a flop. However, among the few people who came to listen to us were Dani and ... Paul Cons! I gave a mix tape to Dani, who handed it on to Paul Cons. I then went on holiday and forgot all about it. Two weeks passed. When I got back home, my answering machine was crammed with urgent messages from Dani, which began quite politely but ended up full of expletives. In short, he was asking me to call him back, so I did and was rewarded with a meeting with Paul Cons the very next day.

The meeting was over in a flash. Paul Cons told me that he wanted to put together a weekly night to attract the in-crowd, with performances from northern comedians and 'caliente' music. He was looking for a DJ. I was one of the five people up for the job; each candidate had to send him a mix tape. I shut myself away in my room for the next few days with mineral water and chocolate and came out with a seriously funky 90-minute-long mix tape. I sent the tape, waited for what seemed like an eternity, and then finally the phone rang. It was good news, 'Hey frog-gy-boy, it's Paul Cons. Are you still interested in the job?'

The night, called Zumbar, was scheduled for Wednesday and I was the resident DJ along with DJ Jose. I called myself DJ Pedro to fit in with the 'caliente' theme. The first Zumbar took place on Wednesday October 7, 1987, under the watchful eye of a giant bull's head that was suspended above the dance floor. Paul Cons aimed to seduce and impress a trendy crowd with the decadence of Zumbar. As far as the music was concerned, we had a free rein. We could play anything. It could be cutting-edge or a bit cheesy, as long as it was good.

For a young guy like me, my first DJ set at the Haçienda was an immeasurable source of stress. I didn't get a wink of sleep the night before. There was no doubt about it, I was petrified. I arrived at the Haçienda at opening time, as white as a sheet. The Haçienda staff all wished me luck. I went into the DJ booth, and there before me were two Technics MK2 SL1200. I had never seen decks like these at such close range. There was even a pitch control to speed up, which I had never tried before. I was trapped up in the booth with a bad bout of stage fright, while down below me people

were dancing. I just stared at them. I tried several times to find what I wanted to play in the records that I had so carefully prepared beforehand. Then finally I took the plunge. My nerves soon gave way to euphoria.

About halfway through my set, I played Pump Up The Volume by M/A/R/R/S, a track that heralded the musical revolution already underway. M/A/R/R/S was made up of Dave Dorrel, Martyn Young (Colourbox) and DJ C.J. Mackintosh. Pump Up The Volume was a heady mix of the latest sampling technology, house rhythms and pop vocals with a repetitive gimmick, 'Brothers and sisters, Pump up the volume, You're gonna get yours!'

The easily recognisable sound of the Akai S1000 sampler, one of the most important machines in early house music productions, can be heard on this track. This was pure UK-style dance music with chart-topping potential. In hindsight Pump Up The Volume was far more than just a dance floor hit. It is a prime example of what was being played throughout clubs in the UK in the late 1980s. There are samples from Ofra Haza, Criminal Element Orchestra (Put The Needle To The Record), Public Enemy (You're Gonna Get Yours) and James Brown. And all this in one track. Pump Up The Volume reached Number 1 in the UK charts in September 1987. It was one of those records that you could play several times over in one night without the public ever getting tired of it.

Despite my nerves on that first night, it was an amazing experience for me, and a huge success for Paul Cons. However, as everything he touched turned to gold, nobody wasted too much time handing out praise.

I had reached a milestone and it was then that I realised that my whole life was geared towards music. Everything else in my life was falling apart. I'd split up with my girlfriend, and as a result was no longer working in her sister's restaurant, but in another restaurant about 40 miles outside of Manchester. I was working 15 hours a day, five days a week, while still DJ-ing at Zumbar on Wednesdays and going out the other nights. I missed the Mud Club but I had found a new home at the Haçienda.

Nobody really imagined making a career out of DJ-ing back then. Only a few people such as Mike Pickering, Dave Haslam and Graeme Park, idolised in the north of England, were actually making a living out of their art. All the other DJs I knew also had day jobs. But I longed to be a DJ; I was obsessed with the idea. Not a part-time DJ like at Zumbar, even if I did put my whole heart into it and took the job very seriously. I wanted to make a career out of DJ-ing.

One night instinctively lead to another, friendships were made (some quite superficial, but that's part of the game) and I gradually became an integral part of Manchester and its nightlife. I truly believed, without a shadow of a doubt, that I could make it happen. Yet up until the early months of 1988, house music and techno were still something of a mystery to white kids. When they started showing an interest in house music, it got huge. It was like a hurricane sweeping across the country, alongside another driving force that was quite literally mind-blowing. The drug ecstasy had arrived in the UK.

Ecstasy hit the UK at the end of spring 1988, coincidentally at around the same time as acid-house, a sub-division of house music. Acid-house was characterised by the inimitable sound of the Roland TB-303, an electronic drum machine that produced acid bass lines. Tracks by DJ Pierre and Sleazy D still contained a few voice samples, but the purely instrumental sounds were soon to take over.

Within three weeks, acid-house was to become the new buzzword for a whole generation in the north of England. Rare groove and soul had become too slow, old and flaky, and great classics such as Maceo Parker's Across The Tracks that had been played incessantly over the last few years had suddenly become obsolete. By around April or May, the first acid-house compilations, released by labels such as Trax and Gherkin Records, reached the record shops on Oldham Street. That was when it all changed. Middle-class white kids started pouring into the Haçienda, and it was to be the end of nights with a mainly black clientele with their dance styles and dress codes. Within a few weeks, jackin' had almost completely disappeared from the Haçienda's dance floor. The new crowd, rushing on ecstasy, danced with their hands in the air, screaming their heads off.

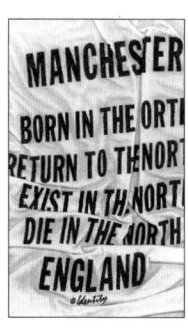

Manchester was also invaded by a new style called scally. It was all about oversized clothes and big printed t-shirts. The word 'scally' was to become synonymous with Manchester's youth. It was used to describe a fashion, heavily influenced by the hippy movement, as well as a way of life and a type of music. A whole new trade of t-shirts emblazoned with logos began to appear with statements such as 'Born in the north, Raised in the north, Die in the north', or, 'Jesus had long hair too'… The northern youth, predominantly students, regarded these t-shirts as a humorous and cheap way to create their own rebel identity. It was no coincidence that the t-shirt became the uniform of the 'Summer of Love' in 1988. Scallies would wear sun hats on their long-haired heads. Some even carried inflatable bananas under their arms to throw at each other at clubs and football matches.

Ecstasy swept away everything in its path. Its impact on Manchester was huge, crossing all social barriers. Although Manchester had a reputation as a violent city, this one drug resulted in thousands of clubbers, whether inside the Haçienda or out dancing in the countryside, sharing a rare collective experience whose magic still resounds today. The arrival of ecstasy also changed the language. People invented daft expressions such as 'I'm cabbaged', 'I'm shedded', or 'Top one, nice one, get sorted'. The influence of ecstasy on the public mood was noticeable by a lull in violence in the football stadiums. The supporters would take pills, and instead of lacing into each other they'd have their arms around each other's necks.

While the national press was asking itself why there had been such a big change in attitude within football stadiums previously blighted by violence, all hell was being let loose at the epicentre of northern clubbing, the Haçienda. The doors opened at 9pm, and by 10pm there would be a queue of about 1,500 people quivering with excitement to be let in. They had it in writing: 'Admission £1.50 before 11pm, £2.50 after'. By 11pm, the place was jam-packed. By 11.15pm, the crowd was bare-chested. By midnight, the heat and condensation were such that the first drops of warm, salty sweat would begin to rain down on the dance floor.

Every club night in the UK had its own ritual, and the Haçienda was no different. For the last 20 minutes, the DJ would only play classics. You could feel the tension building up. When the music stopped at five minutes to two, the crowd felt incredibly frustrated. However, this frustration urged them to savour every minute that they had left. It was at that exact moment that you could reach out and almost touch the energy. It was almost religious, like a ritualistic mass. Every night built up to that last moment, five minutes before the end when, after a moment of silence, the DJ would play the last record, Someday by Ce Ce Rogers. As someone who loves dancing, I swear that at that point the whole club was experiencing pleasure close to an orgasmic high.

As soon as the clock struck two we had no choice but to stop the music, The Haçienda's main lights would be switched back on … what a comedown! From high up in the DJ booth we could feel people's disappointment as they were stopped in their tracks. However, it was precisely the compulsory closure of clubs at 2am that made UK nightlife so legendary. There were, of course, alternatives such as illegal warehouse parties, organised on the outskirts of the city where every kind of music came together: reggae, house, electro and US hip-hop. And be they black or white, students or scallies, they all converged with the same purpose, to carry on partying until dawn. The anarchic and positive spirit of warehouse parties, which involved finding and taking charge of a makeshift venue for several hours, laid the foundations for what a few months later would become the first rave parties.

The way I saw it, living up north, the impact of house music upon the south of England was not the same as in the north. Of course, it still found fertile ground in London and took hold during the Summer of Love in 1988. The DJ and club promoter Nicky Holloway had been organising trips for clubbers to the party island of Ibiza since 1984. In 1987, a handful of the Ibiza contingent were making their way back with pockets stuffed full of ecstasy. Alongside the DJs Danny Rampling and Paul Oakenfold, Nicky Holloway organised the first house nights in London at the Watermans Arts Centre, a stone's throw from Heathrow airport. Then, on Danny Rampling's initiative, the same team started Shoom. Probably the most emblematic and extreme of all London club nights, it exploded onto the London nightlife scene. More promoters started to surface in 1988 creating other nights, including Westworld, Delirium and Spectrum.

London-based pirate radio stations were also making a huge contribution to the rise of house music. They were the nerve centre, acting like a barometer, constantly monitoring new music trends. Their impact on British club culture was paramount. Thanks to the former pirate radio station Kiss FM, founded by Gordon Mac and Norman Jay in 1985, resident DJs Judge Jules and Paul Trouble Anderson broadcast house music to the masses. House music had now spread its roots right across the UK. There were clubs, DJs, music, radio programmes, and all were poised to experience the first Summer of Love.

On May 21, 1988, on the eve of the first Summer of Love, the Haçienda was celebrating its sixth birthday. For the event, a huge ghost train was installed just in front of the club. I was celebrating my first year as resident at Zumbar and was invited to DJ, recognition that I had now been truly accepted as part of the family. At midnight, while Mike Pickering was playing, they staged a breathtaking firework display inside the club. Then it was Graeme Park's turn to take the decks.

For the last few years, Graeme had been a major figure on the club scene in Nottingham (another northern stronghold), and was also a Haçienda resident. Arguably one of the greatest UK DJs of the 90s, he had an outstanding mixing technique – an amazing capacity to choose exactly the right record for the right moment and the ability to stay incredibly focused whatever happened. I remember one night when we'd had a lot to drink; he was mixing when, just as he was coming out of the mix, he mistakenly took the needle off the record. Dead silence. He just looked at the crowd, put the needle back on, started the record up again masterfully scratching over it, and then threw his arms up into the air. The crowd went wild.

On the night of the Haçienda's sixth birthday, once again, Graeme Park did the most amazing set. At 2am, when the lights came back on and the music stopped, a deep rumble seemed to be surging through the earth's crust; it was the roar of thousands of clubbers heralding the first Summer of Love.

However, a simple phone call was about to put an end to my British escapades and change my life forever. It was a very ordinary day, and I was working at the restaurant when my mother rang to tell me that I had been called up for French National Service in Paris on August 1. I had never replied to the official letters and now I was being called up and there was no getting out of it. My world was falling apart. National Service … fuck!

July 1988; after only 10 months, Zumbar was getting ready for its last dance. For the occasion, the Haçienda had invited the prestigious UK magazine *ID* and the DJ Mark Moore. Mark Moore! The wizard from the Mud Club. The first DJ that I was a true fan of. An artist to whom I owed everything during my time in London, who'd taught me about whole areas of music that I'd never known existed. And that night, I was to play alongside him. Him being there was quite an event in local history. Not because of his undisputed talent, or the fact that a famous DJ was coming to town, but simply because it was exceptionally rare at the time for a DJ from London to be invited to play in Manchester.

The last Zumbar was a huge success. That night, Mark Moore told me that about two months later he would be playing at the Palace in Paris, as guest of honour at one of the Pyramid parties organised by a London-based sound system. I was about to ask him if he would be kind enough to put me on the guest list when he said, 'You should come along and play some records … '

The following Wednesday, the first Hot party, a new concept organised by Paul Cons, went down a storm. Manchester was at fever pitch. The Summer of Love was in full swing and I was feeding off the amazing energy, knowing that at least I'd be able to take that back to France with me. But everything happened so fast that I didn't really have time to think about it. After the third Hot party, I got down to organising my departure. As I packed up my things, it was as if the wind was carrying Manchester's positive energy all the way to my house.

As consolation, and because I had the distinct feeling that my savings were not going to be much use to me stationed in Montlhéry with the Regiment of Chad, I splashed out on my first pair of Technics MKII turntables. I left for France at the end of July 1988 and all I took with me were my decks, my records, a few mix tapes and an Acid Trax t-shirt.

2

french kiss

I am the youngest son of a family of fairground people. My father would buy music for his rides, so I always remember there being lots of records at home. He had a friend called Monsieur Fournier who worked at CBS records in France and would come round to our house with boxloads of records, including Earth, Wind & Fire, Trust and Santana LPs.

By the time I was 10, my bedroom looked just like a nightclub. My bed and my desk were pushed up against the wall to make more space. In the middle of the room I had strategically placed records on the carpet to create the dance floor that had a capacity of about three, maybe four, people.

It was a proper mini-disco and I had all the right gear. There was a strobe light, coloured spotlights on the walls, various lamps around the room for atmosphere and a mirrored disco ball on the ceiling. With the flick of a switch the disco ball would slowly start to rotate with the spotlights angled towards it. I would stand behind the DJ booth that my dad had built for me facing the empty dance floor, surrounded by piles of records and tapes, turntables, amplifiers, microphones and a mess of grey cables. When I switched on the machines, hundreds of little white stars would dance across my bedroom walls. With or without music, the disco ball was on every night.

The dance floor was only used on special occasions. Needless to say, mostly by me. It was kind of difficult to be on the dance floor and take care of the music at the same time, but I was dying to see how other people reacted to what I played. So I decided it was time to search out an audience among the neighbours in our block of flats in Bougival. Sometimes my mum stood in for the audience, along with a couple of neighbours. But most of the time, due to lack of interest, there was no one at my club and I used to shut myself away in my room, working hard for an imaginary crowd. The lights would be flashing and the music on full blast. I would be standing behind the turntables and smiling to myself, imagining the crowd screaming with pleasure with every new record.

This could go on for hours. Every now and again I would step out onto the dance floor to gauge how powerful the record was and check the sound levels. I'd often forget about my DJ role, in what was the most underground club in Bougival, and get carried away dancing in a style that could only be described as a cross between rockabilly and funk. These late-night antics would come to an abrupt halt when the parent police burst in and told me to stop the racket. Deflated, I would switch off the music and put the bedside light back on, apologising all the while to the imaginary crowd, 'Sorry everyone, closing time, police orders. Thanks now, goodnight.'

For bigger events, my club was open to everyone regardless of age or creed. During family gatherings, friends and relatives were all invited in to have a boogie on the dance floor in the confines of my bedroom venue.

So as you can see, this fascination with music goes back a long way. When I was eight years old I began recording cassettes for my friends at school. Just listening to music wasn't enough anymore, now I needed to share it with others. I was completely obsessed with music. When I was 12, I'd wait for my parents to fall asleep at night, then tiptoe into the living room. Kneeling there in the dark with a pair of headphones on, I'd search the airwaves hoping to discover the latest imports on pirate radios such as Radio 7. I would leave blank tapes recording for hours, cramming them with new releases from the States. I'd sit listening with a pen in my hand, writing down the names of every group and every track played, feeding my insatiable appetite for black American soul, funk and disco, and getting better acquainted with electro-rock.

On the first Saturday of every month I would watch the television show *Sex Machine*, part of *Les Enfants du Rock*, which was presented by Philippe Manoeuvre and Jean-Pierre Dionnet. They were the first to introduce me to the world of Prince and a whole galaxy of funk from Minneapolis. When the Walkman came out, I spent every waking hour with a pair of headphones stuck on my head listening over and over again to the tapes of US imports I'd recorded.

One day, I heard that Yannick Chevalier, a well-known disc jockey, was starting up a DJ school near Paris. I asked my dad if he would enrol me, but he would hear nothing of it. I knew that I wanted to make people dance, and to be able to make this happen I was going to need more than one turntable. So I asked my parents if they would buy me another one and a mixer – the basic DJ gear.

When I was 14 (and *radio libres* was at its height), a friend and I set up our very own pirate radio station, Radio Teenager. Every Friday night, we did a four-hour broadcast from my friend's house in Le Pecq. We also did the music at all the local parties. On Saturdays, I secretly took the train into Paris to Champs Disques, the only record shop selling imports at the time. I spent every last penny of my pocket money in there. And on Sundays, instead of playing football, I spent my afternoons hanging out in kids' discos listening to what the DJs were playing.

That I wanted to be a DJ was already quite clear in my mind, although back then I had no real idea of what that meant. I thought it boiled down to playing the best music you could, with a certain amount of style, and watching a happy crowd grooving away on the dance floor. I would shut myself away and mix for hours on end. When I closed my eyes the music

▶ Playlist
TEENAGE YEARS
Bon Rock And The Rhythm Rebellion
Searching Rap

Unlimited Touch
I Heard Music In The Street

Katmandu
The Break

Tom Browne
Funkin' For Jamaica

Sinnamaon
Thanks To You

Shock
Let Your Body Do The Talking

SKYY
Skyy Zoo

Gino Soccio
Remember

Edith Nylon
Femmes Sous Cellophane

Taxi Girl
CherchezLe Garçon

Soft Cell
Tainted Love

took over, I was no longer in my bedroom but inside a club. My club. All those hours that I spent working on my mixing technique and all those tapes I made for friends at school, and their friends, were motivated by one thing: the hope that one day one of those tapes would fall into the right hands, giving me the break I needed.

Decades on, when I'm inside a club with the strobe lights flashing and the disco ball slowly turning reflecting its galaxy of tiny stars across the walls, and I hear the sound pushed up loud and watch the crowd react, I still feel deeply moved. All these elements that make a club take me back to the first time I experienced a disco as a child, one summer night in Italy. I must have been about 11, and we were on a family holiday near Rimini. That night my parents and I dropped off my elder brother in front of a discotheque called La Baia Imperiale. A huge billboard at the front boasted 'Seven dance floors – Seven themes – Open-air bar'. From where we were parked, not far from the entrance, we could see the lights, strobes and disco balls flashing in time to the music and lighting up the night sky. As my brother got out of the car, I could hear the music from one of the outdoor dance floors. The DJ was playing the first few bars of Donna Summer's I Feel Love. Sitting in the back seat listening, I began to sing along in broken English. My excited, clammy hands gripped the car door as I leant my head out of the window, desperate to get a better look at where this fantastic music was coming from. A gigantic halo of brightly coloured lights surrounded the club. It was magical, dazzling. The following day, I raced around the tourist shops buying up Baia Imperiale stickers with Marilyn Monroe on them. The impact that those 20 seconds would have on me would last forever. As for the stickers, they ended up stuck on my cheap bedroom furniture, my school books, my turntables, and even on the Garnier bathroom mirror, and were the only tangible things that remained of that night in Italy that fuelled my life-long passion to be a DJ.

Years later, when I'd be playing the right record at the right time, giving everything I had to the crowd, doing everything I could to make a connection with them, I'd think, 'This is what I have always dreamt of, how I've always wanted to feel'. Because, as the years went by, something else beyond the simple pleasure of playing records had become apparent to me. I could take the crowd to another level, surprise and enchant them with different textures of music and awaken in each one of them the primal urge to dance and be free.

You don't need to be a born leader to be able to do this, you just need to feel and build a connection with the people on the dance floor. The relationship that develops between a DJ and the crowd is a complex one.

The DJ picks up on the atmosphere inside the club and the energy generated by the music, lights and people dancing. For that special alchemy to work, certain elements need to come together: a temporary abandonment of the rules of society, a visceral need to dance, and a sense of letting go, and with this people will experience an amazing range of emotions. It's as if an electric charge begins to flow and the DJ controls its intensity and where he wants to take it. The music becomes a journey. In these moments of grace, taking the needle off a record is like a bolt of lightning striking dead 500, 1,000, or 50,000 people in one go. On the other hand, even a great record played at the wrong moment can instantly wipe out the story that the DJ had been skilfully telling to the crowd. The only true secret to DJ-ing is the ability to share.

When I left Manchester at the end of July 1988, armed with two Technics MKII turntables, a couple of bags full of clothes and several boxes of records, I moved back into my childhood bedroom in Bougival. It hadn't changed much since I'd made it my club 15 years earlier. Posters of David Bowie and Marilyn Monroe still covered the walls. My ancient turntables and the disco ball were still there, and even my old records were still in their wooden crates: Barry White, Earth, Wind & Fire and Ted Nugent (nobody's perfect!). And an overpowering smell of furniture polish filled the room.

I slumped onto my single bed and started looking through old *Actuel* magazines I found in a cardboard box. Then I went over to my DJ booth. I flicked on the switches, spotlights flashed and the disco ball started to rotate. While the amplifier was warming up, making a quiet fizzing sound, I started digging through my old records. I pulled out a single from the Casablanca disco label, produced by the German musician Giorgio Moroder in 1977. It was Donna Summer's I Feel Love. I took the record out of its plastic cover, wiped it carefully with my shirtsleeve and put it on the turntable. The needle crackled as it settled into the groove. As the first notes filled the room, I turned the amp up to full volume. For the next 11 minutes, a rhythm somewhere between the chug of a train and a disco bass line filled the four walls. And as the demonic groove of I Feel Love took hold, I got onto the dance floor, threw my arms in the air and sang along at the top of my voice.

On August 1, 1988, I began my National Service with the Regiment of Chad in Montlhéry where I was to spend the next six weeks in training. I wasn't happy about it. Thanks to one of my mother's well-connected friends, I was soon transferred from Montlhéry to Versailles to serve as a waiter in the officers' mess. I was saved, I felt as if I'd been rescued, and on top of that I was allowed to go home every night. Nevertheless, I still felt trapped and didn't hold out much hope for the future. Several weeks went by. One day, I explained to my senior officer, who was quite a nice guy, that I had a house in Manchester and needed to earn money to pay the mortgage. As a result, he gave orders that from then on I was to be in charge of the music for all future receptions held at the officers' mess.

These events regularly attracted over 200 officers who came to drink, unwind and listen to Mylene Farmer records. But there always came a point in the night when they were too drunk to choose the music they wanted to listen to. So I would start to play some house music, including underground hits from Chicago such as Can You Feel It by Mr Fingers and tracks from Royal House. It's funny to think that high-ranking officers were among the first people in France to dance to house music.

In September 1988 I set foot in the first club in Paris to host acid-house nights. The Rex Club on the Boulevard Poissonière, is underneath the cinema of the same name, only a few hundred yards up the road from the legendary Palace. The Rex Club had a reputation for being more of a rock venue, but I'd never been inside. I was curious to find out what it was really like, so one night after a hard day's work at the officers' mess, I headed for the Rex. Little did I know that this club would become such an important part of my life.

I made my way downstairs, which led to a long dark room with low ceilings. I walked past the low-lit bar into the heart of the Rex Club. I could make out people dancing as the lights swept past them. I tentatively made my way towards the half-moon-shaped dance floor. At one end was a stage framed by heavy crimson curtains. The sound system was set up to play rock music and had very little bass and lots of medium. Flashing strobe lights gave the impression that everybody was dancing in slow motion. To the right of the dance floor was another room with several alcoves and a few tables, a chill-out space. The bar there was quieter so people could get away from the blaring sound system before going back to the dance floor. The DJ booth was situated in between the two rooms, like an imaginary frontier. I realised that the Rex had the same layout as the clubs I'd known in the UK.

Within a few years the Rex Club would become a beacon for Parisian nightlife, leading the way in house and techno. People remember the Rex for the risks it took and the unwavering belief it had in this music. My own personal fate and that of so many other DJs and musicians was closely linked to the Rex. However, before we move on to this next chapter, let me tell you a bit more about the history of the Rex.

Christian Paulet had been the heart and soul of the Rex since 1984, when he was taken on as stage manager by Garance Productions. The

original plan had been to create a Parisian version of the Cotton Club. They had a big band playing jazz with the musicians all lined up on stage, but the concept never really took off. However, alternative rock was gaining ground in France and the Rex decided to go down this route instead. Soon there were a regular three concerts a week with bands who later became household names like the Red Hot Chilli Peppers, the Rita Mitsouko (the Rex hosted their first ever concert), Suzanne Vega, Tower of Power, Chris Isaak, and even Prince did an after-show party there. By 1987, the Rex had a solid reputation and every band with a tour date in Paris looking for a 400-capacity venue played there.

Christian quickly outgrew his role as stage manager and began overseeing gigs at the Rex. In 1987, the cinema above the club started holding evening screenings. Sound checks posed a problem because the noise filtered upstairs. Meanwhile, Garance Productions had just bought the Elysée Montmartre, a large concert venue on Boulevard Rochechouart, and so decided to pull out of the Rex. Christian Paulet suggested that he take over the running of the venue but he wanted to start afresh. He set out to see all the main club promoters in Paris, asking them if they would be interested in organising regular club nights at the Rex. They all said yes. The Rex was still known predominantly as a rock venue, but as the number of rock concerts slowly dwindled, Christian started scheduling theme nights several times a week. There were rock nights, dub nights, hip-hop nights, etc. ... all taking place under the same roof and in the same week, each with their own crowd.

Then one day a couple of London club promoters, Kevin and Barbara, came to see Christian about organising an acid-house night at the Rex. Christian had never heard of acid-house, but as they seemed professional and regularly organised these kinds of parties in the UK, he accepted. The first acid-house night at the Rex was called Jungle. The Rex's logo didn't feature on the flyer, just the address and the name of the night. According to Christian:

> *'That night was unbelievable. No one in Paris had ever come up with something as crazy as that before. It was really wild but the atmosphere was amazingly friendly. I'd never seen anything like it ... the energy, the crowd and the atmosphere that night. There were a lot of gay men, people in fashion, and media types. It was über cool. I suppose, they were all people at the forefront of the movement in France. They obviously already knew what acid-house was and were in tune with what was going on in the UK. A lot of them had been to London and had seen the beginnings of acid-house there. These promoters had come up with a*

new way to party, when everyone else was running out of ideas. With acid-house came a whole new dynamic, and people were getting excited about going out again. It had a profound impact on me, but back then I never imagined that house music was going to change the history of the Rex so dramatically. All I saw was that the crowd was changing and that the music was new and fresh. It was enough for me to justify opening up the Rex Club to regular house music nights.'

In the spring of 1988, house music established its first residency in Paris.

In September of that year, another Parisian nightclub, the Palace, experienced a similar club-night revival. This club embodied all the decadence and excess of the 80s, and was synonymous with a certain avant-garde. From behind its deep red façade on the Faubourg-Montmartre, the Palace ruled Parisian nightlife throughout the 1980s, thanks to the visionary Fabrice Emaer. Andy Warhol, Mick Jagger, Diana Ross and David Bowie all went to the Palace to have fun. Iggy Pop or Serge Gainsbourg could be found at the end of the night drowning their sorrows along with the rest of them. Nights like these regularly featured in Alain Pacadis' gossip column in the newspaper *Libération*. Kenzo, Karl Lagerfeld or Yves Saint Laurent would put on outlandish fashion shows and costume balls that brought together 'le Tout-Paris'. Grace Jones would hang out with her groupies there while the next generation of French artists, including the likes of Taxi Girl, Jacno and Patrick Eudeline, would get together for regular punk nights. The original DJ at the Palace was Guy Cuevas. He was one of the first to explore New York nightlife. He must have gone to the Loft and to Larry Levan's club, Paradise Garage, to have brought back a sound that was specific to New York, a mix of soul, funk and disco (the origins of garage). Cuevas introduced the Palace to this new music. Later on, Thierry Belfort and Didier Dart took over as the in-house DJs, bridging the gap between the disco years of the early 80s and the beginnings of house music.

But by 1988, the golden years of the Palace were over. After Fabrice Emaer's death in 1983, Paris nightlife changed drastically. All that remained of the club's glory days were memories. So it was in this gloomy state that the organisers of Jungle launched a second weekly acid-house night, but this time at the Palace. The night was called Pyramid, to mirror their night with the same name at the Heaven club in London.

I turned up at Pyramid with a bag of records to see Mark Moore who was playing on the opening night. He kept the promise he'd made to me in Manchester and let me DJ during the warm-up slot. The predominantly

▶ Playlist
NEW YORK CLASSICS
Double Exposure
Ten Percent

War
City Country City

Roy Ayers
Running Away

Carl Bean
I Was Born This Way

The Salsoul Orchestra
Ooh I Love It

Loleatta Holloway
Love Sensation

Ecstasy Passion And Pain
Touch And Go

Barry White
My Sweet Summer Suite

gay crowd went wild and danced as if they were already familiar with house. House music had only just arrived in France so I had a huge advantage. I had been there when it had started in the UK. This was an opportunity not to be missed.

At the end of my set, Kevin and Barbara asked me to play for a couple more hours at the end of the night, and to become the resident DJ playing the opening and closing sets. I decided that it was time to leave 'DJ Pedro' from the Haçienda behind and have my own name, Laurent Garnier, on the flyers. After that night I had my first short article in the magazine *The Face* and that, coupled with being offered a residency at Pyramid, constituted a second key moment in my career.

Mark Moore had been the special guest for Pyramid's first night, but it was another English DJ, Colin Faver, who became the resident DJ. Every Tuesday I would play the warm-up set and the last couple of hours. Word soon spread within the gay community and more and more people showed up each week. Thanks to the British input and to house music, the Palace was now rising from its ashes. Paris now played host to two acid-house nights a week. There was Pyramid on Tuesdays and Jungle on Fridays, where I also became the resident DJ alongside Colin Holsgove.

From then on things started moving quickly. By association with Pyramid and Jungle, my name became known on the gay scene. The bosses of the Palace put me in charge of the music at the Gay Tea Dance on Sunday afternoons, alongside Didier Dart. Since my teenage years I'd come to know the gay scene quite well – my brother, who owned a restaurant, would make me work there on the weekends, promising me that he would take me out after work to the underground gay clubs in the capital. So working at the Gay Tea Dance was easy for me as I found myself within a community that I was familiar with.

Every Sunday at 3pm the doors would open for the Gay Tea Dance and 2,500 men wearing skin-tight t-shirts would descend on the Palace, ready to party to the end. Initially, the gay crowd were the only people interested in dance music, so that's mostly what we played, whether it was house from Chicago or early techno tracks from Detroit. The crowd also loved acid-house and those Sundays were far from days of rest. I thrived in this environment and learned how to play the crowd. When the dance floor at the Palace went wild, it was like a game to me. I used to call it 'letting the dogs out'. I played the records that made them go wild and their job was to react.

I was working more and more regularly. When the Palace closed on Sunday evening at the end of the Gay Tea Dance, I would head off to DJ at another club, which meant I was now playing a total of 14 hours

▶ Playlist
PYRAMID

Inner City
Good Life

Kraze
The Party

The Minute Man
Bingo Bango

Ten City
That's The Way Love Is

Hashim
Al Naafiysh

▶ Playlist
JUNGLE

Mantronix
King Of The Beats

Ann Clarke
Our Darkness

Phase II
Reachin'

Baby Ford
Oochy Koochy

Todd Terry
Bango

every Sunday. From the Palace, I would go straight up rue du Faubourg-Montmartre, then up rue Notre Dame de Lorette, rue Fontaine until I hit Place Blanche. And there, on the edge of Pigalle, right next to the Moulin Rouge, was a white floodlit wall with an inscription in black lettering: La Locomotive.

I had met Hilda, the artistic director at the Locomotive, at one of the last Zumbar nights in Manchester. She had suggested that I get in touch with Fred Bolling, the club owner. Fred was a bit of a tough guy. Our meeting was very brief, and Fred said in an off-hand way, 'You want to play at the Loco? Alright, let's see what you can do with your shit music.'

The Locomotive, an amazing club, was established in 1960. The actor, André Pousse, was the host at the neighbouring Moulin Rouge, and would organise parties at the Locomotive for the under 20s. While maman and papa were at the world-famous cabaret, the Moulin Rouge, their kids would be going wild next door at the Loco. But the 60s were a long time ago, and now the Locomotive was a mammoth three-floor rock club frequented by thugs, skinheads and punks. Once past the very long bar on the ground floor, you got to the first dance floor, which could hold about 800 people. It resembled a modern-day arena with people pogo-ing like crazy. The DJ booth was situated in the middle, several feet off the ground. In one corner was a staircase that led down to a second room in the basement. This room was smaller and industrial in design, with metal pipes running across the walls and ceiling and large copper panels. Two floors up by another staircase was a third, much smaller room, which had a bird's eye view of the main dance floor.

I'll never forget my trial run at the Loco. It was a weeknight and every single kind of punk and rocker you could imagine were in there. I started the set, gradually steering the music towards acid-house. Everything was going well. Fred, the boss of the club, was on the door and he'd had a mini-speaker installed above the main entrance so he could keep tabs on the music being played in the main room. At one point I put on the acid remix of Mory Kante's afro-beat track, Yeke Yeke, which had recently entered the French charts. Given the number of skinheads that hung out at the Loco in those days, it was pretty dangerous to play anything that might sound the slightest bit African. Fred came charging up to me shouting: 'Are you out of your bloody mind playing African music in here? You'll get yourself killed!'

I pointed to the crowd going wild on the dance floor and said, 'Look at them, they're loving it.'

▶ Playlist

GAY TEA DANCE

Joe Smooth
Promised Land

Ten City
Right Back To You

Corporation Of One
The Real Life

Sha-Lor
I'm In Love

Phortune
String Free

They gave me my residency that night. From then on, during the week, I played a mixture of rock and house music, and, every Sunday, Hilda gave me free rein to play acid-house in the basement.

Hilda knew exactly what was being played in Manchester. She organised the first ever house night at the Locomotive, using Manchester as the inspiration, on February 25, 1989. DJs Graeme Park, Jon Dasilva and Mike Pickering were invited to come and play in Paris for the very first time. I was in charge of the basement room. The Manchester night was a big success and brought in a clientele that would never have set foot inside the venue had it not been for that event. They were a mixed crowd, gay and straight, just out to have a good time. This was another critical turning point.

It was at the Locomotive that I met Eric Rug for the first time. Eric was already one of the resident DJs when they took me on. He was a prominent figure on the Paris nightlife scene, but had taken an unusual route to get there. He had lived in Berlin and had been DJ-ing at the radical punk club, the Rose Bonbon, near the Olympia. Eric knew everything there was to know about music. He knew the rock scene like the back of his hand, and as soon as house music hit Paris, he became one of the very few DJs to take a real interest. We soon became friends and would often DJ together on the same nights. Before long, we decided to pitch a new night to the Locomotive called H30. The aim of this night was to attract a different crowd to the Locomotive by playing the best in house, techno and new beat. Eric Rug played new beat, a kind of synthetic industrial-sounding techno pop from Belgium, whereas I played mainly house and techno. Fred gave us the go-ahead and scheduled our club night for Wednesdays.

French Kiss was the big track back then. It symbolised everything that was innovative and uplifting in house music. Produced by Lil Louis, a DJ from Chicago, the record came out of nowhere and went straight into the French charts. Lasting 11 whole minutes, it was one of the first ever minimalist tracks with a repetitive loop. The tempo slowed right down in the middle until almost coming to standstill to make way for the sounds of a woman's cries of pleasure. Then the tempo started to build again slowly, like a machine picking up speed, before reaching its original tempo. It was nothing short of revolutionary.

French Kiss was one of a kind. Its explosive success transformed the musical landscape of Europe, and alternative versions of the track started cropping up all over the place. I remember a gay version where the woman's screams of pleasure were replaced by that of a man. There was even a cover version produced by a group of French musicians that got into

▶ Playlist
H30

Humanoid
Stakker Humanoid

D-Shake
Technotrance

KLF
What Time Is Love?

Bam Bam
Where's Your Child

Lil Louis
French Kiss

the charts at the same time as the original. French Kiss was *the* hit. You could play it five times over in the same night and hear the crowd roar with pleasure each and every time.

Eric and I regarded H30 as a place to let off steam. Sometimes we would grab the mike in the middle of the set and stir up the crowd if they weren't reacting enough to a tune we loved. In the UK there was a tradition of MCs (Masters of Ceremonies) whose job it was to charge up the atmosphere. We were doing the same thing, in our own way, à la française, as we shouted into the microphone.

H30 was the result of several months of hard work, during which Eric and I worked tirelessly to establish a house night in a punk club-which wasn't known for being open-minded. Each week there was added pressure as, despite the fact that we played house music to a mainly gay crowd, the punks and skinheads still turned up. To avoid any confrontations we were very careful not to play any new beat tracks that skinheads seemed to identify with. Front 242 and Nitzer Ebb are key examples of that particular category of harsh dance music.

Gradually, the boundaries between different genres of music began to diminish and even the most reluctant clients warmed to house music. Gays, skinheads, hipsters, rich kids and rockers would all dance to tracks such as Blue Monday by New Order.

A house music scene was beginning to take root in Paris. Some of the first DJs to start playing this music were Cyril Gordigiani, Olivier le Castor, Jerome Pacman and Guillaume la Tortue. The first French house record was How To Do That by Jean Paul Gaultier, with a video directed by Jean-Baptiste Mondino, but when it came out the press simply reported it as 'odd but interesting.'

The first records by French artists were released with little ado on Manu Casana's Rave Age label. The record shop Caramel began importing and distributing dance music. Yet only a couple of French journalists, Didier Lestrade and Vincent Borel, were paying any real attention. Apart from them, the media treated dance music with distaste, as nothing but a passing fad.

If you look at the history, the first real interest shown in dance music in France was only very slightly later than in the UK. But the way the music was received on either side of the Channel was radically different. In the UK, bands such as the Happy Mondays incorporated dance music rhythms and culture into their pop songs, which resulted in dance music being broadcast on national radio via their chart hit, Hallelujah. It was the same with Unbelievable by EMF. In France, dance music was for gay people, and rock fans just laughed at it. They even said it wasn't music

at all. The clubs didn't believe in it and paid no attention. It felt strange defending a style of music that other people dismissed.

Whereas in the UK everyone was into acid-house, in France it was a slow-burn. But it was this music that brought us a new crowd – people came to the clubs to dance, not just to chat someone up.

As I'd taken no leave since I'd started, my National Service came to an end two months early, in June 1989. I felt like I hadn't slept properly in years. I bid my farewells at the Locomotive. At the Palace, the British promoters were going to stop Pyramid. At the Rex it was the same. On June 19, 1989, I packed up my records, my two Technics turntables and a couple of suitcases of clothes, shoved them into the boot of my car and headed back to Manchester. All I wanted was to get out of France and never come back. Paul Cons had promised me a Saturday night residency at the Haçienda as well as a job at Dry Bar as soon as I was back in town. For the past few weeks I had been getting news of another wave of energy building in the north of England: the second Summer of Love was about to hit Manchester.

Letter of reference:

I, Frederic Bolling, hereby declare that Mr Laurent Garnier worked as a Disc Jockey at the Locomotive discotheque, 90 boulevard de Clichy 75018 Paris, from September 1988 to June 1989.

He carried out his job in an exemplary manner, taking his role very seriously, gracing us with his good nature and demonstrating outstanding musical creativity.

He has greatly contributed to our club and to its reputation. I am certain that in the future he will continue to enthral clients and be an asset to any club who is lucky enough to employ him.

Paris, June 1989
Frederic Bolling

Monsieur GARNIER Laurent

CERTIFICAT DE TRAVAIL

Je soussigné BOLLING Frédéric, déclare par la présente que Monsieur GARNIER Laurent, a travaillé à la LOCOMOTIVE discotheque sis au 90 BLD de Clichy 75018 PARIS, en tant que DISC-JOCKEY et
ce de SEPTEMBRE 1988 à JUIN 1989.

Il y a travaillé d'une façon exemplaire non seulement par son sérieux et ses qualités humaines
mais aussi par sa créativité musicale.

Il nous a beaucoup apporté, a contribué au renom de la LoCOMOTIVE et, continuera j'en suis sur,
à enchanter les clients et le patron qui aura le bonheur de l'employer.

Fait à paris, le 19 juin 1989.

BOLLING Frédéric,
Gérant.

42.57.37.37
R.C. PARIS B 338 706 047
SIRET 338 706 047 00010
APE 8605

LA LOCOMOTIVE - 90 Bd de Clichy, 75018 PARIS TEL. 42 55 87 39
SOCIETE A RESPONSABILITE LIMITEE AU CAPITAL DE 240.000F SIEGE SOCIAL: 12 RUE CHABANAIS, 75002 SIRET: 338706 047 00010 RC: 338 706 047

3

live the dream

I took the motorway from Paris to Calais, got on the ferry, crossed the Channel and headed north towards Cheshire. My clothes, records and decks rattled around in the boot of my Nissan as I headed up the motorway. I got off at the exit to Altrincham and passed underneath a large sign welcoming visitors to Manchester – or, in my case, welcoming me back. I went straight to my house and found the tenants had left it in a complete state. So I had a shower, a couple of hours sleep and got back in my car and headed into the centre of Manchester for my first night out there in months. After a couple of drinks at the pub, and a short walk through the city, I could already feel a change in the atmosphere. Things were not as I had left them.

In less than a year, acid-house had spread throughout the north of England. It had grown from an elite phenomenon into something global. The British music industry, known for its quick thinking, had taken on board this new style of music and made it readily available. The fashion for baggy clothes, previously confined to Manchester, could now be seen in every town. The Smiley, a round yellow face with laughing eyes and a big smile, fashionable in the 70s, had made a comeback. It was everywhere, on badges and t-shirts, as if to say: 'I'm part of it'. The music press had given acid-house extensive coverage, followed closely by trend-setting magazines like *The Face* and ID, and newspapers such as *The Sun*, who commented on the changes brought about by this music. Journalists described acid-house, with its bright colours and peaceful ideology, as the natural successor to Woodstock and the hippy movement. The underground tidal wave that had spread throughout the country was now out for all to see and nobody could pretend it wasn't happening. Words and phrases such as 'revolution', 'new generation' and 'cultural phenomenon' were being banded about. The term 'Madchester' was borrowed from the band the Happy Mondays to describe the wild goings-on in this city of excess that had regained its title as one of the capitals on the world-clubbing map.

As soon as I got back to Manchester I was taken on again at the Haçienda. The team was still the same and I was welcomed back like one of the family. On weekdays, I was put in charge of running the restaurant at the Dry Bar on Oldham Street that belonged to Tony Wilson. I only had to go a few hundred yards down the road to find a specialist record shop where I could spend all my pay. I spent every day, night, and weekend going backwards and forwards between Oldham Street and Whitworth Street West.

During the day, The Haçienda had that very distinct smell of old beer and cold cigarette smoke. Each footstep resonated on the empty dance floor. In this temple of light, monochrome by day, echoes of past parties hung in the air. I would stand there and ask myself, 'What does tonight have in store?'

Yet even if the winds of change were blowing all around, UK licensing laws remained unchanged, and clubs still had to close by 2am at the latest. The DJ only ever had four or five hours to play music, and the clubbers knew that the clock was ticking so they gorged themselves on drugs, dancing and having fun as if their life depended on it. At 2am on the dot, the Haçienda closed its doors and a couple of thousand sweaty clubbers emptied out onto the pavement and hung around in front of the club, making plans to carry on the party.

Manchester found its own solution to satisfy the hoards of frustrated clubbers. In 1988, while I was in Paris doing my military service and honing my DJ-ing skills, the arrival of ecstasy and house music had altered the nature of warehouse parties and had made way for the beginnings of raves. Completely illegal (well, that was half the fun), raves were organised in a spirit of good will and cooperation, which made them so infamous. The essence of raves was freedom: the desire to dance all night long. A group of people had thought long and hard about the problem and asked themselves: Why not think big? Why not put a sound system out in the open, in the middle of a field, and play loud music all night so everyone can enjoy it?

First, let's go back to 1988 in London. Tony Colston-Hayter, a young club promoter and playboy, had discovered acid-house at Shoom. He spotted the extraordinary financial potential that acid-house presented and went on to organise the first big raves in the UK. His first event, called Apocalypse Now, took place at Wembley Studios in August 1988. Tony invited ITN news to come and film the event. By going public, he put the backs up of all those involved in the acid-house scene and infuriated the authorities. After this first success, he organised Sunrise, but realised that the police were an obstacle to his ambition. In spite of this, he carried on organising events, and masterminded an intricate game of cat and mouse. The location of the venue was kept secret until the doors opened. The ravers had to call an info line to get directions. In October 1988, he organised a rave in Buckinghamshire. The ravers danced out in the open, surrounded by fairground rides, and discovered a young DJ from the Midlands who had moved down to Brighton, a certain Carl Cox. Thanks to Tony Colston-Hayter and his Sunrise events, the UK moved into the era of the 10,000-capacity rave.

During the second Summer of Love in 1989, the raves taking place in the north of England had not yet been transformed into huge moneymaking enterprises, and still kept their spirit of one-off parties. Thousands of people gathered in one place, having got the information from a very basic flyer (just the name of the party and the date and no mention of any DJ's names) handed out after the clubs closed. An army of DJs played one after the other in no particular order, slamming music out of the immense speakers plonked on the ground. They played everything: acid-house, house, techno, hip-house (a hybrid of hip-hop and house) and chart hits, surrounded by a battery of lights that were bright enough to draw in space ships. When they were not dancing, the ravers threw themselves onto bouncy castles or huddled on the fairground rides. As time went by and a structured network began to take shape, raves became less and less spontaneous. The most elaborate events boasted security staff, bars and food stands.

In Manchester in 1989, the meeting place for ravers was often a motorway service station. From here, an endless stream of cars followed each other for hours on end through the countryside; a giant traffic jam at 4am on a cold, foggy morning, which for anybody watching was an extraordinary sight.

Whichever way you drive out of Manchester you are in the middle of nowhere within 15 minutes. All around are fields and hills and … but wait! Over there! What's that? … a party … a fucking huge party!

It's no exaggeration to say that the first rave I ever went to in the UK was a massive shock to the system. Joy. The rave was called Joy. That night, in August 1989, changed my conception of partying forever. It was a complete nightmare to get there. Dani and I spent over two hours stuck in traffic and getting lost down muddy tracks looking for the rave. All we had for directions was a flyer. We finally pulled up on the brow of a hill. It was pitch black outside, but down below was a green fog through which we could make out hundreds of parked cars. I caught sight of the silhouette of a couple of ravers making their way through the dark down a steep path. We followed them until we found ourselves in a deep valley. From there we could make out the unmistakeable sound of huge speakers that screamed:

booooooooooooom!

My eyes lit up, my throat went dry and my hair stood on end. Everything was saturated in colourful light. It was as if we were being sucked in. I could feel my skin tingle as the ecstasy rushed through my body, travelling from the tips of my toes to the top of my head. I let out a 'Huuuuuuuuum. Aaaaaaaaargh. Pfouuuuuuuuh. Ohlalalalalala. Ffwwwoouuuaaaarrrhhhhh.' And then I realised that the green fog was nothing to do with the two 'magic pills' that Dani and I had taken. 'Fuck mate, look at that laser!'

The organisers of Joy had rented the same sound system as U2 for their recent concert at Wembley Arena. At about six in the morning as the sun came up and rays of light began to light up the ravers' faces, one of the DJs played Why? by Carly Simon. At that moment, an engine could be heard in the distance and as the sound got closer, an aeroplane appeared through the clouds just a few hundred feet above our outstretched arms. It seemed to slow down for a moment to salute us and then disappeared.

Would Carly Simon ever know the power of her song? That thousands of ravers shouted and screamed every time it was played? Would she know that from that moment on, in the north, it was impossible to end a rave without her song, Why?, being played as a last goodbye?

After Joy and the explosion in 1989 of the second Summer of Love, raves were taking place every weekend. We knew that we were part of something new, but we were unaware of its impact. Our heads were not straight enough and we did not have the necessary distance to realise that this was a nationwide phenomenon, and that it was not the first time something like this had happened. A similar fervour had taken hold but in another place and at another time, a whole generation ago. As they say, history repeats itself in a 'cycle of 30' years. Raves and acid-house were the natural heirs of northern soul. An invisible thread linked two generations from the 50s and 60s to the 80s and 90s. It was a renaissance, an echo in time.

But before telling this part of the story, it first needs to be put into its historical context. Manchester was the first city in the UK to embrace the Industrial Revolution. In fact, by the middle of the 19th century, Manchester was one of the most prosperous cities in the world. Factories lined the outskirts of the city, and between 1820 and 1830 over 800 warehouses were built to store and manufacture cotton. It was a golden age. The north of England, with its successful commerce, was able to liberate itself from London's dominance.

A different England was developing in the north, and its cities were thriving on this new economy. Liverpool became a major port, where cotton arrived from America and slaves passed through from Africa. Sheffield became a leader in iron production, Birmingham centred upon engineering, and Manchester and the county of Cheshire boasted 90 per cent of the world's cotton manufacturing.

As these industries developed, an influx of migrant workers from Ireland and the UK's poorer rural areas considerably increased Manchester's population. Thousands of new houses were built to cater for an ever-growing demand. In time, thick smog hung over the city and the walls were covered in soot. Young men clocked in at the same factory as their elder brothers, fathers and uncles. And all these people needed some kind of entertainment. So, Manchester spawned its own nightlife scene, fuelled by alcohol and colourful local characters. But soon it was not enough to just go out at the weekend, and, with the arrival of cinema at the turn of the century, about a hundred picture houses opened all over the county, coinciding with an influx of new music.

The first black American jazz bands came to the Rainy City in the 1920s. Manchester became an El Dorado for jazz artists, free from racism and harassment and the poor conditions back home. To satisfy the ever-increasing demand, new concert venues were built to house this new music from America, and it generated a dance music culture that developed into a huge craze. Nightlife became the city's new attraction.

In 1930, industry in the north started to stagnate, as Manchester was hit by the recession. The cityscape changed. Factories were abandoned, and deserted warehouses were commonplace. In 1948, the Rainy City was looking to the future with the creation of Manchester Mark 1 (the first electronic computer with an index register), and the area of Moss Side developed into a playground for partygoers, with its bars and night-clubs. By the middle of the 1950s, R'n'B records were being imported from the US in enormous quantities to satisfy an ever-growing demand from the working-class kids who worshipped soul music and spent their whole week's pay in one weekend.

By 1960, Manchester's youth were enjoying some economic wealth. Manchester boasted one of the most vibrant nightlife scenes in the country. Beatnik coffee shops were the nucleus of social and intellectual life, and clubs such as the Twisted Wheel, the Plaza and the Oasis played host to the city's nightlife. The music was also changing, and the kids were turning their backs on American jazz in pursuit of something harder, funkier and wilder. While the clubs played chart hits – the Shadows, Cliff Richard and the Beatles – a group of DJs broke away in search of something else. Thanks to them, Afro-American music became the word in the north. Elvis, Nashville and the white American dream took a back seat. The Stones and the Beatles could be heard blaring out of radios, but were inconsequential as people headed out for a weekend of serious dancing.

Rock was now the predominant musical style, but in Manchester people were going wild about rare soul tracks recorded almost a decade before. In the white working-class suburbs, people were dancing in over-heated venues to singles recorded in the 60s by mostly forgotten black artists. The 1970s was already experiencing its own retro movement! This movement had a name: 'northern soul'; black soul music from America, idolised by the youth of the north of England.

▶ Playlist

NORTHERN SOUL

Don Thomas
Come On Train

Robert Parker
Let's Go Baby

Clarence Murray
Don't Talk Like That

Jackie Lee
Would You Believe

Big Al Downing
Medley Of Soul

Gloria Jones
Tainted Love

R. Dean Taylor
There's A Ghost In My House

Edwin Starr
Agent Double-O-Soul

Several clubs were at the heart of the northern soul movement, and just the mention of their names conjures up images of legendary nights: the Twisted Wheel in Manchester, the Mecca in Blackpool, the Casino in Wigan, the Torch, the Catacombs, etc.... These are the clubs that made northern soul legendary. Northern soul pushed things to new limits and made new demands on DJs, forcing them to redefine their art. It was no longer good enough just to pick out and play any old funk track. The music had to be raw-edged, sexy and powerful, and literally sweep you off your feet.

On top of this, tracks had to be rare. Rarity became the ultimate criteria, and brought with it a series of specific demands. Whereas at first the public appreciated a DJ because he rocked the dance floor, he was now being judged on his ability to source and play rare tracks. As a result, northern soul DJs spent a lot of time hunting down rare white labels and previously unheard of music. A story went round about a Jamaican DJ in London called Count Suckle who was the first to import 'cover-ups'. This involved ripping off the stickers in the middle of the record so that the public and other DJs couldn't identify them. DJ Farmer Carl Dean did this with northern soul tracks. Soon every DJ was trying to keep ahead of the game and find new ways to keep the identity of his records secret. It was at this time that the first bootlegs appeared, alongside a wide range of other inventions that included faking the recording's reference number.

Via the northern soul movement, DJs instigated a craze for the secrecy, excess, dancing, very loud music in the clubs, and rare records that were shared among like-minded enthusiasts fleeing the mainstream. Every weekend, hundreds of people travelled for miles along England's outdated road system (there were no motorways in the 50s) just to party. Thus, northern soul invented the spirit of rave. Its followers went all out. A whole generation after northern soul, Manchester would experience a second revolution – house music – and with this, the north continued to cultivate that same fervour.

I only played at the Haçienda once a week on a Saturday – the rest of my time was spent either working at the Dry Bar or partying. Paul Cons wanted to replicate its success at other clubs and so entrusted me with a new night he was organising in Blackpool, a seaside town situated about 40 miles north of Manchester. Blackpool's youth lived in an environment overshadowed by unemployment, drugs and depression. This was England's unglamorous equivalent to Cannes, strewn with derelict funfairs and amusement arcades. Nothing much had happened there since northern soul fever, and in the 60s a Rolling Stones concert caused a riot.

But during that summer in 1989, a night out in Blackpool promised something different, another world, and was incredibly exciting. The crowd that gathered at the entrance of Frenzy included people who had travelled over 100 miles to get there. Once inside the venue, a former cinema, they raced against time to have as much fun as they could, dancing and taking drugs. The number of ecstasy pills taken at those parties was frightening. People were desperate to get the most out of their time there and, once inside, they got stuck in.

I teamed up with Steve Williams, a DJ from the Thunderdome events organised by the Spin Masters (part of 808 State). They were considered to be the underground alternative to the almighty Haçienda. From 10.30pm to 1.50am, we carefully built the atmosphere and the tempo of the music until people were ready to explode. Ten minutes before the end, we played big classics, sending the crowd wild. Sometimes it reached such a point of hysteria that we could have played anything and people would still have hung off the lights and blown foghorns until they collapsed with exhaustion. Yet they always managed to keep going for the final push. As they reached their arms in the air, condensation dripped from the ceiling… then 2am struck and the music stopped. The crowd stood with tears in their eyes clapping for about 15 minutes, begging us to play one last record. I had witnessed real madness that night in Blackpool, but there was more to come when a certain Mike Knowler invited me to play in his Liverpool club.

In 1989, Liverpool was the perfect illustration of an industrial city that had been hit hard by unemployment. It was very different from the picture-postcard image of the Beatles era. The only thing young people had to look forward to was going out, and the only thing they had to be proud of was their reputation for being hardcore partygoers.

Liverpool was home to the club Quadrant Park, a 2,500-capacity venue whose reputation for excess was legendary throughout the north. It also had a reputation for being dangerous, but, if anything, this only added to the excitement. At the end of my first night at Quadrant Park, I saw the bouncers throwing someone off the first-floor balcony. He landed in the middle of the dance floor, 12 feet below. I later found out that the guy in question had tried to stab one of them in the stomach with a broken bottle. The bouncers didn't hesitate. They got hold of him, threw him over the balcony and then gave him a good beating once he'd landed on the dance floor. One of the bouncers tried to explain to me, 'The problem is, if we don't come down hard on him now, tomorrow he'll be back here to shoot us!' Although Liverpool seemed like quite an edgy place at that time, as a DJ, playing at Quadrant Park was a unique experience.

▸ Playlist

FRENZY

The Doc
Portrait Of A Masterpiece

Orange Lemon
Dreams Of Santa Anna

Slaughterhouse
The Funky Ginger

Heavy D & The Boyz
We Got Our Own Thang

The Back Room
Definition Of A Track

E-Zee Possee
Everything Starts With An E

Stetsasonics
Talking All That Jazz

Mister Fingers
I Have A Dream

I remember playing a track there by Elevation and seeing the crowd almost spontaneously combust. Even the sound of their foghorns couldn't drown out their hysteria. A packed-out Wembley stadium couldn't make as much noise as the 2,500 people inside that club. When the crowd went for it there was a real sense of coming together; it was mind-blowing to watch them. From the DJ booth, you could see guys diving off the first-floor balcony into a sea of people below, girls dancing in just their bras, and hundreds of bare-chested people rubbing up against one another while their shouts of joy drowned out the music.

In 1989, to make it as a DJ you had to stand out. I was honing my own style, drawing on my experience in Paris, Manchester, Liverpool and Blackpool. English DJs were mainly playing British techno and piano tunes, but I preferred to play a mix of new beat, techno and ghetto house from Chicago – a mix of minimal funky house with sexually charged lyrics. In France, I played to a predominantly gay crowd who went wild for the 'Fuck me, fuck me, till I start to scream' lyrics. But in England it was a different story. When I first played those kinds of tracks, the crowd stopped dancing. But, despite being a bit prudish at first, the British soon found their sense of humour and would laugh at records with words like, 'Slap your ass and move … bitch!' The biggest risk was to play 666 by Demis Roussos and Vangelis' band Aphrodite's Child at Quadrant Park. It sounded like the Greek actress Irene Papas was having sex with the devil. I remember being really scared of this record when I was a child, 666 being the number of the devil … At Quadrant Park, playing records like 666 helped me make a reputation for myself as a European DJ in the UK. My name started to get known, and I got more and more bookings at clubs and raves.

Summer '89. The second Summer of Love was in full swing, raves were happening all over the place. I was approached by a promoter to play at a rave in September, about 25 miles outside of Manchester, somewhere off the motorway. Once I had finished my Saturday night DJ slot at the Haçienda, I hooked up with Steve Williams, and we headed for the rave, following the directions on the flyer. We pulled into a layby where a circus tent had been erected. The sound system was loud enough to wake the dead. We made our way past the queue, said hello to the organisers, bouncers, and a couple of people we knew and made our way inside the tent. There, right in the middle of it, among the gyrating bodies of hundreds of people dancing, stood a gigantic polystyrene cut-out letter 'E'.

The party had already been going for several hours. Steve played his set and then handed over to me. The decks were just balanced on a trestle table on the dance floor, inches away from 800 hardcore ravers. The hours flew by, and there I was dancing bare-chested behind the decks, screaming like a lunatic, when suddenly the police stormed in. They seemed to be heading straight for me. As shouts of 'The party's over!' could be heard over the loudspeakers, a police officer shone a torch in my face as if to point out the culprit responsible for this mayhem. He told me to stop the music; there was no way I was going to argue. Then a senior police officer took me aside and said, 'Who is the organiser? Who is the fucking organiser?' I tried to explain that I was playing for free for a promoter that I had never even met before, but before I could finish he gestured to a colleague, 'Book him … now!'

This was my first ever experience of a raid, and it was good and proper. There were dogs, walkie-talkies, flashing blue lights, the works. Once they had taken off my belt, my watch and my laces, I was thrown into a cell for the night. I was coming up on ecstasy, and was by then completely off my face. Steve Williams was locked in the cell next to mine. He squeezed his head up against the bars and kept laughing and mumbling, 'Hey, I'm off my face man. I'm rushing!' A few hours went by and then a police officer came to take each of us in turn to a soundproofed interview room with a cliché one-way mirror. It was time for questioning. I was completely out of it and couldn't stop laughing at the detectives who were trying to conduct the interview, when in walked the chief superintendent. He stood in front of me, looked at me hard, and asked me very seriously, 'What was that letter E in the middle of the dance floor?' I took a deep breath and tried to come up with an acceptable explanation that would get me out of there. 'It was Eric's birthday,' I said. The superintendent tried to remain calm, patient and understanding, but I could tell he was ready to explode, 'It was what?'. 'Yeah, yesterday it was Eric's birthday.'

I had missed the first Summer of Love because I was doing my National Service. I lived the summer of '89 to the full. But I knew deep down that as long as I remained in the UK I would always be regarded as an exotic creature. I decided to go back to France where I knew that, even though I would have to fight 10 times harder to get my music heard, I could make something for myself. And I was sure that, by doing this, I would become more than just an exiled 'froggy DJ' for the British. The plan seemed simple enough, but putting it into action was going to be another story. First, I was going to have to stop working in restaurants to be able to devote myself 100 per cent to DJ-ing. I made a couple of phone calls to the Palace and the Locomotive and was welcomed back with open arms: 'Yeah, you can come back and play your shit music if you like!'

I only had a few days left in Manchester, just enough time to pack my stuff, say my goodbyes and go mental one last time … My brother,

Thierry, came over from Paris in his pre-war van to help me take back all my belongings.

It was a Saturday night, my last night DJ-ing at the Haçienda. At two in the morning, about 15 of us climbed into the back of Thierry's clapped-out van and set off to a rave called Live the Dream, guaranteed to be one of the highlights of the second Summer of Love. The inside of the van was a fog of sweat and spliff smoke. We soldiered on, on yet another two-hour magical mystery tour, to try and find the rave (we went the wrong way, got lost, turned around, then again ...) and made it at last to the 'final frontier', where we could make out the shapes of thousands of ravers, a couple of tents, and the groan of several different sound systems. We all piled out of the van, already in an advanced state of debauchery, and stumbled through the countryside. Steve Williams and I headed straight for one of the tents where we were supposed to be DJ-ing. My brother, who I had left with a few scally friends of mine, was experimenting with every new drug under the sun. Having swallowed a cocktail of acid and ecstasy, he experienced the most mind-boggling trip of his whole life, a sort of Alice in acid wonderland.

As the sun came up, the heavens opened and it poured with rain. Drugged-up ravers, soaking wet and covered in mud, were running wild round the site, trying to leap up and touch the hot-air balloons that were sailing up through the dawn sky. My brother was floating somewhere between the hot-air balloons and the grassy meadows, his last two functioning neurones having been zapped by the rain, damp grass and dawn light.

Suddenly, out of one of the enormous speakers came Why? by Carly Simon. The wind seemed to carry her question right across the fields, up into the universe and straight into my brain. 'Why ... oh why ... tell me please, Carly, why do I really want to go back to Paris?'

4

got the bug

On the day I got back to Paris at the end of September 1989, I made the decision never to go back to being a waiter again. At that time in France, DJs were generally regarded as night-time employees. It was still very difficult to find enough regular work to make a decent living. As soon as I was back in town, I went straight to the Locomotive. They put me in charge of the music for their Saturday rock night. I also went back to working at the Gay Tea Dance parties at the Palace on Sunday afternoons. Philippe Corti, recently appointed creative director at the Palace, had been entrusted with the job of trying to restore some of the past greatness that had given the club its name. Nightlife in the 80s had been all about money, sex and celebrity, but things had changed, and Corti had to be inventive and create new concepts on a tighter budget.

Philippe Corti was a legendary shaker and mover. He was a DJ, promoter and influencer. He had been responsible for organising the wildest parties in the south of France since the early 80s. Wherever he went, his reputation as a party animal preceded him. His party tricks included being able to scratch records with his penis, organise waltzing contests in the middle of a night, and be thrown head first out of nightclubs. Corti was a believer in the 'out for a laugh' brand of DJ-ing. He was the kind of person to kick a DJ off the decks if he felt 'this ain't fun'. Once, during the highly respected DMC mixing championships at the Arènes de Nîmes, he took to the decks, pulled out a single by the deceased French pop star Claude François, put it on and turned up the volume. The audience was dumbstruck. When Philippe Corti was appointed creative director at the Palace in 1989, it was a turning point in the club's history. As, aside from the Gay Tea Dance every Sunday (the Pyramid parties were long forgotten), there were no other exciting or risqué events happening at the club.

Corti came to see me to offer me the job of resident DJ at the Palace alongside a young hip-hop DJ, David Guetta. David had instigated a hip-hop night called Unity at the Rex club alongside Sydney, another renowned hip-hop DJ. Guetta had a unique talent that enabled him to be part of an ever-growing hip-hop movement, while simultaneously nurturing his love for all that sparkles. We worked together behind the decks at the Palace and played everything from Fight The Power by Public Enemy to Promised Land by Joe Smooth. It was November 1989. The club started to regain its popularity, attracting a crowd of gay and straight men and women, and a generous sprinkling of celebrities and starlets. But the magical atmosphere of the past had vanished.

I was determined not to lose touch with what was going on in the UK and to keep up my residencies on the other side of the Channel. So every

Repérages

Philippe Corti au Palace

[Photo François Dymont.]

Philippe Corti, le disc-jockey vedette du Papagayo, le club de Saint-Tropez, vient de signer un contrat avec le Palace pour animer chaque jeudi, vendredi, samedi et dimanche des Corti's Folies. Première ce soir.

Friday morning, just as the Palace was about to close, I would grab the microphone and shout out to the 10 or so people left in the club, 'I've got my car outside, and my records. I'm heading for the UK in 10 minutes. Who wants to come?'

More often that not, three drunken strangers would stumble into the back seat of my ravemobile and I would set off once again for the UK, happy to drive the 500 miles to get there. First stop; first gig: Portsmouth on the Friday night. Straight after the gig, without a wink of sleep, I would head up to Manchester. Same thing all over again. On Sunday morning, while listening to the recording of my set from the previous night, we would drive up to Liverpool for the final stint at Quadrant Park. On Sunday evening, completely shattered, our t-shirts stained with sweat and beer, our hair glued to our heads with a mixture of sweat, cigarette smoke and other unidentified chemical substances, we would clamber back into my car littered with crisp packets, drink cans and cigarette butts, and drive all the way back to Paris, via the Hovercraft. I kept up this gruelling routine for the next four years or so.

Since I had been away on National Service, a house music scene of sorts had taken shape in Paris. One of the first to openly support dance music was an associative gay radio station called FG 98.2, run by Henri Maurel, which was broadcast throughout Paris. As house music was played mainly in gay clubs, it seemed logical that it would filter through into the radio programmes scheduled on the station formerly known as Frequence-Gay. This was thanks to the likes of some of the pioneers of house music in Paris such as Guillaume La Tortue, Jerome Pacman and Saul Russo (alias Doctor Beat) who ran a record shop called BPM. In 1990, Radio FG's programmes were aimed at a gay audience. There were debates, explicit call-in talk shows, as well as programmes on art, literature and contemporary culture. Musically, the station didn't have one clear directive – they played a bit of everything (indie, rock, disco, house); it was all for fun.

Another early supporter of house and techno was Radio Nova. For over a decade, this Parisian radio station had been a staunch defender of the avant-garde, more than any other French media. Radio Nova was started in 1981 by Jean-François Bizot as a laboratory for innovation, fuelled by his own creative vision. Nova uncovered new sounds and styles, with a particular penchant for soul and black music, playing the latest records, encouraging eclecticism and offering a platform for new urban trends. Nova was a world of its own. Let's not forget that it was from the very same offices at number 33 rue du Faubourg Saint Antoine that Bizot had launched the magazine *Actuel*. The arrival of *Actuel* was a bombshell to the French press. It introduced several generations of readers to the notions of gonzo journalism and modern-day tribes.

Through *Actuel*, Bizot had succeeded in redefining the nature of a magazine. Radio Nova was *Actuel*'s on-air counterpart. Following its creator's impulse, and taking inspiration from the street, Nova upheld a policy of cultural excellence that was perceived by some as fashionable elitism. Nova became a place for experimentation and was open to everything new. It played an important role for an entire generation when other national radio stations simply pandered to young people's tastes. Nova welcomed into its studios those who were at the forefront of creativity. You could tell that this was no ordinary radio station just by the atmosphere within the studio. The people who worked at the station were not your average nine to five office workers. Oh no. This was a place where energy was generated and shared. This was a place that had neither obligations nor censorship. The people lucky enough to work for Nova were expected to give their all, and in exchange, they benefited from unlimited freedom of expression.

The first time I set foot inside Radio Nova, I was invited by Loïk Dury, the music programmer. He was a true man of radio, culture vulture and nightlife aficionado. He was also a huge fan of all styles of black music. Loïk was very interested in house music and played it on the radio. He invited me to come in and mix. I liked the feel of the Nova family. They didn't look anything like the slick media types that you often come across at radio stations. Here, culture didn't take a back seat; it was considered something worth fighting for. I met so many people there with true passion and profound cultural knowledge. People such as Remy Kolpa Kopoul, a human encyclopedia of jazz, Brazilian and Latino music; Bintou Simporé, the leading lady of world music in Paris, DJ Gilb'R the magnificent, Ariel Wizman the agitator, Dee Nasty the godfather of French hip-hop, Lord Zeljko the reggae pioneer … my first invitation from Loïk Dury developed into a weekly residency. The name of my show was Paradise Garage. The concept? Carte blanche.

One evening, a rather drunk man staggered into the studio. He had a wild look in his eye, a cigarette in his mouth, his clothes were dishevelled and his hair all over the place. He stood staring at me without saying a word. I carried on with my show and took hold of the microphone to announce the record I was playing, when I heard someone grumbling from just behind me, 'You don't know how to speak on air. What a load of shit. You'll have to learn.' And that was the first time I ever met Jean-François Bizot, a living, breathing, rock 'n' roll Encyclopedia Britannica, if that exists. Over the next few years I would move back and forth between different radio stations in the capital, but I will always consider Nova to be my true home, in honour of the spirit of Jean-François and his team.

In 1990, Eric Hautville and Joachim Garraud (who, 10 years down the line, would write several hits with David Guetta) went one step further to getting dance music onto the airwaves by launching a 100 per cent dance music radio station called Maxximum. With substantial financial backing, this Parisian radio station exclusively broadcast dance music from pioneers such as LFO and Orbital to the more commercial sounds of Adeva and Blackbox. I was given my own show on Saturday night entitled Rave Max, which consisted of four hours of the latest house and techno. I recorded the show at home on a Revox tape-to-tape, and stuck to the simple rule of never playing the same record twice.

As a result of the increasing amount of dance music being played in the clubs and on the radio, the demand for house music grew bigger, and now most dance music being produced worldwide was readily available to us via a network of independent record shops in Paris: BPM, USA Imports, Danceteria and TSF. Meanwhile, two journalists, Didier Lestrade (*Libération* newspaper and *Gai Pied* magazine) and Vincent Borel (*Actuel*), were increasing the visibility of dance music and drawing in a wider public by writing in-depth articles on dance music culture.

I still had my residencies at the Locomotive and at the Palace, which guaranteed my place on the Parisian nightlife scene, but it was no longer enough. What I really wanted was to have my own night. Not another residency, but a night where I could have total freedom to do what I wanted and develop a real relationship with a crowd and create a family. Doing your own night is a bit like having friends over for dinner, just sweatier. You carefully prepare everything in advance, hoping to please your guests. Inevitably, you also have to be prepared to lose money if you want to do things properly, as everything costs money, whether it be inviting a DJ from abroad, giving out mix tapes or renting the sound system and the lights. The problem isn't really finding the right place to do it, but finding the right club owner who is willing to take the risk. I have always preferred to work with people who have been willing to lose money in order to build something bigger and better. In the end, everyone is happy. If there is one thing that the public appreciates, it is that the event they are part of is genuinely authentic.

And me, what do I get out of it? Loyalty, trust and love. Music aside, this is the true motivation for any DJ. It's something that money can't buy.

I had a very clear idea of the kind of night I wanted to create. I wanted it to be like a UK night, along the same lines as those I had experienced in

Manchester. Saul Russo, the owner of BPM, put me in touch with a very small gay club just up the road from his record shop on the rue Keller, called La Luna. I decided to go along and found myself inside a small, dark, two-storey venue with low ceilings, packed with gyrating men. At a squeeze, the downstairs room could probably hold about 150 very slim people. It was exactly the kind of venue that I was looking for. I introduced myself to the boss, Christian Vannier, and persuaded him to let me have a trial run the following Wednesday. I decided my night would be called Trax. Flyers were handed out in all the record shops and bars in the Marais.

The first Trax night took place on November 30, 1989 and drew in La Luna's regular gay crowd. Soon the night also began to attract a group of straight English students, both men and women, who quickly became regulars. Among them was a discreet young English student with an inimitable hip wiggle who would one day be my wife. Trax offered a unique formula: an English-style club in Paris. Word got around and the night took off. Guest DJs included the Mancunians Jon Dasilva, Graeme Park and Steve Williams. The Happy Mondays organised their after-show party at Trax, and groups such as Candy Flip, Man Machine and Dream Frequency played live gigs there. Throughout the night, graffiti artists and performers had free reign to do what they liked on the walls of the club and on the dance floor.

I spent every weekend in Liverpool or Manchester, where I was also able to promote my night with the help of DJ friends who agreed to come over and play, and encouraged ravers to make the trip over too. Needless to say, the size of La Luna's reputation was out of kilter with the capacity of the club. The ravers who turned up at rue Keller expected to find a club that could hold 2,000 people. Once, I even overheard someone say, 'Ok, so this is the entrance but where is the actual club? Well, this is it.' That's what made La Luna so special.

What happened next as a result of my night Trax had a domino effect. It was at La Luna that I met the very influential fashion photographer, Jean-Claude Lagreze. He was a disciple of Suzanne Bartsche, empress of the New York drag queens. Inspired by Suzanne Bartsche's wild happenings, Jean-Claude Lagreze introduced Paris nightlife to the New York phenomenon of gogo dancers and drag queens by launching his own night at the Locomotive called French Kiss. Guillaume La Tortue and I were the DJs at these wild parties put on by Lagreze. On the first night, an extravagant and deliberately shocking performance unfolded in front of a cool crowd of fashion types, gays and trendsetters, as well as the odd confused-looking rocker. Jean-Claude Lagreze then decided to take

▶ Playlist

LA LUNA
Homeboy Hippy & Funky Dread
Total Confusion

S.H.I.E.L.A.
Mr Policeman

Man Machine
Man Machine

Shades Of Rhythm
Sweet Sensations

Ce Ce Rogers
Someday

Dream Frequency
Live The Dream

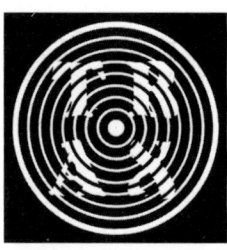

TRAX DERNIERE
Jeudi 12 JUILLET 23 H
EN CONCERT EXCEPTIONNEL

DREAM FREQUENCY
(LIVE THE DREAM)

D.J. : LAURENT GARNIER

Entrée 30 F avec présentation de ce carton.

LA LUNA
26, rue Keller Paris - Bastille

the concept of his night and transport it to the Baia Imperiale in Rimini. Thanks to him, I found myself back in the place of my childhood dreams! The lasers, I Feel Love, the Marilyn stickers that I had stuck everywhere… the Baia had been the first club ever to have made the hairs on the back of my neck stand on end. But nostalgia has a tendency to exaggerate feelings, and once I was actually there I realised that this club represented everything that I hated: a club with chandeliers and people dressed up to the nines…

It was during the French Kiss night at the Baia that I met Fred Dumelie, the boss of the An-fer Club in Dijon. He wanted to revamp his rock club and so asked me to come and DJ. I accepted. I arrived in Dijon in June 1990 and discovered the two different floors of the An-fer club. On the first floor was a dance floor the same size as the Rex, while upstairs was a much smaller room, away from the commotion. I quickly got to know the staff, including the lighting guy, Tonio, who would later become a techno DJ. That night I played my records and made no concessions. The public were very sceptical and stood holding their beers while requesting U2 and the Cure. Within the first hour the crowd had gone from 800 people right down to 100 or so. The only people left were a handful of curious clients. It was a flop. Fred came to find me, apologetically, 'So?' I was a bit pissed and replied, 'I'll do it every month if you like!' I would go back to the An-fer once a month for the next five years.

Back in Paris, Trax had been a very popular night. When a party has got to the point where it has achieved what it set out to do and kept its promise, it is time to stop. Trax played its last night in July 1990. Soon after, I left straight for Ibiza for the first time ever to join DJ Sasha at the Re-Live the Dream rave. The headliners were 808 State. They were a group from Manchester, founded by the visionary Gerald Simpson (A Guy Called Gerald), Martin Price (owner of the record shop Eastern Bloc and the label Creed) and Graham Massey. In the summer of 1990, 808 State were surfing the wave of their huge hit Pacific State.

The vague memories that I still have of that trip to Ibiza have blurred into one giant hangover. Four days, head down, raves, beaches, clubs. The second Summer of Love was not far behind us and the sweet smell of acid-house was still very much present. Ibiza was overrun with hoards of English clubbers desperate to experience the Ibiza they had heard so much about: the party island.

When I got back, it was time to take stock. With one booking leading to another (the domino effect), in the space of one year I had achieved my goal: to make a living from DJ-ing, to create my own night and to be an active player in the development of the dance music scene in Paris. As far as I was concerned, DJ-ing came before everything. There was no room (and no time!) for anything else. Yet, in spite of night after night spent DJ-ing, in spite of my hectic private life (in no particular order: my love life, friends and family), in spite of the miniscule sums of money that I was earning, in spite of the state of my flat jam-packed with records, in spite of my poor diet of macaroni cheese, and in spite of zero sleep, I was happy! What could a 24-year-old want more than doing what he loves most and watching his life take shape? Nothing! Hey, my child-hood dream was coming true! In three years I had gone from being a footman to being a DJ playing five nights a week. You soon get used to all the rest; the fragmented social life; the constant feeling of being in a different time zone to everyone else. At seven in the morning, walking out of a club after a full night's work, I'd look at people heading off to another day in their office job that they couldn't give a shit about and think, 'Hey guys, I'm off to bed!'. I was even able to brush off any con-cerns expressed by my family about my choice of career as I was now financially in-de-pen-dent! No mum, it wasn't just a phase!

I threw myself head first into this newly acquired freedom, and those around me just had to put up or shut up. I was a cocky little sod and was often heard saying, 'They'll just have to get used to it.' That is, until I met my wife-to-be. It was only then that I realised that love cannot grow with such a narrow view of life. It takes a good deal of self-sacri-fice to be a part of a DJ's life. The women and men who have been in this situation know exactly what I am talking about. A DJ is never there at the weekends and always works on public holidays. A DJ's apartment is packed full of records. Their hours are terrible, unless of course you like being woken up at 7am by someone stumbling in, stinking of cigarettes and telling you he loves you. I thought that this predicament must be the same for any night worker, I don't know, barmen, bouncers, truck drivers …? But then again I've never met a truck driver who finishes his shift at 6am, arms in the air, drunk on tequila, playing Can You Feel It in front of a crowd of screaming gay men, people on ecstasy, and doe-eyed girls smiling at them … Everything is there on offer to tempt a DJ and it's sometimes difficult to avoid nightmare situations.

One night at La Luna, a guy came up to me: 'My name's Maurice. I organise parties in New York. Everyone knows me there. You must come.' And I said, 'Yes.' Like every other European DJ at the time, I dreamt of going to New York. There are so many legendary stories about New York that DJs know of, so many not-so-distant memories that people love to share with us: Larry Levan and Paradise Garage, David Mancuso and The Loft, and the origins of New York disco nightlife. Everything happened quite quickly. I left for New York with the intention of playing at three parties. I paid for my flight. Maurice said he would pay me back once I got there. I was young and naïve and didn't see it coming.

I landed at Kennedy airport and no one was there to meet me. I called Maurice. He was still in bed. 'Oh yeah, I partied last night, you woke me up, damn it. Right, well don't move, I'm coming to get ya.' I waited nervously for two hours at the airport, sitting on my record box. Finally Maurice turned up, looking like shit. 'Listen man, I didn't get you a hotel. You can come and sleep at mine. It'll be cool.' We got into a taxi and headed for Greenwich Village. He pointed to his building and showed me my room, which was the size of a cupboard and was infested with cockroaches. It also stank of drains. I said to him, 'Listen Maurice, I don't mind sleeping at your place tonight but tomorrow you've got to get me a hotel.' He muttered, 'Don't worry, it'll be cool. The parties are going to be great. By the way, could you lend me a bit of money? I have to pay for the posters. I'll pay you back, don't worry ...'

I thought this was odd but the day went by and we hung out in Soho ... he still hadn't reimbursed me for my plane ticket. My money was running out, and by that evening I had nothing left. Maurice acted as if nothing was up, 'Tonight, there's a party, we'll do some promotion there. It's cool ...' But it wasn't cool. That night we walked to a club in Manhattan and stood outside for ages. The doorman stood holding the rope looking at the crowd. He picked whoever he felt like out of the crowd and let them in. He purposely overlooked people who had been standing there for hours in the freezing cold and let in whoever he wanted with a supercilious nod of the head ... how ridiculous! Several hours went by and I was beginning to get the feeling that Maurice didn't really know anyone in New York. By some miracle, we eventually got into the club and then it all became clear. Maurice knew no one and there were no flyers and no posters announcing our party. There was a surreal performance taking place on stage. A group of actors dressed in 17th-century costumes were acting out a scene from Peter Greenaway's *The Draughtsman's Contract*.

We wandered around the club for about two hours before going back to Maurice's shitty apartment. When I woke up the next morning I found him rifling through my bag. I realised that Maurice was a complete liar and a cocaine addict to boot. When it finally came time to go and DJ, I found myself at Nell's playing in front of a crowd of no more than 30 people. I was bored out of my brains, when a young bald guy came up and started talking to me. His name was Moby and he had his own record label, Instinct Records. His single, Go, was a hit in Europe. Moby stayed all night at the club and invited me to visit his studio the following day. We left the club at dawn as good friends, and I went to spend the night in a hotel, paid for by me. I couldn't bear another night at Maurice's.

The following day, things didn't look much better. Another party was planned that night at Nick's Groove. I got to the club at 10pm to be told that the party had been cancelled. Big problem. Maurice was avoiding me and there was no sign of my money or my return ticket. I thought that this kind of asshole only existed in a bad movie. There was still a third party to go to at a club called the Red Zone, a huge club that held at least 2,000 people. I couldn't work out how a loser like Maurice had managed to get me into such a big venue; in fact, I didn't really want to know. I was just hoping that party would be a success and everything else would just become a bad memory.

On the night of the party there were more DJs in the DJ booth than people on the dance floor. There were probably about six people there. Moby was there again. The owners of the club put a stop to the party at 2am. I began to look everywhere for Maurice. I was not the only one looking for him, the other DJs and the club owner also wanted to get hold of him. But surprise, surprise, Maurice had disappeared.

I found myself out on the street, alone, sitting on my box of records with my suitcase and no money and no ticket to get back home. I was fucked. I was already imagining the worst-case scenario, being attacked and robbed by a gang, who would leave me for dead on the pavement to be finished off by a pack of wild dogs ... Then I saw a guy looking at me from the other side of the road. I held my breath. The guy came up to me, smiling and told me that he was in the club ('Oh really, I didn't see you.'). He realised the situation I was in and offered to put me up for the night and lend me the money to buy a ticket to get back to Paris. That guy saved my life. The least I can do is to dedicate a few lines to him as a way of a thank you.

I got back from New York completely broke. Everyone asked me how it went, 'It was shit! I got taken for a ride by a complete asshole. I'll never set foot in that s***hole of a city again ... ' But at least I had learnt the rule of survival for a DJ: never go anywhere without first booking your return ticket and a hotel, and always have money in your pocket.

With the help of Jean-Claude Lagreze, my different DJ residencies, and the growing reputation of La Luna, I was getting more and more work, inside and outside the traditional club circuit. For example, I was booked to play at Elton John's birthday party at the Pré-Catalan and to open for Deee Lite's concert in Paris. Deee Lite were topping the international charts with their song Groove Is In The Heart and wanted me to play the warm-up set before their concert at La Cigale, in November 1990. Deee Lite were from New York. Their music was influenced by hip-hop and house and they wanted the warm-up set for their concert to include a French hip-hop group as well as a DJ. This was unheard of in France at the time, as hip-hop and house (the former being labelled 'music for criminals' and the latter 'music for gays') were considered to be two movements diametrically opposed. Yet both these movements had the same roots; the German group Kraftwerk were as much as an inspiration for Afrika Bambaataa's *Planet Rock* as for Detroit techno musicians.

Supreme 93, later to be known as NTM, were chosen to be the opening support act for Deee Lite. As Joey Starr and Kool Shen took to the stage, the atmosphere in the crowd was tense. The B-boys and gays were careful to stay clear of each other. Once Supreme 93 had finished their set, the hip-hop crowd all walked out en masse. By the time I began playing my first house record, the crowd was exclusively made up of gays and trendsetters.

I was convinced that house music needed to be heard in the French provinces too, so starting in November 1990 I exported the night I organised at La Luna to a club in Dijon. New Age, my night at the An-fer, attracted a new crowd to the club, but didn't go down so well with the existing clientele: 'Can you change the music? Have you got any Simple Minds?' Having worked at the Loco, I was well acquainted with this type of punter and knew how to win them round by playing tracks by Manchester pop bands like the Stone Roses, EMF and Happy Mondays, all bands with their roots in UK rave culture. (The rhythm on these records was four by four, but there were big guitar sounds so rock fans could still get into it.) Then I would lead them towards more electronic-sounding dance music, light years away from the world of fringed leather jackets and greasy hair. During the second month of my New Age residency, I found out that a group of people were coming back again and again from nearby Besançon, bringing more and more friends with them each time. These people refused to leave until I'd played my 'acid naze' set at the end of the night. It became a sort of ritual with me, drunk as a skunk, pulling out a record from the club's own collection, scratching over Mort Schumann's Allo Papa Tango Charlie, grabbing the microphone and shouting, 'Bring me a beer!'

After several months' residency, the crowd at the An-fer were all avid fans of house and techno. The An-fer had made a successful transition. One night, a guy came up to me in the DJ booth and asked, 'Have you got any Beatles?' I couldn't believe it. I stopped the music, took hold of the microphone, and pointing straight at the guy I shouted, 'Guess what this guy here just asked me to play … the Beatles!' Everyone in the room began to boo, 'Shame on you', 'loser', shouted the 800 or so partygoers. The guy in question stared straight at me and mouthed, 'You mo-ther-fu-cker.' He probably went home and listened to *Let It Be* over and over again on his stereo to calm down. No one ever asked me to play the Beatles again.

Word soon got around about the success of the An-fer. As a result, I started playing more regularly around the country – in Montpellier, Marseille, Lyon, as well as in other far-flung places where techno was unheard of. It was at this time that I became acquainted with Alexandre Herkommer, an eccentric young guy who organised gay nights in Switzerland. He invited me to DJ at the MAD club in Lausanne, a club whose reputation was on a par with that of the Palace in its heyday.

The MAD (Moulin-A-Danser) was started in Geneva in 1984 by Pascal and Monique Duffard, bona fide members of the Flower Power generation. Pascal had been a concert pianist as a child and had once accompanied Gilbert Becaud on stage, and Monique was a woman of the world. The Duffards had been extremely clever and had managed to find a loophole in Swiss law which exempted them from having to obtain a costly alcohol licence. Swiss nightlife is subject to strict controls, but the couple realised that there are fewer restrictions when a venue is subject to the 'private circles' law. Each client had a member's card obtained after paying a yearly subscription fee that gave him/her free access to one club night every weekend as well as around 25 concerts per year (The Communards, Nougaro, Bashung, Magma, La Mano Negra, Django Edwards, etc.). The MAD then moved from Geneva to an old station warehouse in the Flon district in Lausanne. Pascal Duffard signed a contract with LO (who managed the Flon district) which stipulated that his was to be the only venue in the entire area authorised to have two turntables. And that was that! In 1987, LO had plans to build a station where the MAD was housed so the club was moved into a four-story factory right in the centre of Lausanne. It was a gigantic warehouse. In the basement was a small room, the Parlor. On the ground floor was the main room, a multi-purpose venue with a capacity for 2,000 people. On the first floor there was a cinema and a chill-out room, equipped with beds. And on the second floor was a restaurant and offices.

Like Paris, the Swiss gay scene embraced acid-house, adding a touch of extravagance. House music first made its mark in French-speaking Switzerland in 1987. The first house nights took place in Montreux casino with the American DJ Tony Humphries. A local DJ scene then emerged led by DJs such as Mandrax, Djamin and Willow. Neighbouring Italy played a big part in its success, and clubbers travelled back and forth between Lausanne and Rimini. Parties took place on top of mountains (the only way up was via a ski lift) and in warehouses. With the arrival of the first wave of the acid-house movement, in 1988 the MAD changed its music policy to make room for house and techno. Maurice Béjart's dancers, who trained nearby, regularly went to the MAD to give spontaneous performances. And Susan Bartsche organised parties with more than a hint of scandal.

I arrived in Lausanne on December 16, 1990 and played to a very enthusiastic, energetic crowd. At the end of the night, once the MAD had closed its doors, I was told that the owners wanted to see me upstairs in their office. I went up the stairs, walked passed the beds in the chill-out room, past the restaurant, and stopped for a moment in front of the empty cinema. I finally found the office, where the Duffards, both dressed all in white, were expecting me. We were just through with the introductions when I suddenly felt a massive ecstasy rush ('Fuck, it's already been half an hour!'). We carried on talking politely and I tried to keep a lid on things. They paid me and I thanked them, trying to suppress a huge rush of enthusiasm. I said goodbye and went back downstairs, pretty pleased with how I'd managed to pull it off and act normal.

I met the Duffards again at the MAD the following month, when I went to begin a monthly residency in Switzerland. This was the beginning of my regular toing and froing between Paris – Dijon – Lausanne, which would continue over the next few years. Monique and Pascal were there to welcome me when I arrived and suggested, with a kind smile, that I let them pay me before the party this time. 'It will be easier for you, Laurent.' As they say, you can't pull one over on two pioneers of the Flower Power generation.

From June 1990, smileys, imported from England, began to appear in France. Techno was in demand. There was a host of newcomers on the scene and Paris had a burgeoning underground rave scene. That summer, two promoters, Luc Bertagnol and Manu Casana, organised techno events inspired by UK raves at the Fort de Champigny and the Armenian College. From one party to the next attendance tripled, going from 600 people to 2,000 in the space of three months. On December 8, Maxximum radio organised its first big rave at Le Bourget with guests including LFO and Nightmares On Wax. Not long after, Parisian raves found a new home on an industrial estate in one of Paris' communist suburbs, Mozinor.

In the 1960s, Mozinor was built as the first multi-level industrial zone in Europe. The huge ramps that gave lorries access to each level of this giant network of warehouses were still in existence. A terrace was built on the roof as a place for workers' families to come and relax at the weekends. During the week, the kitchens on these terraces were used to prepare food. But this ambitious project never came to much and so Montreuil council took over Mozinor and forgot about it.

Meanwhile, a guy called Eric Napora, who ran his own catering business and organised events for private businesses, was on the lookout for new venues. He came across the top floor of Mozinor. He thought the place was amazing and seized the opportunity to turn it into a business. At the end of 1990, Eric Napora rented out one of the rooms on the top floor of Mozinor to Luc Bertagnol for a rave. The event wasn't as successful as had been expected. The promoters lost money but Napora, captivated by what he had seen, offered them a deal. He would write off the money they owed him in exchange for organising raves together at Mozinor. Bertagnol and his team already had a powerful promotional tool for their events, a mailing list that dated back to their first rave at the Fort de Champigny, guaranteeing the right kind of people. Their first joint event took place in early 1991. Success was immediate. For the second event the organisers opened the terraces and 2,400 ravers turned up! Not long after, in order to keep up with demand, the organisers opened up all the other adjacent rooms on the top floor.

Between 1991 and 1994 the production budget tripled. A sound system was shipped in from Holland; lights were brought in from Germany; DJs came from all over Europe. Extra special attention was paid to production design. All this was done within a strict legal framework. Cosmos Factory Ltd applied for and obtained a licence to sell alcohol, hired professional security firms and informed the local council of every event.

But the fact that these events were legal didn't take away from the magic. Ask anyone who has ever been to Mozinor to describe what it was like and you'll see how just one night can have an impact for life and remain in someone's heart forever. The two resident DJs, Jerome Pacman and Francesco Farfa, played music all night long until midday on Sunday. An 80-year-old neighbour came to dance among the ravers. People would set their alarms at 8am and head for Mozinor with croissants and fresh fruit. Others stood on the roof of Mozinor, their faces lit by the morning sun, as they watched the rest of the city sleeping.

I have to say that I wasn't really welcome at the parties organised by the duo Casana/Bertagnol, whether in Champigny or at Mozinor. It's funny really because they considered me a DJ on the gay scene, whereas at La Luna and the Palace, the gays were always complaining that I let too many girls in. And if it wasn't the old 'gay' excuse, I was subject to

various onslaughts about my UK connections: 'Keep doing your thing with the gays and the Brits and keep out of our way!' The message was clear. Up until then I had never come across any hostility, but I was cast aside by a group of people who I had never even met before and who held unjustified prejudices against me. Of course, it hurt at the time, but over time you develop a protective shell. The dance music scene in Paris was microscopic and yet people were already at each other's throats. Talk about being open-minded! I find it strange, this typically French attitude. As soon as someone tries to build something and develop their career they are immediately labelled a sell-out. France must be one of the only countries in the world where success is considered suspect. Everywhere else, local artists are supported by their community and their country first. But you just have to learn to deal with it.

I still had in the back of my mind the images of the performance I had seen on stage in the club in New York. I suggested to the Palace doing a night like this and calling it Oz. I also wanted to bring with me a young, shy, music-mad student who I had met at La Luna, DJ Deep. The first Oz party was held on May 23, 1991. During the first part of the night a curtain was drawn across the stage with a laser projecting a ticking clock. At 1.30am precisely we opened the curtain to the music from *The Wizard Of Oz* and *2001, A Space Odyssey*. The stage filled with smoke from a smoke machine and, as it cleared, the crowd saw a tableau of paper flowers and paper faces designed by an English friend of mine.

But the Palace had recently changed hands and once again found itself in serious financial difficulty. In 1991, the club was forced to close for a few months, so Oz was transferred to an old punk nightclub, where punters smashed the washbasins with their heads as they listened to the Sex Pistols. Back then, the club was called Le Rose Bonbon. It was situated on a street not far from the Olympia. But once its two founders, Eric Rug and Fred Bolling, left to take over La Locomotive, the Rose Bonbon was turned into a gay club. At number 6, rue Caumartin, Le Boy opened its doors and would become the best gay club in Paris throughout the 1990s.

A wide staircase led down into the club. Downstairs, the bar ran along the right-hand side of the club and the dance floor was a semi-circular shape. At one end stood a stage. The DJ booth was situated at the opposite end of the room and was so far away from the dance floor that it was difficult to see what was going on through the mass of hundreds of sweaty bodies. Le Boy was a sanctuary where anything could happen. There were no taboos. Every single night it was packed until 7am.

Every weekend, the clientele from Le Boy would swarm to the Bocaccio club on the French-Belgian border, to dance alongside hundreds of other

European clubbers who came to party non-stop from Friday through to Monday. The resident DJs played new beat as well as dark, moody techno tracks fresh out of the recording studios of Belgium. They had their own special way of making tracks into overnight hits by playing them at least 10 times the same night, so people would hear the same track once an hour. It was very clever. By the time anyone had extracted themselves from this clubbing inferno they knew the track list by heart. Once back in Paris, Le Boy's clientele would expect the resident Belgian DJ, Marco, to play the same tracks and create the same torrid atmosphere as they had experienced at the Bocaccio.

In September 1991, the first Zoo night at Le Boy presented a style of house and techno that was very different from the banging new beat sounds that the club was used to. Using Oz as a model, the DJ booth was moved on stage to make the DJ the centre of the party. The night was interspersed with on-stage drama – at 1am the curtain behind the DJ would open to reveal domestic scenes of home life that were in stark contrast to the highly charged atmosphere on the dance floor. While the crowd were going crazy on the dance floor, a seedy middle-aged couple sat on the stage in their dressing gowns watching TV, knitting and reading quietly. My brother Thierry Garnier was responsible for the fantastically kitsch set design, and the crowd loved it.

In 1991, techno spread right across Europe. All over France people were about to experience their first illegal parties, the Belgians were leaders in the production of raves, the Swiss were on the verge of organising massive techno parties. From Frankfurt to Berlin a wind of euphoria was blowing across Germany, while in the UK the rave scene still kept getting bigger. This was another turning point in history as, at this time, techno was going global and it was no longer just about the music; it was now also about business, gangs and the police.

total confusion

5

Every month it was the same story. Friday morning at the crack of dawn, while everyone in Paris was queuing at the bus stop or rushing for the metro, I would emerge from Le Boy, loaded down with my record boxes, my clothes stinking of cigarettes. I'd chuck the boxes into the boot of my ravemobile, change into a clean t-shirt, jump into the car and switch on the engine. My ears were still buzzing from the music that had been belting out of the club's speakers. I hadn't slept in almost 24 hours.

Meanwhile, on the other side of the Channel, more wild nights were on the cards.

Madchester was about to reinvent itself and change once more.

In most UK cities at the time, different gangs ran their inner-city region. It was all a question of territory and had nothing to do with either race or religion. Up until the end of the 1980s, gang violence in Manchester was confined to three areas: Moss Side, Salford and Hulme, but spared the residents of these neighbourhoods. But in the summer of '89, the impact that acid-house had on the UK clubbing scene created a huge new market for the drug Ecstasy. The gangs got involved in dealing, hoping to gain control over the drug market, leading them right to the doors of the clubs.

Due to its popularity and its pivotal role in Manchester's nightlife, the Haçienda found itself in the eye of the storm. The club watched on helplessly as their clients were subjected to increasing violence, racketeering and intimidation. Before long, the people in charge of the club were under threat too. The area in and around Whitworth Street West was getting dangerous. Within the space of a few months, the whole atmosphere in the city centre had changed to one of guerrilla warfare. Every weekend things got a little edgier. Cars were set alight, scores were settled on the pavement and shots were fired at the bouncers if they dared refuse entrance to a gang member.

At a loss as to what to do and faced with this brutal upsurge in violence, Manchester police ordered the Haçienda to refuse entrance to any dealers or drug takers. This was a complete waste of time as nothing could stop the explosion in rave culture: an estimated 90 per cent of people in clubs were taking ecstasy. Aware that trying to keep people away wasn't the answer, the police sent a report to the local authorities stipulating that drugs were being openly sold at the Haçienda and that the only way to put a stop to this was to close the club down. In response, the Haçienda pointed out that they were the victims of the violence linked to drug trafficking and that closing them down was not the way to deal with the problem; what they needed was help from the authorities, not sanctions.

They gained the support of Manchester City Council and with the help of George Carman, one of the UK's leading lawyers, the Haçienda won their case. To prove their determination in the fight against drugs, the Haçienda put up signs all over the club stating, 'Drugs are not permitted on these premises.' They also adopted a stricter door policy, demanding that each person carry student ID on Thursday nights and tried, in vain, to refuse entrance to gang members. Because of the club's efforts and show of goodwill, and because the police had lost their case, the police lost interest in what was going on at the Haçienda. The chips were down and things were going from bad to worse. It all came to a head in the winter of 1990 when, during an argument inside the club, a gang member pulled out a gun and held it to a client's head. The management were so shocked by this event that they closed the club temporarily in January 1991.

To stop the club being completely overrun by drugs and violence, secret talks were held between the Haçienda and the most fearsome of all gangs, Salford. Tony Wilson's answer to critics was, 'If we have to put up with people running around inside the Haçienda with guns, let's be sure that the security staff have even bigger guns than them.' Metal detectors were installed at the entrance to the club to try and stop anyone getting in with a weapon. But they were discreetly switched off by security each time a member of their gang turned up. Things didn't look good. The Haçienda reopened in May 1991. The club's three legendary DJs, Dave Haslam, Mike Pickering and Graeme Park, were back behind the decks, but the magic seemed to have gone for good.

By now, all the clubs had to deal with these problems at the door. They all had metal detectors installed and hired 'special' security staff. Tensions were running high, but the public weren't bothered. They were out of control. The cocktail of music and the increasing amounts of ecstasy they were taking had sent them to a different reality. Each night it was as if anything could happen, good or bad. These were exciting, hedonistic, reckless times … people in the UK were dancing with the devil.

I had kept up certain routines from my time up north. Whenever I was booked to DJ in the UK, I'd stay at Sasha's house. One of the guys who often hung out at the house was a guy called Ian. Ian was 19 and was a member of the Salford gang … I was on quite good terms with him and remember one time when my ravemobile broke down he lent me a car he'd 'borrowed' so that I wouldn't miss my gig at Quadrant Park. I had no idea of the long, dark road that he and his gang mates were going down. One day, they held up one of Sasha's housemates, a promoter. In doing this, they brought trouble into a house that up until then had been spared any problems. Another time, Ian came down to the Haçienda and got into an argument with one of the bouncers. He pulled out a knife, stabbed the bouncer in the gut, and went off to dance as if it was nothing. A week later he bought himself an Uzi. No one will ever really know exactly what happened that night. Did the gun go off by mistake? Did Ian really empty a whole cartridge full of bullets into his girlfriend, keeping the last bullet for himself? They were both found dead. They were 20 years old, and their baby witnessed the whole ordeal.

Madchester became Gunchester.

It was not only the north that was affected. Since the explosion of raves in 1989, the south of England had also fallen prey to gangs due to the large amounts of cash being generated at events attracting up to 10,000 people at a time. Unscrupulous promoters teamed up with the gangs. When they weren't dealing in ecstasy at raves, they were coming up with all sorts of scams to get rich. And so appeared a spate of phantom raves with flyers announcing the best UK DJs. Tickets were sold in advance and, come Saturday night, groups of ravers could be found scouring the countryside looking for a rave that never existed. Another tactic was for the gangs to place their own members in among the security. Their job was to extort a copious share of the profits from the organisers.

The police showed little interest in these swindles as they were trying to cope with a much bigger problem. Drugs and raves had decentralised Saturday nights-out and partygoers were deserting the city centre. Every weekend, people migrated from the cities to raves in the countryside, which was a source of serious concern for the authorities. They saw it as dangerous or, even worse, subversive. The police authorities sent a memorandum to local councils allowing them to relax drinking laws, which up until then had been incredibly strict, with the aim of regaining control over Britain's youth. But this didn't change a thing. So, with public opinion weighing down on them, the police proceeded with their first spectacular clampdown. Two people who were responsible for organising an illegal boat party in Greenwich were arrested and found guilty of 'conspiring to manage premises where drugs were supplied'. They were both given very harsh sentences, six and ten years, respectively. The case was widely reported in the UK press, launching an anti-rave witch-hunt.

Following the deaths of two young ravers in 1989 from an overdose of ecstasy, Margaret Thatcher's Britain was up in arms, so the police scaled up their anti-rave clampdown. The government created a special unit made up of 200 police officers called the Pay Party Unit whose mission was to gather information on raves. From then on, party organisers and police authorities were locked in a power struggle. Tony Colston-Hayter,

the Pay Party Unit's bête noir, went as far as creating membership cards for his events (turning them into private gatherings) so as to lawfully avoid any accusations of organising illegal gatherings which concerned every house and techno event on UK soil.

Faced with the ever-growing rave phenomenon, the Pay Party Unit tried out several different game plans. Initially they decided to try and break up the rave scene by openly discouraging ravers, hoping to put them off. So when they weren't taking down signposts, they were organising phantom raves. They would lie in wait for the ravers at the address given on flyers, paid for by taxpayers' money, and when the first carloads of ravers would arrive they would shout into their megaphones, 'Go home! There's no rave here!' Yet it was going to take more than that to stop rave organisations. By now, they were using new technology, including mobile phones and info lines to inform people about their events. But the Pay Party Unit continued laying on the pressure to put a stop to events.

By 1991 the undercover war between the government and the rave scene was at fever pitch. The Pay Party Unit had all they needed at their disposal to eradicate raves, putting all new projects at risk. Rave organisers found themselves at a dead end. Now considered outlaws, not only were they being coerced by gangsters but they were also being persecuted by government.

It was in this context that Paul Shurry's organisation, Universe, emerged. Having spent the past few years dodging police vetoes, Paul and his team of associates, who came from the free party scene, were tired of this system that was forcing them further and further underground, so they decided to structure themselves. To ensure some kind of protection, Paul Shurry teamed up with Roger Spurrell, captain of the Bath rugby team (1991 UK Champions), who was well connected with some of the highest officials within the British police authorities. With Spurrell at his side, Paul Shurry thought that he would be protected from any extortion or police pressure. However, just one week before the first Universe rave was supposed to take place, Paul Shurry was kidnapped from the centre of Bristol in broad daylight and was held captive for several hours. Who were his kidnappers? The promoters of a rival rave organisation, Perception, who demanded a share of the proceeds from his event. Paul Shurry bullshitted them saying, 'I only look after booking the artists, I don't manage the money side,' and sent them off to negotiate with Roger Spurrell.

A meeting was set up on site in the dead of night on the eve of Universe. Spurrell turned up along with another member of the Bath rugby team, who also happened to be assistant chief constable of the Avon and Somerset police force. A very big fish! Shurry couldn't believe it! The gangsters and police officers seemed to know each other and were even on first name terms ... it was surreal! A tacit agreement was reached that night, but in spite of it, the next day Perception went ahead with their counter-rave and sold over 8,000 tickets 30 miles up the road from Universe.

I played at the first Universe event. Having driven for several hours from Manchester to get there, I arrived at the site near Bath with Sasha. Like Carl Cox, Sasha's DJ career had taken off with the rave scene in the south of England. His reputation as a DJ had gone from strength to strength. Sasha didn't have a driver's licence and he loved to party hard, so promoters were never quite sure whether he'd turn up or not. When Paul Shurry booked me to play at Universe he made it very clear that, as no one had ever heard of me in the south, he was giving me the chance to DJ on condition that I was to drive Sasha there and he would arrive fit for work. Mission accomplished.

Despite Perception's counter-rave, the first ever Universe was a success. Four thousand five hundred people turned up. Sasha played on the main stage and I played in one of the smaller tents. I was very excited and also very aware how important it was for me to make my mark. I put a lot of energy into my set, mixing house, techno and new beat, a far cry from breakbeat that was becoming the official UK rave sound. My set went down well and I was booked to play at the following Universe event. Once Sasha had finished his set, the promoters invited us to go along with them to the after-party that had been organised in a beautiful spot, on the edge of a cornfield. From 7am onwards, groups of ravers, scallies and travellers arrived from Universe and Perception alike, to dance to the sounds of the DIY sound system and discuss the laid-back friendly atmosphere at Paul Shurry's raves. For once you had paid your entrance fee, everything else was free (drinks, fairground rides, activities, etc.). Universe made their first big splash.

A year later, Paul Shurry organised Mind Body Soul which attracted 7,000 people, and was given the highly prized 'Rave of the Year' award by *Mixmag* magazine. On the back of this new-found media credibility (the British press being very powerful, as we know), Universe obtained the Holy Grail for a rave organisation, an entertainment licence, allowing them to organise an event for 25,000 people. Thus, Universe became Tribal Gathering. The concept was simple: a rave organised like a festival.

In 1992, cracks started to appear in the UK rave scene. Clubs began to be a serious alternative venue, as raves were becoming more and more commercial and less appealing to real ravers. Several DJs decided that it was time to move back to working in clubs; they were starting to get fed up with the police harassment, intimidation from gangs, never-ending scams of certain promoters, and the lack of interesting music being played. With the help of the press, some of these DJs were making a name for themselves despite the relative anonymity of raves, and were on their way to becoming stars. They included Carl Cox ('The Three Deck Wizard'), Sasha, and Paul Oakenfold.

I had regular DJ gigs in the north, and witnessed a battle-worn UK scene struggling to find new impetus, away from the sound of happy hardcore and dodgy dealings. Drugs had wiped out all the good things about raves and all the rave kids seemed to be interested in now was an unhealthy competition to see how many ecstasy pills they could down. Music had just become the pretext. Parties were reduced to one topic of conversation: 'How many are you on?' I had never had much to do with that way of thinking. I tried to protect myself from this and concentrate even harder on the music.

Aside from a few events (Universe being one example), the essence of house had been lost somewhere along the way to moneymaking and violence. I was starting to travel a bit further afield and was in search of somewhere new, where genuine passion came before business and where I could find a fertile terrain for house and techno to plant its roots.

Since 1992, people in Paris had been hearing rumours of a new sound from Berlin and Frankfurt: German trance. Keen to experience a night out in Germany, I accepted an invitation to DJ at a 4,000-capacity rave in a warehouse on the outskirts of Munich. The public there had never heard of me; they were there to listen to the head honcho of the German techno scene, Sven Vath. Over in Germany, Sven was the charismatic leader of the techno generation.

Born in Frankfurt, Sven had taken his first steps as a DJ at his parents' pub, where his father had given him a slot on condition that he memorised the entire family record collection, dating from the 60s and 70s. Before the first rumours of acid-house hit Germany, Sven Vath was already a national hero. He had been resident DJ at Dorian Grey in Frankfurt (the first club in Europe to have a sound system designed by Richard Long, who had been responsible for the sound at the Paradise Garage and the Sound Factory in New York), and had been bitten by the techno bug when he first heard the album *Computer World* by Kraftwerk. Blown away by the groove and the precision of what he heard, Sven decided to make the leap from DJ to recording artist. He joined forces with the future members of the group Snap! to create OFF (Organisation

For Fun), a cross between Depeche Mode and Kraftwerk. In 1985, OFF released their single, Elektrica Salsa. They quickly achieved international success with this record, which paved the way for other German electronic pop bands such as Falco, Spliff and Déjà Vu. In 1987, the German music industry was ready for something new.

As the first American house music records began to trickle into German record shops, new DJs such as Westbam in Berlin and DJ Talla in Frankfurt began to emerge. Sven left OFF, and his routine of regular TV performances, to immerse himself fully into the world of clubs behind the decks at Dorian Grey. In 1988, along with a couple of associates, he bought his own club, Omen, where he implemented an eclectic music policy. By the following year dance music was pouring into German record stores at an unprecedented rate. Crate loads of new beat, acid-house and techno records arrived each week. By now it was possible for a DJ to play an eight-hour set made up entirely of new tracks, without ever having to repeat himself. At Omen, Sven put on the first ever house-and-techno-only night in Germany and called it Let's Sweat, Keep Your Body Wet, and every Friday night people came from all over Germany to be there. In the meantime, there was a buzz in Berlin about another night called UFO being organised by two DJs, Westbam and Dr Motte.

In July 1989, four months before the fall of the Berlin Wall, Dr Motte and DJ Kid Paul had a mad idea to rent a truck, stick a sound system on it, and drive down the Kurfurstendamm, one of the main streets in Berlin. The word soon spread among the Berlin house scene, and for four hours, 150 ravers danced behind a truck through the city centre. Their motto was definitely very hippy sounding: 'Peace, Love, Unity and Respect for one another.' That day, the Love Parade was born.

On November 9, 1989 the Berlin Wall came down. Techno became the soundtrack of German reunification. Techno was passionate and modern, it was about having fun and dancing, and it expressed better than any other music the spirit of communion that was gripping Germany.

Spurred on by Sven Vath, the Omen posse hooked up with key players on the Berlin techno scene to organise a free party called Freedom. The message was clear. In East Berlin, huge warehouses belonging to the ex-DDR (Deutsche Democratic Republik), situated at the heart of what was once the East German Politburo's HQ, were commandeered for techno events. Everything seemed possible now. The Berlin police, under government orders, let parties take place. A wind of change was sweeping across Germany, and Berlin was at its heart.

In 1990, demand for techno in Germany kept growing. That year, Tresor and E-Werk, two now-legendary clubs, opened in Berlin. They were the first clubs in Germany to invite American DJs such as Blake Baxter and Jeff Mills to come and play. But without any homegrown record labels or producers, Germany was lacking its own personal vision of techno. That was until Sven Vath set up Eye-Q, one of the first German techno labels, and then went on to create Harthouse Records, signing tracks produced by young artists who were regulars down at Omen. Meanwhile, Sven Vath was also back in the charts with his new band, Barbarella. Artists from the Berlin techno scene, whose records were being released by Harthouse, were also starting to reach a wider audience. Within a few months, Berlin and Frankfurt had become a hotbed for German techno, with each city boasting its own style and musical identity. At the Omen, Sven Vath launched 'The sound of Frankfurt', a mixture of techno, new wave and electronic pop, and went on to define the colourful sounds that would characterise German trance. Meanwhile, in Berlin, one half of the scene was developing a taste for a more raw, visceral sound while the other half was developing a taste for happy trance at times verging on tacky. These different styles co-existed happily, and there was no rivalry between the two cities. That was until the German monthly techno magazine *Frontpage* decided to adopt the same marketing methods as the UK press and create a rivalry between cities and artists. Whereas in the UK press there were stories about London vs. Manchester or the Rolling Stones vs. the Beatles, *Frontpage* dreamt up competition between Frankfurt and Berlin.

In 1992, Mayday, the first major German rave, saw 6,000 people flock to Berlin. The people witnessed a classic example of a German techno rave with lasers, an almighty sound system, giant screens and the first ever computer-generated 3D visuals (techno's take on psychedelic imagery). Sven Vath turned up with the rest of the Eye-Q/Harthouse teams wearing t-shirts bearing slogans such as 'Frankfurt Posse' and 'Don't Mess With Frankfurt'.

The simultaneous arrival of raves and ecstasy had a phenomenal impact on Germany's youth. Raves became a popular form of entertainment without any trace of subversion or objection from the German authorities to whom the promoters paid their taxes. With no obstacles in their way, an industry began to flourish: fashion got its foot in the door with companies designing new trancey clothing lines for die-hard ravers; drinks companies invested huge sums of money to ensure that their brands were affiliated with the techno movement.

Germany owed part of this cultural and economic shake-up to the invention of trance; a colourful, psychedelic and utopian offshoot of techno that united all of Germany's youth, bringing down barriers and slowly emerging as the cultural determinant of a nation. German techno artists became huge stars. Previously, it would have been unheard of for a German DJ to headline a festival. As a result of this interest, both of Sven's labels became known worldwide. Several rave anthems emerged during this period, including Vernon's Wonderland and Hardfloor's Acperience, confirming German savoir-faire and the sound of Frankfurt as an international reference for techno. The UK magazine *ID* wrote about the sound of Frankfurt, and techno labels such as Warp and +8 held parties at Omen. Underground Resistance (Detroit's best-kept secret) performed live at the Omen for the release of their album *Accident In Paradise*. Sven Vath was heralded as 'Kaiser Techno' by the British press.

From 1992, international DJs flocked to Germany while, simultaneously, the German underground techno scene was growing, with new artists like DJ Hell and Maurizio and new clubs like the Warehouse in Cologne. Meanwhile, in Manheim, Stefan Charles created the Time Warp rave organisation. In reaction to the immensity of Mayday, Stefan wanted to reintroduce a club atmosphere into raves. He programmed international DJs, little known by the German public (Josh Wink, Carl Cox, Juan Atkins, Richie Hawtin, Speedy J), who came and played alongside the big German stars such as Sven Vath, Cosmic Baby, DJ Dag and Mark Spoon.

I became a regular on the German nightlife scene. I happily played in both clubs and raves and preached techno even in the remotest towns. Then, one day, Sven recommended me to the organisers of Love Parade, and in July 1993 I found myself in Berlin for the very first time. I discovered an exciting, open-minded, friendly city. I sensed a real quality of life and an energy that seemed to make anything possible. Berlin was the cultural exception in Germany. During the period of transition since the collapse of the wall, Berlin had experienced troubled times. Among all the enthusiasm, the tension was palpable. The inhabitants had been scarred by a series of violent demonstrations. Berliners had had to fight to open up to the modern world and the city was united in a desire for everything new. I spent the night before the Love Parade at E-Werk, a club where 3,000 people came together to experience techno's communicative energy. There I met most of the Berlin dance music scene who explained to me what I was in for the following day, the fifth Love Parade.

I had such a surprise when I saw 200,000 people in broad daylight dancing behind dozens of floats through the streets of Berlin. In the space of a few years, Love Parade had become a major event in Germany. It was mind-blowing yet it still felt spontaneous. DJs came with their records, met quickly with the organisers and played for free on the many floats. And once the Parade was over, they would start up again, in one of the many raves that were organised in the 10,000-capacity warehouses in East Berlin. At the end of that Love Parade I was invited to DJ at E-Werk where I had spent the previous night as a punter. E-Werk was a DJ's dream. The ultimate Berlin club. In addition to the sheer size of the place, the sound system had been designed to ensure perfect listening conditions. Dozens of plaster cast statues of the great figures of the Berlin techno scene overlooked the dance floor. Everything was designed so that the thousands of people plunged into the darkness of this warehouse could enjoy an environment that was the perfect middle ground between a club and a rave. Big sound, big venue, big parties in peaceful harmony. This was the kind of thing that I had been trying to create in Paris, and here it was, just like that, with no special effort. I went back to France with a lasting vision in my mind: 3,000 people dancing wildly, hands up in the air, ready for anything as long as there was good energy and music to dance to.

Germany and the UK (in spite of their cultural differences) were the two leading countries in Europe for dance music. France had far fewer claims to the international dance music scene. There was little happening in clubs or raves in France that could measure up to what was going on elsewhere in Europe, and up until then there had been no techno artists to make their mark. This was not helped by a disregard for techno, which discouraged any initiative there might have been.

Tackling this scepticism was as intimidating for me as the idea of rebuilding Berlin!

6

wake up

A real turning point in my career came when I began making my own music. Thanks to the first records I released, I was invited to travel abroad, first to Germany and then further afield.

I first met Ian Bland, alias Dream Frequency, in 1989 at a rave, Live The Dream. In the months that followed, Ian released a track that became a massive underground hit, Live The Dream. As a result, Ian was playing live at all the raves in the north of England. I bumped into him one night in 1990 at Quadrant Park. We spent all evening talking and Ian invited me back to his house ('You can't sleep in your car mate!'). His spare room had been turned into a home studio, typical of that first generation of dance music producers, with an M1 keyboard, an Akai S1000 sampler, a 16-track mixer, and various other machines. All his machines were linked up together with miles and miles of cables. I was fascinated, and asked him to switch on his studio equipment and give me a demo. We ended up making a track together, a blend of new beat and techno composed in a hurry. I finally went to bed at around midday once we had finished recording the track on tape. I fell asleep on the sofa in Ian's sitting room with his dog Casey curled up next to me.

When I woke, I glanced at my watch, and went to wake Ian. We stumbled into my ravemobile and drove to Eastern Bloc. I bought around 30 records, and when I felt I had the owner's full attention, I took out the tape, 'Could you put this on?' As soon as the track ended the owner said he wanted to sign it to his label. At first I thought he was taking the mickey, but he was very insistent and so we signed a sort of contract. A three-track EP was released three weeks later on Creed Records under the name French Connection. Back then all you had to do was rustle up a house track for it to be signed to a label – as long as you weren't expecting any money, managers or lawyers to be involved.

I headed back to Paris with my first EP tucked under my arm. I played it in all my DJ sets, especially at La Luna. One night, I met Eric Morand, a young label manager who was working for Barclay, a subdivision of Universal. Eric was a regular at La Luna. I often bumped into him at after-parties without ever really speaking to him. But when we eventually did speak, we realised that we had friends in common, Didier Lestrade and Vincent Borel.

One of Eric's main roles at Barclay was managing the French distribution for the UK label FFRR. This included raising the profile of various bands in France, such as Orbital, that I loved. I somehow found out that Eric was planning to release a record for the clubs to promote Orbital, but that he hadn't included the track Belfast. As far as I was concerned, Belfast was a classic. I played it in all my sets. Eric had already suggested once or twice that I drop by his office just a few blocks away from the Place d'Italie. I decided that this was a good opportunity to take him up on his offer. So I just turned up at Barclay unannounced and marched straight up the stairs to Eric's office. A secretary ran behind me calling out, 'Mr Morand is in a meeting, you can't go in ...' But I marched in, stood in front of Eric and blurted out my well-rehearsed diatribe about the incompetence of major records labels with regards to dance music. I told him that he was making a huge mistake with Orbital and that major labels didn't have a clue about house, etc. Basically everything I had been bottling up came out. We argued for a while, with Eric shouting, 'What's it got to do with you?!' He was sitting squarely behind his desk while I stood blocking the exit. After a while we both calmed down. I sat down and we carried on talking normally. Once our meeting was over, Eric kindly gave me a few promos and showed me out. The story could have ended there with Eric thinking, 'What a pretentious little shit!' But Eric didn't harbour ill feelings towards me and carried on coming down to La Luna. We became friends, and one day I played him the track I'd made with Ian Bland. After a few minutes silence, Eric told me he thought the track wasn't bad and said he would play it to his boss, Pascal Negre. But Pascal Negre put an end to any idea I might have had: 'It sounds like Jean-Michel Jarre. It's crap!'

Barclay only had very short-term objectives for dance music in France. However, Eric wanted to get more involved in developing French dance music artists, so he left Barclay to head up a dance music department for the FNAC (Fédération Nationale d'Achats des Cadres) group. His new job came with a guaranteed free rein and full financial backing. This was relatively unheard of. Eric's plan for FNAC Dance Music Division was to produce French house music artists. He wanted to give his artists time to develop their projects in the hope of achieving international success. This strategy had rarely been seen in France before. This was a country that, in the past, had rarely managed to find an audience for its music abroad. In order to achieve his goal, Eric Morand wasn't banking on a sudden change in attitude towards French artists, but on the FNAC's logistical strength and their ability to export finished product. This was in stark contrast to all the other record companies at the time, and particularly the majors, who relied upon their international counterparts to consider licensing their product for release abroad. The FNAC was able to sign an artist, record them, and then promote and distribute their release nationally and, more importantly, internationally. What was their secret? They were financially autonomous and artistically independent.

I became very involved with Fnac Dance Division. Not only because Eric Morand was a friend, but also because I felt it was important for me to learn the ropes of the music business and to be part of a musical family. I had no official role to play within the label, but I listened to each new track fresh from the studio and tested it out on the dance floor. I would then report back to Eric with my thoughts on the track and how the crowd reacted.

As Fnac Dance Division was getting going, Eric brought up the subject of the first track that I had recorded with Ian. He wanted me to go back into the studio again and be the first artist to release a track on the label. As far as I was concerned, French Connection had just been a one-off. Up until then, I had only ever thought about making music for fun. The only thing I was really interested in was the dance floor. But Eric didn't give me much choice, 'Here's a return ticket to the UK. Now go to Ian's studio and get to work!' I didn't argue and dutifully set off to Ian's the following week. Ian and I shut ourselves in his studio. We had a laugh and mucked around with his studio equipment, but in the five days I was there we managed to produce four tracks. One of the tracks, Join Hands, was in the vein of Someday by CeCe Rogers. Another track we did, Storm, was inspired by Detroit techno. The other two were a mix of Chicago and UK dance music.

As soon as I got back I went straight to the Fnac offices. I was nervous about how Eric would react. I remember apologising to Eric for having made tracks for a laugh, having a go, just for fun … Eric listened to the tape from beginning to end in complete silence. I was feeling increasingly anxious, when the music stopped and Eric said, 'It's good. I'll have it … on one condition – that you sign it under your real name and that your name appears on the cover.' An argument ensued, 'No! It's underground! I don't want my name anywhere on it!' Eric finally managed to persuade me. The record was released under the name Laurent Garnier and Mixmaster Doody (Ian was under contract with a UK label, that's why he chose a pseudonym). It was the first record ever to be released by Fnac Dance Division, in December 1991. Fnac Dance Division then went on to sign two other artists: Ludovic Navarre, who had already released several Belgian techno records under the name of Sub System, and Shazz, a producer who was a huge fan of house music and a regular at La Luna.

Eric Morand also signed a deal with Warp, a pioneering label of bleep music (techno made in Sheffield), to oversee their promotion and distribution in France. As dance music only really existed on 12-inch vinyl, Warp stood out by releasing one of the first ever techno albums (on CD!) by LFO, a duo from Sheffield led by Mark Bell.

In the space of a few months, Morand had put together all the necessary elements for the label to take off.

The rapid evolution of Fnac Dance Division coincided with the arrival of the first radio station in France entirely dedicated to dance music. At the beginning of 1992, when Maxximum closed down, Radio FG overhauled their entire music output. Programmes exclusively targeting the gay community were put to one side, as FG reorganised itself into an underground dance music radio station. Music programming was handed over to the cream of Paris' dance music DJs (DJ Aquarium, Sonic, Armand, Pacman...) and the weekly programme, *Rave Up*, presented by Patrick Rognant, reported on what was happening on the rave scene. As the first large-scale techno events were being organised, it seemed legitimate for Radio FG to be the media partner of choice.

Alongside *Libération* newspaper and the rave promoter Happy Land, Fnac Dance Division organised a rave at La Défense on January 18, 1992. LFO headlined the event. The rave at La Défense was to be one of the first major big-budget underground events (not a paradox!) to be organised. The rave, which took place in an exhibition hall underneath the Grande Arche de La Défense, was openly promoted. *Libération* printed several full-page adverts, flyers were distributed and FG ran a radio advertising campaign. For one night, all the different dance music factions in Paris put aside their rivalries and worked together as a team. Four thousand ravers came to see LFO. That night, LFO proved that a techno group could perform live and create something musically outstanding on stage. A lot of LSD was circulating that night. During the concert the atmosphere was so extraordinary that I've never really experienced anything like it since. When LFO played an amazing version of their hit track LFO you could feel the atmosphere becoming that bit more intense because of the drugs. The duo picked up on the energy and stretched out the studio version of their track, experimenting with it like never before, improvising long acid breaks, getting the crowd begging for more as they held a wavering chord for several minutes before launching into a heavy, funky rhythm sending the crowd crazy...

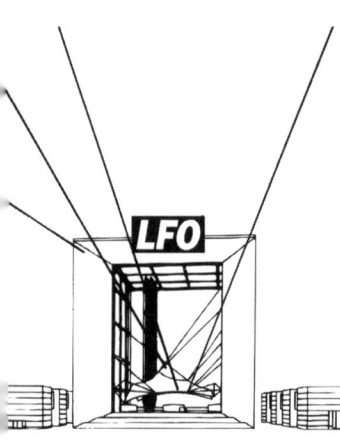

That night, a group of 40 English ravers had come over on a bus from Nottingham especially for the event. They took over the dance floor, going mad like they were back home. One of them had been so scared of being caught by customs on the way over that he had swallowed his entire supply of ecstasy at the border. He was in a complete mess. When he arrived at the venue he went straight into the middle of the dance floor, got undressed and lay down among the sea of legs. When he finally got up, he raced outside onto the plaza in front of La Défense, naked. The police arrested him and put him in a police cell for 48 hours. Needless to say, the bus went back to the UK without him.

Paris still didn't have a major weekly house or techno night. Nightlife was in a sad state of affairs. It had been hit hard by AIDS, as well as a lack of funds. Le Boy and the Palace were closed. The word on the street was that the Home Office had had it in for Le Boy for a long time, firstly because it was a gay club right in the heart of the smart Madeleine district and, secondly, it was packed every night until midday the next day, so it's maybe not surprising that it got up some people's noses.

Paris nightlife was in the authorities' bad books, whereas everywhere else in Europe, nightlife was booming again thanks to dance music (trance in Germany, techno and hardcore in Holland, new beat in Belgium and breakbeat in the UK). In Paris, there was not one club where you could go and listen to house or techno (just a few events dotted here and there). The Rex was trying hard to reinvent itself as its traditional clientele was losing faith.

It was at that time that Eric and I decided to organise the Wake Up parties. We were perhaps being a bit over-ambitious as our aim was to really shake up Paris. But how were we going to get people interested? How were we going to persuade people to come to our parties week in, week out? We started by asking ourselves what we felt was missing from the club nights we attended. Our musical idols were American? OK. The first thing we had to do was to invite DJs from Chicago and Detroit to play at our night. All that was left to do was to persuade Christian Paulet. We needed to choose our words carefully: 'Christian, it's wicked news, Derrick May and Kevin Saunderson have agreed to come and DJ. Are you in with us?' Then followed an embarrassing silence. Apparently Christian Paulet didn't know who I was talking about. 'Christian, it's like saying that we've got the Beatles and the Rolling Stones both playing on the same night at the Rex! So?' Christian got behind the idea, even thought it was going to burn a hole in his pocket, because he understood one of the key rules of nightlife: a club that doesn't take risks is a club that dies.

So … in 1992, Wake Up took a risk every week by inviting a DJ from abroad while maintaining a modest door fee and banishing any guest lists. In contrast to what had been the norm in Paris since the 1980s, i.e. free entry to clubs, everyone who came to Wake Up had to pay an entrance fee. Every Thursday, the team (Eric Morand, Philippe Seguineau – our great doorman, DJ Deep and myself) were stationed at the Rex club. Eric was at the door and spent most of his time explaining to the clientele that, yes, they did have to pay to get in because there was

an international DJ, and on top of that the cost of hiring lasers and extra sound. And all of that cost money!

'Giving' was the golden rule at Wake Up. For the first two anniversary parties we pressed a limited edition record to give to each punter. We also regularly gave out fresh fruit, sweets, freebies and even free candyfloss. All of this was just for fun and to create something memorable. But the real gift that Wake Up gave to its punters was bringing DJs from all over the world, living legends whose names sent shivers down people's spines. Most of these DJs had never set foot in France before. From the first official opening party on May 21, 1992 with DJ Deep, Wake Up became a second home to artists from Chicago and Detroit. Derrick May and Kevin Saunderson came to play on June 25, 1992, followed by Jeff Mills, Lil Louis and Ron Trent.

It was during these parties that Eric and I realised that there was a huge difference between the impact the music produced by these American artists was making in Europe and how they were perceived back home. When Ron Trent, the man behind the classic track Altered State (which he wrote when he was only 14), came to play at Wake Up, he had absolutely no idea how much people in France adored his music. When DJ Pierre, the official inventor of the acid sound, came to play in Paris on September 17, 1992, he couldn't believe that the DJs at FG radio were playing Chicago house all day long, and were so excited at the idea of their master playing in Paris a few hours later at the Rex. A close relationship began to form between Paris, Chicago and Detroit. A loyal crowd of clubgoers who no one ever saw the rest of the week would turn up every Thursday night, without fail, at the Rex. Wake Up became the meeting place for all those involved in Paris' dance music scene: Guillaume La Tortue, Olivier Le Castor, Scan X, Loïk Dury, Eric Napora, and the staff from FG. Week after week, the Rex slowly underwent a transformation. Even the bar staff started dancing behind the bars, happy to see such a friendly, enthusiastic clientele taking over their club.

Around that time, I travelled a lot between France and England. I started a new monthly residency in Birmingham on top of the residencies I already had in Manchester and Liverpool. In Birmingham, I got to know a mad group of clubbers, one of whom was called Dominic and worked in a recording studio in Stoke-On-Trent. After the club we would go back to his studio, close the door and switch on the machines. From these sessions came my second release on Fnac, Stronger By Design, which came out in September 1992.

Simultaneously, Eric Morand was defining a strategy for the label, and in November the Fnac Dance Division went on the road travelling

around France in a van equipped with a sound system, lights and studio equipment. The Respect For France tour included six dates: Rennes, Strasbourg, Toulouse, Dijon, Lille and Montpellier. Shazz and Deepside (Ludovic Navarre's solo project) played live, and in between the concerts I DJ-ed. Eric Morand, who was behind this promotional campaign, had a hard time trying to satisfy everyone. First there were the club owners, who still believed that house music was confined to gay clubs. Then there were the promoters, who were unsure of this new type of event. And then there were Shazz and Ludovic, who had never played in front of a live audience before, and the clubs that didn't have a clue about house music. Not to mention the nasty little surprises that always pop up on these kinds of tours. For example, in Rennes, we played in a club called Pymps the day after Beaujolais Nouveau arrived. The club's regulars had obviously stayed at home, too hungover from the night before. A predominantly gay crowd took hold of the club that night, and the atmosphere was wild. The cash desks were overflowing, but the club owner still took Eric aside shouting hysterically, 'You've introduced debauchery into my club! What is this music? What is your problem?' But, overall, we were made to feel welcome everywhere we went. The Fnac Dance Division's Respect For France tour never once got a mention in the local press, but that didn't matter to us at the time. For the first time in history, a French dance music label had taken to the road, to meet and seduce the public, to promote their music, and strengthen the relationship between the artists while eating sandwiches and drinking cold cups of coffee at motorway service stations.

Respect For France laid the first foundations outside of the capital, and only time would tell if this tour really had any impact.

The weekly Wake Up nights were our laboratory – the place where we tested our latest creations. Derrick May was our guest when I played the track Acid Eiffel for the very first time. I'd written it and recorded it onto DAT the day before, along with Shazz and Ludovic Navarre. We were all in the DJ booth, staring at the crowd, waiting to see their reaction. They seemed to like it. Derrick, too, liked what he heard, 'What is this shit, man?' I replied, 'Oh, just something I did with Shazz and Ludovic Navarre for fun.' He stared at me, 'You don't make music for fun, man!' He began his DJ set and when he finished he told me he wanted to release Acid Eiffel on his label, Fragile Records, no less. One of the most legendary techno record labels in Detroit was going to release a track made by three Frenchies 'for fun'. Derrick kept his word, and Acid Eiffel appeared in record shops stamped with the label F, for Fragile. Fnac Dance Division was starting to forge links with artists from Detroit.

Acid Eiffel had not yet been released when Eric and I headed to New York for the New Music Seminar, a music industry event that had decided to embrace dance music. Anyone who was anyone in the dance music business was there. The programme was simple: serious business in the day and partying (where networking continued – after all, this was the United States) at night. It was not uncommon to bump into Carl Cox, Ritchie Hawtin, Sven Vath, Derrick May tearing off to their next meeting. It was all about business, so it was full on. But it was there that we could see which artists and which labels had a long-term vision for dance music.

During the New Music Seminar, a conference was held on the subject of Detroit techno. Juan Atkins, Blake Baxter and Derrick May sat facing a room full of journalists, record label owners, DJs, producers and side-kicks … The discussions degenerated when Juan Atkins got angry, 'You haven't understood a thing about techno. Instead of talking about it, come to Detroit and see what's really happening, assholes!' Great atmosphere!

Eric and I went to many meetings, some more successful than others. When we met up with the people from the Canadian label, +8 records, their agent accompanied the two founders, Ritchie Hawtin and John Acquaviva. We were severely put to the test as he interrogated us about our abilities. We left the meeting suffering from nervous exhaustion, but had managed to sign a contract stating that Fnac would oversee the distribution of +8 records in France. Our next stop was the Nervous Records office. In 1992, Nervous was *the* record label, the jewel in the crown of the New York underground house scene, and home to producers such as Josh Wink and Masters at Work. The meeting was typical of the disregard the Americans had for European music (except for the UK, of course). Nervous regarded Fnac as a way to get their records released in France, but when it came down to asking them to listen to our productions, the person we were in the meeting with changed from being quite a nice guy to extremely patronising. He half-heartedly listened to our tracks, obviously not in the slightest bit interested, and ended up saying, 'You French, what you're missing is the sound. You don't know how to produce records. That's shit, all of it!' We got the same reaction from Strictly Rhythm and Eight Ball, both independent house music labels like Nervous. The only person to show any genuine interest in our records was Larry Slick, a dance music journalist who wrote a highly respected column in *Billboard* magazine (the bible for the American music chart). Towards the end of the New Music Seminar, he wrote a review of a Fnac Dance Division record in *Billboard*, and people finally started paying us some attention.

However contemptuous, the American labels were right about one thing: the sound, or to be more precise, the quality of the pressing of French dance music records. It was a real problem. The pressing is the key to the success of a track. When a track is mastered, it is the equalising process that determines the final sound of the record. It determines the grain and depth of a record before it finally goes to be pressed. Back in 1992, there was nothing in place to enable the release of a great dance music record in France. To master a record you first need a sound engineer. But all the guys that we were dealing with (the majority had a rock background) had never had to master this style of music before. As soon as we tried giving them directions on how to do it they stared at us blankly: 'What? You want the kick drum in the foreground? You can't do that!' On top of this, the CD, since it first appeared in 1985, now dominated the market. Vinyl had been massively pushed aside by the music industry. So when, in 1992, Fnac Dance Division brought up the subject of releasing records on vinyl, stating that vinyl was a fundamental part of dance music's identity, people laughed. Only one pressing plant in the whole of France was still pressing vinyl, so to press records, we had to work with pressing plants in Holland and Germany.

When we got back from New York, the general outlook was not very encouraging.

The international music market was not interested in our records – 'You're good at perfume and food … but music? Forget it!'

In France, the mainstream media and general public weren't particularly interested in house and techno, either. We heard the same old thing: 'It's not music.' Sales were so poor that when a Shazz single sold 300 copies it was hailed a success.

Dance music had no image, and the artists hid behind pseudonyms. Anonymity was considered one of the elements of dance music: who cares who I am, just listen to my music. However, Eric Morand was convinced that the best way to reach a wider audience was to put a face on this music. He decided to use the promotional tools of a traditional record label: press shots, artist biographies, careful record sleeve design, etc. In contrast to dance music's hardliners, the Fnac Dance Music Division bet everything on visibility. For these reasons, and because we wanted to produce and distribute our artists abroad, Fnac was considered a commercial label (or less politely 'a sell-out') by some people on the French scene – for the most part, rival groups of promoters who had become masters in the art of bad-mouthing. In a nutshell, it wasn't going to be easy.

Yet the contempt in which we were held by those abroad as well as our own fellow countrymen went from being a cause of suffering to our driving force. We were convinced that our records were good and that our approach was honourable. But sales didn't follow, which in the long run would threaten the sustainability of Fnac Dance Music Division. We needed a big hit, and quick.

I began work on a new track at Ludo's house. One evening we switched on the machines. It was one of those nights where everything just came together. There were no technical hitches and the inspiration just seemed to flow. Everything was clear and simple. Once we had finished the track, we recorded it onto DAT and I went home to bed. The following day I played my new track on FG, where I had been asked to do a radio show again. I explained to my listeners that I liked the track, that it had been finished the night before and that it still did not have a title. One listener left a message on the FG minitel: 'The track is beautiful, it sounds like someone breathing, call it Breathe.' In the end I called the track Breathless. It landed on Eric Morand's desk. Verdict: 'I need a B-side.'

So back I went to Ludo's. The Wake Up club nights had been a great success. I wanted to do a track for all those people who had been loyal to us. In my mind, the UK was still the leader in dance music, while the growing dance music scene in France was being eaten away by in-fighting between promoters, DJs and labels. What did I want to say? 'Wake Up!' It was time to stop squabbling and consider house and techno as a global movement. A kick drum from a TR-909, a bass line straight out of a TB-303, a sample of my voice saying 'Wake Up' in a loop. Then Ludovic added tons of filters to make it sound like a beast growling from the depths of his throat: 'Noooo moooore sleeeeepiiiiing wouaaaeeekh uuuppp.' The next day a new tape arrived on Eric Morand's desk. He listened to it and said no. He didn't like the growling beast. No problem, we went back to the studio. Fnac Dance Division released the definitive version of Wake Up in April 1993. It became an overnight hit in Germany. Warp then licensed it for the UK. Finally people were tuning in to French house music. All of a sudden we were being approached by foreign media and record labels. We knew we had to take advantage of this sudden interest to make a difference, so Fnac Dance Division manufactured a series of jackets emblazoned with the logo: 'We give a French touch to house.'

I was still playing raves in the UK every other weekend and regularly saw my friends from Stoke-On-Trent. Our first track had sold 2,000 copies in France – not bad. One drunken evening we came up with the ludicrous idea of starting our own band called the Moose Posse. There were no obligations, we just locked ourselves away in the studio, smoked a lot and laughed hysterically. We also had crazy face-pulling competitions with our hands on our heads, fingers spread out like Moose antlers yelling, 'Mooooossse!'

Only then would the Moose Posse switch on the machines and get to work. Our goal: to write the perfect soundtrack for a herd of moose crossing the Arctic tundra. In July, under the name Alaska, the Moose Posse released Lost In Alaska on Fnac, the story of a young moose who gets lost in the North Pole and almost freezes to death while searching for his friends. Just as he is about to give up hope, he finds his herd. The story ends with them celebrating his return with a party to end all parties!

Following this record, we were asked to take part in a series of remixes of the track I Believe by Kevin Saunderson, to be released on Network. We got hold of the different parts of the recording: the voice, the rhythm section and the melodies. During a Moose Posse session we came up with a remix that was way, way off the original. A sort of long, trippy journey with moose lowing in the distance, nothing to do with this 'oh-so-holy' track from Detroit. The next day we gave the off-the-wall remix to the person in charge at Network, who pulled a rather strange face when he listened to the track but promised to forward it to Kevin Saunderson. Kevin liked it and gave it the go-ahead. The 'I Believe Laurent Garnier Frenchman In Stoke-On-Trent Ambient Chill Baseroom Mix' was released on Network in September 1992.

In the space of a year, Eric Morand's Dance Division signed a few more French artists (notably Scan X and Lunatic Asylum, Fnac's rave recruits) as well as the Dutch label Djax Up, which was enjoying a lot of attention thanks to the huge success of Speedy J's single Pull Over. Djax Up joined Warp and +8 as part of Fnac's platform for distribution. But, in early 1993, the first signs of problems with Fnac Music's financial health began to show, and Eric Morand's artistic freedom was at risk as sales figures were poor. These uncertain times coincided with the release of The Meltdown by Lunatic Asylum. The track was an overnight hit on the rave scene and, for the first time for a French techno production, it was also a hit in the clubs of Paris. The Meltdown was such a big hit in raves in Germany that it entered the German charts in the first week it was released. This resulted in Fnac being named Label of the Month in *Frontpage* magazine, the reference for dance music in Germany.

Following this spotlight on the label, Fnac artists found a second home in Germany, which was in the midst of a trance explosion. Not so long ago this would have been unheard of. In return, Wake Up welcomed a host of German artists, such as Sven Vath, Paul Van Dyk, Pascal F.E.O.S; English artists such as Carl Cox, Colin Dale, Black Dog, Darren

Emerson, Luke Slater. And, as ever, artists from Detroit such as Stacey Pullen, and Derrick May's protégé Kenny Larkin, who had recently released two albums *Azimuth* and *Metaphor* on Warp and R&S.

I was more than just interested – I was obsessed with Detroit techno. When Kenny came to play at Wake Up I questioned him for hours about everything to do with Detroit: my heroes, what the city was really like, the music, everything I could extract from him to fuel my dreams. But Kenny went one step further. He invited me to stay with him in Detroit and meet my mentors: 'Anytime, Laurent.'

In life, you have to take an opportunity when you see one and grab it with both hands before it's too late.

final frontier

7

'Like Detroit, techno is a complete mistake. Like closing Kraftwerk and George Clinton in an elevator with just a sequencer for company.'
DERRICK MAY

'We created tomorrow and live in your imagination. We will never die.'
UNDERGROUND RESISTANCE

My plane landed in Detroit at around 5pm local time. I was questioned several times over at border control without really knowing why. Eventually, the US immigration officer got bored and stamped my passport. I passed through customs and stepped outside through the security doors.

I jumped into a cab and gave the driver Kenny Larkin's address. He was waiting for me at his house in the white suburbs of Detroit. The taxi pulled away and sailed onto the ring road. Once we had crossed the invisible boundary into 'downtown Detroit' I began making out the city's wide avenues. It was getting dark. The headlights faintly lit the decrepit walls lining the streets. Buildings resembled crumbling mausoleums. In the distance I saw two towers bearing the letters G and M. The taxi driver pointed them out to me as if proudly showing me the ruins of a local monument, 'You see right there, that's General Motors!' On top of the steel and glass towers, the red and blue letters overlooked the down-at-heel city.

In the taxi, I was trying to recall when I had first heard the name Detroit. Was it in the 90s, via techno? Or through Motown soul? Soul and techno: two by-products of the same story of suffering and sincerity. One thing is for sure, I have always associated Detroit with music. For the likes of me, having grown up with music, Detroit is the mark of quality, whether experimental jazz or rhythm 'n' blues, the invention of futuristic funk by George Clinton or the cries of anger of MC5 and The Stooges, and, of course, the unforgettable sound of Motown.

The US itself seems to have a hard time remembering Detroit as a musical guiding light, whereas in Europe Detroit is regarded as a city overflowing with innovation, groove and perfection. And for people like me, Detroit is the birthplace of techno, a place of hardship, where jazz, the last great music of the century, underwent a change and evolved into electronic music. Techno can be considered the urban continuation of jazz. Be it John Coltrane or Derrick May, their obsessions are the same: space, time, groove and unfathomable melancholia. I was in Detroit for a special reason, to soak up the vibes of the city and to meet my techno heroes. I hoped to reach the purity and great sadness that permeates the music and understand why Detroit's music exudes such emotion, so much hardship, so much experience and so much beauty. I had expected to arrive in a rundown city and have a hard time getting to grips with the mystery that is Detroit. I had planned on questioning everyone I met there and interpreting every sign. But instead, all the answers could be found just by looking at the history of the city.

Like Manchester in the early 1800s, during the golden age of the British Industrial Revolution, Detroit also became the great American city of industry. Several thousand blue-collar workers came from all over the US to work at the Ford automobile plant, while the black workers were confined to the foundries. Greek immigrants founded Greek Town and the first black community within the city settled in a ghetto known as Black Bottom. It was there, on Hastings Street, that the first temple of the Nation of Islam was built.

In 1932, after the Wall Street Crash, Detroit was nicknamed the 'green city', as there were more trees per square kilometre than in any other city in America. World War II marked the second golden era for Detroit, a.k.a. Motor Town, as it became 'democracy's arsenal'. B52s were built in the Ford factories and army tanks at Chrysler. Then jazz appeared and the Black Bottom ghetto was knocked down and replaced by a motorway. In 1959 Motor Town gave birth to Motown, the cultural pride of the black community. Then the battle for civil rights broke out in the US, and in July 1967 Detroit experienced three days of bloody rioting. Then began the city's slow downfall. It began with the closure of automobile factories. The white community fled to the suburbs and the ghetto grew bigger and bigger. And finally, in the 1980s, there was an explosion in drug abuse, especially of crack, in these same ghettos.

Detroit techno music tells the story of all of this hardship. And within this music one can feel the life force that refuses to be put down. Words are of no importance. Everything is expressed within a few notes, repeated ad infinitum. Detroit techno is made of metal, glass and steel. When you close your eyes you can hear, far off in the distance, then closer and closer, the echo of crying. Like in jazz and blues, Detroit techno transfigures suffering. This authenticity of spirit has no price.

At the beginning of the 1980s, Detroit was still a sounding board for American record companies. If an artist made it in Detroit, the labels felt that artist could make it across the US; the majors trusted the local Detroit radio stations and their DJs. The influence of Detroit radio DJs would play a critical role in the future of young artists and the emergence of new musical trends. Today, every single DJ and producer who made up this first wave of Detroit techno artists still talks about Electrifying Mojo's radio show. He was a visionary, who mixed European electronic music with early black music. Mojo was the first to play prime-time Prince and A Certain Ratio, Funkadelic and Kraftwerk, Visage, New Order, Pet Shop Boys, the B52s, Falco and even the French violinist Jean Luc Ponty. Everyone agrees that Mojo was the person who created the framework on which to hang Detroit techno.

In the middle of the 1980s, another DJ appeared on the Detroit radio scene, known as The Wizard. His technique, innovation, knowledge of mixing and the mystery that shrouded his true identity resulted in him becoming a legend within the city. Almost 20 years later, Jeff Mills still remains The Wizard. The current hip-hop generation in Detroit grew up listening to him. And to this day, on the rare occasions that Jeff Mills performs in Detroit, you will still find hip-hop fans at his gigs who would never normally venture into techno clubs. It's not rare to overhear in a conversation, 'Eminem and his posse came down to listen to The Wizard' or, 'The Producer Jay Dee and the group Slum Village were at the venue'.

Jeff Mills is undoubtedly one of the most important and creative music producers of the last 15 years. He is a visionary, a leading light in the world of techno, and a master DJ (as one would use the term master craftsman). You only have to see Jeff playing across three record decks to be mesmerised by his feline movements, not to mention the inimitable way in which he plays rough, minimal, funky music. Here, Jeff Mills will serve as our guiding voice and describe Detroit in the early 80s; a city struck by crises, which, in the space of a generation, changed from a city of abundance to an urban nightmare, giving birth en route to the final musical revolution of the 20th century: techno.

JEFF MILLS:
'In 1979 I was 16. My older brother had been a DJ for several years. He let me practise at his place, on his gear. At around the same time we both began sending mix tapes to radio stations in Detroit. It wasn't really something people did back then. On my brother's advice I must have sent about 15 tapes in just one year to the station WDRQ, but never got a reply. When my brother decided to stop DJ-ing he gave me all his records and his equipment. I set it all up in my bedroom and started practising for several hours a day.

'Between 1979 and 1981, the first hip-hop sounds started filtering through to us from New York via Chicago. It was the beginning of a street culture made up of dance, graffiti, rap and DJ-ing, with some incredible inventions like scratching. Hip-hop was both a global and a community culture, created by and for the ghetto: "For Us By Us". On the East Coast there was Grandmaster Flash and DJ DST; on the West Coast Dr Dre and DJ Yellow; in Florida and in Mississippi there were Bass stations, radios playing the beginnings of electro and Miami Bass. But at this time, videos showing DJs mixing didn't exist, and in Detroit it was impossible to get hold of any information to find out how these DJs were scratching and making these sounds. Rumour had it that if you wanted to scratch faster you had to wear surgical gloves. Within a matter of days every DJ in Detroit was wearing white latex gloves.

'The more I heard from New York, the more I got into DJ-ing. I studied every piece of information to do with music that I could: the label bosses, the musicians who were in, the remixers, scratching patterns … In Detroit we grew up with music. From as young as 14, kids were going to mobile discos for teenagers. Every age group had their own parties. When I was 17, I started getting DJ work at mobile discos.

'Then my brother introduced me to some influential people on Detroit's nightlife scene. These people could help me develop my art, teach me how to play records in a club and make a selection of music suited to an older crowd. My brother arranged a meeting at a downtown club called Lady so I could audition. As I wasn't yet the right age legally (21) to be allowed into the club I had to sneak in through the back door and scramble up into the DJ booth without being seen by security. It wasn't yet 10pm and the club was already packed. The bosses and the resident DJs came into the DJ booth, "OK, show us what you can do". I started off my set with a move that they had never seen before. I put the needle on the first record in the middle of the break and then played a second copy of the same record from the beginning. I won my ticket to play the week after. The bosses agreed to take me on and teach me the ropes. I learnt how to make a track popular with the crowd (play part of the record, take it off, play it again an hour or so later to build a hit), I learnt what kind of records I should always have in my boxes to adapt to any given situation, I learnt which records were good for transitions, etc. … . Basically, I learnt about the psychology of the dance floor; training that a lot of DJs and musicians from Detroit have never had.

'Despite my youth, within the space of a few months, I was given three residencies in three Detroit clubs. In one of them, the UBQ, they were organising the after-party for Prince's Purple Rain Tour, which was in town for seven dates. As luck would have it, WDRQ radio decided to broadcast the after-party live on air. I received instructions to only play music associated with Prince (Sheila E., Vanity, Tiles, etc.). It was my first time on the radio. I was really excited and prepared my set several days beforehand. Just as I was about to start my set the radio DJ asked me, "What's your stage name?" And I replied, "My best friend calls me The Wizard". And so she announced, "Now, live on WDRQ, it's The Wizard!" The next day I found out that WDRQ had achieved their best audience figures in months. I was called in to the radio station to be interviewed with a view to getting my own show and to meet the new programme director. He came from New York and wanted to introduce hip-hop to Detroit by programming a special hip-hop mix show on WDRQ. There were two of us being auditioned. After playing a 15-minute set I got the job. The director took me aside in his office and said, "We know about you already because of all the demo tapes you've been sending us." He opened up a cupboard and there inside I saw all the tapes I had sent in over the years, in chronological order. "We'll teach you the rules of radio." And so I learnt how to edit tracks on tape and how to produce a show. I was given a budget as well as access to their entire record collection. I was allowed to buy all the records I wanted and had carte blanche. For a guy who wasn't even 20, it was an unbelievable stroke of good luck. Faced with a rival radio station, WRDQ needed to head off the competition and the new director was counting on me. "Here's your studio [built specially for me with three turntables], this is your receptionist, and here's your telephone. Now, over to you."

WDRQ gradually introduced The Wizard to their listeners as of November 1982. Their aim was for him to present the big New Year's show, during which he would play for nine hours solid. 'The radio station did a lot of advertising around me. I had to be available to go on-air at any time of day to surprise the listeners. I distinguished myself from the other radio DJs by creating thematic mixes: Michael Jackson vs. Prince, Automobile vs. Motor City, etc. For these shows, I used the radio's archives. I think that my love of concepts dates back to this period.

'To preserve The Wizard's mystery, I wasn't allowed to use the name The Wizard in clubs or to reveal my true identity to anyone. Meanwhile, I continued to play in the city's clubs. At the beginning of the 80s, Detroit had many very talented DJs including Darryl Shannon, Delano Smith, Carl Martin, who, influenced by Electrifying Mojo, introduced new music from Europe, known as synthpop, into the clubs.

'In 1981, a record – Sharevari – was released that would play a pivotal role in the history of Detroit techno. Sharevari was produced by a group

▶ Playlist

DETROIT VIBES

Kevin Saunderson
Rock To The Beat

Blake Baxter
When We Used To Play

Model 500
The Battle

Jeff Mills
The Bells

Mayday
Sinister

Aux 88
Direct Drive

K Hand
I Do

Eddie Flashing Fowlkes
Track One

Kenny Dixon
I'm Doing Fine

Theo Parrish
Walking Through The Sky

Alan Oldham
Engine Float Reactor

Dark Comedy
War Of The Worlds

Dopplereffekt
Satellites

Fade 2 Black
The Calling

of middle-class students from Detroit, two boys and two girls calling themselves A Number Of Names. They were members of a student association (called Sharevari) that organised parties and had made quite a lot of money. They decided to make their own music. They went into a studio, found inspiration in the track Moscow Disco by the Belgian band Telex, and recorded Sharevari. Mojo turned the track into a big hit in Detroit. Sharevari is the very first techno record from Detroit, but as yet nobody had used the term "techno", it simply didn't exist.

'I met Juan Atkins just after the release of Sharevari. He already had his band, Cybotron, loved Kraftwerk, and had released a track, Clear. After Sharevari, his music changed. His band split and the two other band members left for California to make pop music. Juan chose to stay in Detroit. In 1985, he released No UFOs and Night Drive, two amazing tracks that used sounds similar to Sharevari. It was then that everything happened. People began talking about techno, without really knowing where the name came from – but who cared? New music from Detroit now had an identity, a special flavour. Sharevari had been the trigger and Juan Atkins was the first hero of the techno trinity. Derrick May and Kevin Saunderson would follow suit.

'But this small group of people didn't know each other. The city was divided into two: one side was downtown and the other in the suburbs. At the time, there were a lot of parties going on in Detroit, in people's backyards to local clubs. One Sunday night, at a "black night" I was playing, Kevin Saunderson came down to see me. We didn't know each other, as we didn't hang out in the same circles. Several different scenes had sprung up across the city without ever coming into contact. Kevin gave me one of his first records, which he had released under the name Reese & Santonio. He also introduced me to Neil Rushton, the boss of Network Records, the first record label to release Detroit techno in the UK. A few months later, Kevin Saunderson released Big Fun and had a massive hit.

'At that time, I had my own industrial band called the Final Cut. We had made a few records but I felt like I hadn't found the right people to make music with. Then I met Mike Banks.'

Mike Banks, alias Mad Mike, is the true soul of Detroit techno. He is an urban guerrilla, a man haunted by the suffering of his city. Mike has chosen music to fight against the problems of daily life and takes his inspiration from the Afro-American struggle of the 1960s. Mike is a resistant, 'a pure product of Detroit's black culture', as he says.

Mike, a musician, producer and legendary techno figure throughout the world, chose to organise his struggle in the shadows, never giving interviews or wanting to be photographed. Through his record label

Underground Resistance, Mike Banks spreads a guerrilla philosophy whose targets are the major record labels, the American segregationist system, and despair in the ghetto.

From inside the building that houses his record label Underground Resistance, a distribution platform for Detroit's independent record labels Submerge and several studios, Mad Mike pursues his causes – to get young people away from crime and drugs, to rally against the economic disaster that is Detroit – and music.

When he speaks, Mike Banks tells the story of Detroit with a slow, deep 'scarred' voice and relates the history of Underground Resistance.

MIKE BANKS:

'Jeff and I wanted to do great things, like all the kids in this city. We wanted to do something big, be on a major, earn money, be on TV, be in a magazine. All these things are proof of success over here.

'Jeff loved industrial music, and I loved everything Jeff played, as he has the funkiest ear for sound in the world. We met in a studio in Detroit, the United Sound Studio. I was recording with other musicians: Ray (now in Underground Resistance), Mike Pierce and Scott Christers. We were studio musicians, able to play any kind of music: R&B, funk, church music, gospel. Our band had been signed to Motown. But Motown wanted to call us For Girls Only, or something like that, and make a boy band out of us. They wanted us to be dressed like Prince and put on make-up … We were 23 or 24 years old. We thought, "If that's what we've gotta do to make it, fuck that!" Motown broke off our agreement and we became studio musicians for the remainder of our contract. This enabled us to work with George Clinton, David Spradley (who wrote Atomic Dog), Amp Fiddler and the Reverend Thomas Whitfield. Because of our bad experience with Motown, we were left with a bitter taste in our mouths. This is when I met Jeff Mills.

'Jeff also had a bad taste in his mouth. Musically, he was excellent, but things were turning sour with his band the Final Cut. Besides, a black man playing industrial music, it just didn't make sense! Jeff had an amazingly fast way of making music. In contrast, we were used to working up to three months on a song to obtain exactly the right harmonies. This is why Kraftwerk's music was so fascinating for us. We were trying to reproduce their songs on our guitars. We didn't know that it was machines that produced these sounds. When we learned that all these things were done with computers, we started studying the technology. We used our lunch breaks to record. Jeff came and gave us a hand on the edit of a few of the tracks.

'We started to see each other more and work together more regularly. We both liked Public Enemy for the way they refused to play the "show niggers". You know, we the black people, in the USA, we always have to be disguised, to make ourselves up, to be flashy or to play the clown if we want to enter the music business. I came from a family of sportsmen and workers. At my place, we were opposed to this "show nigger" shit! I was educated in an environment that despised fancy clothes, all those pimp get-ups, because living in the ghetto doesn't necessarily mean acting like a pimp. My family instilled one core value in me: work. Pimp, prostitute, dealer, that's not a good model. I became very disparaging of these kinds of people as I grew up. The "showboats niggers", as I called them, were nothing else but cannon fodder. And that's why a band like Public Enemy immediately struck a chord with me. They were so powerful, so good. Their logo was a target with a silhouette in the middle. What they were saying to the white establishment was: "This silhouette, here, it's me, and I put myself in front of the target on purpose. If you have the balls, shoot!". They were taken to court for that.

'With Jeff, we realised we worked well together; we had the same mindset. So we created the UR concept, Underground Resistance. UR came from Public Enemy for the black power, and a love of the German precision of Kraftwerk. When we became business partners, Jeff was at the height of his fame with his radio persona, The Wizard. He started playing Public Enemy on WJLB, the most influential black radio station in Detroit. The bosses asked him to stop. But, hanging out with me, Jeff had become a resistant. He was supported by me and my boys, most of whom were gang members. Jeff ignored the station's warnings. He continued playing Public Enemy, each night, on WJLB. The radio station started to cut back his shows. From two hours, the show was put back to one hour, and then to thirty minutes, until it only lasted fifteen minutes, and at this point, Jeff resigned. It was the end of The Wizard. It was hard for us. And I think it also damaged music's development and expansion in Detroit.

'UR evolved out of this fighting spirit. UR is the continuation of a long struggle and we chose existing technologies to make this struggle move forward. Through UR, we wanted to express everything through sound; no need for pictures. We were against everything you have to accept in order to be famous.

'Jeff and I were studio musicians, and so operated in the shadows. So we decided that if people wanted to meet us, it would be for our music, not to see what we looked like or to check out the colour of our skin. We were just coming out of the 80s, a time when many black artists had

had their noses done or their skin whitened. Fuck that! If a guy doesn't know what you look like, he won't care, as long as he likes your music. It's Detroit and the whole black experience in America that gave birth to Underground Resistance. UR is a prolongation of the incessant struggle in everyday life. I think inspiration goes beyond generations. Jeff and I often talked about that. Our music goes beyond us. Sometimes, I compare music to what a vampire obtains from the blood he sucks: eternal life. The energy we pass on stays behind and can touch people in 200 or 300 years' time. I'm on earth to inspire other people, and maybe people who are not even on earth yet.'

JEFF MILLS:

'At the beginning of UR, Mike and I would meet and discuss what we wanted to do. Derrick May, Juan Atkins and Kevin Saunderson had told us about their bad experiences with European record companies. Big Fun and Good Life had been released on majors and things had gotten nasty. It was perfectly clear to us, we didn't want to work with the majors. We both had experience of deals with majors in which we had been swindled. That is where the name Underground Resistance came from. Literally, to create a resistance to the "overground". Before we started making music together, we first thought about the direction we wanted to take. Our militant approach to techno comes from Public Enemy, but the idea of conceptualising our music came from the radio. If you want a show to become big on the radio, you have to be different, surprise people. That's what we did with UR. I had access to recording studios, I had a good knowledge of sound, and I knew about editing. I could be a DJ for a hip-hop night or a house night. Mike brought soul to our music, and a special way of playing keyboards. He also had a certain knowledge of vocals and introduced patience and consideration into the narration of our tracks.

'All my machines and all his keyboards gave life to an incredibly well-equipped studio. At that time, we didn't work on computers. Our studio was configured so we could work on several songs at once. We had a very simple way of working in UR; we each had distinct roles. First, we ate chicken, and then we discussed what we wanted to do. We wrote the instrumental parts together. Mike played the keyboard parts and then left the studio to allow me time to prepare the mix on the mixing desk. He came back to do the final mix and I finished the track's final edit alone. We worked in this same way from the first UR record, Your Time Is Up, that came out in 1990, until The Punisher in 1992.

'In 1992, we produced a band from Detroit called Members Of The House. The record was released under licence on the UK label React, and, as it did well in Europe, the band was invited to do a show in the UK. The guys from Members Of The House came from the ghetto and they were tricky, so Mike decided to go with them to Europe, while I stayed in Detroit. It was the first time we were separated for more than a week. During Mike's absence, I wrote The Punisher, the first record I made for UR on my own. At the time, Derrick May and Blake Baxter were starting to tour in Europe and sent home amazing news: "I played in Belgium to a crowd of 15,000 people." It was crazy! I had only been to Europe once before and had no idea what was going on over there.

'Meanwhile, Detroit was also changing. It was going from musical fever pitch into a downward spiral. Most of the artists had moved to Chicago, California or New York. Hip-hop and gangsta rap had become huge in Detroit; radio stations didn't play techno anymore. Young people that had no musical background or studio experience were doing mixes on the radio. They didn't even know the difference between hip-hop and gangsta rap. Gradually, gangsta rap imposed itself as the dominant genre and completely changed younger people's mindset. There were more and more drugs and gangs. The streets became more and more violent and the audience less and less open-minded.'

In 1992, Jeff Mills left Underground Resistance, and went to live in New York. Mike Banks continued his struggle and got to work with the younger generation (Drexciya, Aux 88, James Pennington, DJ Rolando, etc.). Yet, Detroit was plunging back into darkness once again.

My taxi drove through a deserted neighbourhood, passing endless warehouses and pieces of twisted and bent sheet metal, shaped by the freezing cold wind. Here was the last tangible evidence of a past era when this neighbourhood would have been Detroit's central food market. I stared at the giant parking lots littered with the remains of abandoned trucks. There was a great sense of loneliness here. Flashes of graffiti stood out against the abandoned vehicles that had been left to rot.

Urban myth says that, at night, the Unknown Writer wanders Detroit's derelict buildings. He walks through abandoned neighbourhoods, stricken areas and ghettos painting his slogans, pamphlets and poems onto the walls. Underground Resistance promoted the Unknown Writer's work, printing his slogans on their records in order to spread his political and lucid urban poetry. 'Do not allow yourself to be programmed'.

A conversation started up with the cab driver. He asked me, 'What are you doing here?' I hesitated before answering, 'I've wanted to come here for a long time, you know … I need to understand a few things.' Silence.

And then he repeated '… a long time,' with a drawling voice. He then said in a low voice, 'So, you've come here to understand Detroit… We're going to make a quick detour; there's something you have to see. It's a few miles from here. Don't worry, I won't charge you, it's on me…' Outside, I could hear bass sounds, but I couldn't tell where the music was coming from. The cab edged its way into the night. Neon lights twinkled. Rows of Baptist churches and weather-beaten houses alternated with liquor stores. Further along, a crack house. I could make out a couple of people moving about in the shadows. For miles on end, the same configuration: church, liquor store, crack house…

Suddenly our surroundings changed and the taxi driver slowed down. The façades of derelict buildings painted with frescos became visible in the headlights of his Ford T. A huge banner hung across the wall of a faded red-brick building stated: 'You are entering the Heidelberg Project peace zone'. Poems advocating non-violence and respect were painted in big letters on the walls, floors and abandoned cars. The cab driver turned at me, 'Here, it's a peace zone. It must be one of the only places in Detroit where people say hi to each other and come to pray. Even the gangs stay clear of this area, you know! That's Detroit too: there's violence, but there's also hope…'

Then the cab pulled away and we drove back through the same derelict neighbourhoods to go back downtown. I could almost smell the death, the drugs, the violence, and the loneliness. This city seemed to live under a perpetual curfew. The centre of Detroit was deserted, except for the area of Greek Town, which houses luxury hotels, restaurants and shopping for tourists. Detroit was a ghost town. The odd pedestrian we came across turned round to check they weren't being followed. In Detroit, cars waiting at red lights keep an eye on people crossing the street, in case they pull out a gun. That's everyday life in downtown Detroit, which runs all the way to the edge of 8 Mile Road.

8 Mile Road is the name given to the ring road that separates two very different worlds. On one side is downtown Detroit where 80 per cent of the black community lives. On the other side lives the white middle-class, free of gangs, drugs and violence. When a car driven by a black man leaves downtown Detroit, passes the 8 Mile road, and heads towards one of the white suburbs, the driver can be sure he'll be followed by the flashing lights of the DPD. Every time, it's the same scenario. The vehicle is pulled over and the driver is questioned ('Where do you live? Where are you going?'), and then he is called to order ('Don't forget to go back home…').

MIKE BANKS:

'It's so stupid what's going on in this city! The desire to do something new is already dead in the water before the plan has been hatched. I can never feel truly happy or satisfied because I know it won't be long before somebody else is shot. If you let yourself be happy around here, something will come along and destroy it. At the same time, I love this city for its special vibe. Nothing is really normal here. For example, if you go buy shrimp, "Hello, a pound of shrimp, please". The guy will answer, "We don't have any shrimp". Yet there's a huge sign saying: "We sell shrimp" right in front of him. But the guy answers quietly, "We don't have any". That's crazy! But I learned to love all of that. It's like church … When I was a kid, I didn't understand a single word the priest was saying. He talked about the struggle between good and evil. I listened to what he was saying and thought, "Yeah, right, you keep talking". But then I grew up, and the theme of the struggle between good and evil came back to me. I realised it was true. It's a vampire world here. Public Enemy wrote Night Of The Living Baseheads, well that's exactly what it is! When night falls, guys come out to find dope. You see them wandering around like vampires looking for blood, hanging out on the streets looking for their next fix. When the sun comes up, they go back into hiding. When the Bible talks about the possessed, madmen who are prisoners of their dual personalities, like Dr Jekyll and Mr Hyde, I swear they're talking about people on heroin. Nowadays, when I go to church, I understand more what the priest is talking about. Because I have lived here and I've grown older and learned not to judge people. As the Bible says, "Don't judge thy neighbour".'

The taxi dropped me off in front of Kenny Larkin's house in the white suburb of Birmingham. In Detroit, Kenny was seen as techno's golden boy. He had trained as an actor and got involved in making music by accident. He had been inspired by Derrick May's music and had signed three albums, including *Azimuth* and *Metaphor*. Both of these albums did well worldwide, earning him a lot of money. For all these reasons, Kenny was criticised in Detroit, but – and this was a problem for his critics – his music was excellent.

After a warm reunion, Kenny told me that a dinner had been organised at Fishbones, a restaurant in Greek Town where several other people were waiting for us. Just as we were about to leave he said, 'Bring your records, – Why? – Don't worry! Just bring your records.' I put my bag in the boot of his car, got into the passenger seat and off we went. We drove towards the lights of the hotels in Greek Town. We walked into the restaurant. The walls were covered in photographs of baseball players and pictures of classic cars built at the Ford factories. At the back of the restaurant, the makers of Detroit techno were all seated around a table. I walked over and Kenny introduced me, and I realised then that this kind of dinner, with all the people on the Detroit scene, was exceptional, maybe even a first. In 1993, it was still rare for someone from Europe to take an interest in Detroit. Around the table were Derrick May, Mike Banks, Kelly Hand (one of the only female producers in Detroit) and Maurizio, a producer from Berlin who had invested in a factory in Detroit that pressed vinyl. They were all very welcoming. I wasn't there to ask for anything, and they knew that. Acid Eiffel, licensed by Fragile/ Transmat, was a rare collaboration between Detroit and Europe. On top of this, Kevin, Mike and Derrick had all been to the Rex. They knew me; they knew I was there for the right reasons. I talked to Mike Banks, who offered to take me somewhere the next day. It was all very mysterious. 'I got something to show you.' The atmosphere was relaxed, we talked about music, of course, and there was a lot of joking around. They joked about people who weren't there, and then the conversation moved onto baseball and I was out of my depth. As the restaurant began slowly emptying, I noticed that no one in the place recognised any of these demigods of techno…

As everyone stood up to put their heavy winter jackets back on, someone asked me, 'Did you bring your records with you?'. I answered shyly, 'Yes.' I got back in the car with Kenny to discover there was a party at a local primary school. There were hardly any clubs or venues where you could organise techno nights in Detroit. Nevertheless, promoters were very resourceful, despite the real risk of the DPD or even local gangs turning up. These events rarely attracted more than 200 people and most of them came from the white neighbourhoods, beyond 8 Mile Road.

I bumped into DJ Bone in the corridor of the primary school. He suggested that I come and DJ with him in one of the empty classrooms. The exclusively black crowd was here to dance and listen to the music. There were no lights, except for the neon light coming from outside. In a word, we were a million miles away from how all those Parisian music aficionados imagined Detroit. Bone played a few records before inviting me to take over. I hurriedly opened my record bag and began my set. I tried my very hardest to get the crowd to come round to me, though I could feel some people looking at me sceptically. As people began to get into the music, their dancing got more flamboyant. Mike was watching on from a corner of the room. I felt like I was really getting somewhere, as the room hit fever pitch. I played a St Germain track followed by Losing

Control by DBX. People were yelling 'Yeaaaaaaaah!' I had been dreaming of this for years! I would have given anything for an opportunity like this, and now here it was! It was like a dream; in fact I really thought I was dreaming … Then, suddenly, a guy stood in front of me and said, 'No more music in here!' Bone stood behind me, not moving. Mike came over quietly. I asked the guy why but he just mumbled, 'Stop the music.'

I was told that the police had arrived. The party was over. People quietly left the room, obviously used to the DPD putting a dampener on things. As Kenny was showing me out and offering to drive me back to my hotel, I heard bass sounds coming from another room at the other end of the corridor where the Canadian DJ Richie Hawtin was playing. I went to find out what was going on and walked into a room full of white kids clearly unaware of any police intervention. Did the DPD really only close one of two rooms? I would never know. I picked up my record boxes, said goodbye to Bone, and went back to find Kenny, who was waiting for me in the hall to take me back home.

The next day, Mike Banks asked me to meet him at the Motown Historical Museum on 2648 West Grand Boulevard. Mike was waiting for me in front of the museum, sitting on the bonnet of his car. He didn't ask me anything about what happened the night before as he walked me up to the entrance. All he said was, 'You gotta understand where you are.' We entered Hitsville, Motown's headquarters, opened by Berry Gordy in 1959. Mike paid for my ticket. 'I'll wait for you outside.'

Within the first few minutes, I could already feel the greatness of the ghosts of the past. People were whispering, like in church. I walked past photographs of Marvin Gaye, the Supremes and Stevie Wonder. I then went inside the recording studio where absolutely nothing had been changed. Inside this very studio, Smokey Robinson, Gladys Knight, the Temptations and Norman Whitfield recorded some of the most beautiful pieces of African-American music. The studio once ran 24 hours a day. This hellish pace of production only stopped in 1972 when Berry Gordy, the big boss, relocated to Los Angeles. I continued my visit along a corridor whose walls were lined with gold records before entering the projection room. I took a seat. Like a perfectly orchestrated partition, a film about the story of Motown started playing on the screen. The images were narrated in a respectful tone of voice. Some scenes were silent, others filled with music. This was a film about pride, ambition and independence. The images told the story of the African-American ideal conveyed by Motown. I sank back into my seat and slowly began to realise the purpose of my visit: to grasp the soul of Detroit through the memories of its most beautiful creation. I understood that the spirit of 'Young

America' was still alive; that, despite countless knockbacks, it hadn't disappeared. And that, 40 years on, we could still find traces of this spirit, in the projects Mike Banks had undertaken at UR. Like UR today, Motown was a record distribution network that protected the independence of the artists from the majors. It was a recording studio (where all the musicians from the label could go) that guaranteed a particular sound. It was a group of accomplished artists who shared the same philosophy. And it had a visionary boss who re-invested all the profits back into his label and back into his city.

Through Underground Resistance, Mike Banks continues to celebrate this great lineage. But UR didn't model its working methods solely on Motown. UR took inspiration from Motown, but then adapted Berry Gordy's model to the realities of a now disillusioned Detroit. It's like a thread running through the years, and a desire to communicate the same sense of urgency. You only have to look closely at UR's work to see a similar driving force to the Motown story. In the music of Detroit there has always been soul and there has always been anger.

If you go out onto the streets of Detroit you will quickly see that Berry Gordy's golden age is long gone. Detroit's artists, the keepers of its soul, have deserted the city in droves. Mike Banks has found a new energy in this desperate situation and is trying to restore hope.

MIKE BANKS:

'For the people of my parents' generation, Berry Gordy was a symbol of hope. That's what the Motown museum represents for me. When you go inside, you realise that the struggle we are having now is the same as in the 60s. But Gordy won his battles without the technology we have. That was an inspiration for me. At Submerge, we have printers, computers and faxes; with all that stuff we should be able to do something! When I see the conditions the Motown musicians had to work in, what limited resources they had, and the impact they had on the world, I think it's amazing! Berry Gordy wanted to conquer the planet with Motown music, at a time when black people were still fighting for their rights. He is a great source of pride for our community.

'But in his system, musicians weren't the most important cog in the machine and they suffered. What happened to them won't happen to artists at UR because I wear two hats: I'm both the CEO and a musician. Berry Gordy was an excellent businessman and I can appreciate the sorts of things he had to deal with. Like, for example, when he had to give the mother of an artist who was on drugs the money the artist had earned … The dark side of success, I sure know what that is. When you

make something of yourself in this city, you have 3,000 unemployed guys after you wanting you to bail them out. But it's impossible! I hear people cussing Kevin Saunderson, saying, 'Kevin sold out, he left to live in the white suburbs of Detroit.' But he didn't have a choice! He was incapable of saying no. Every time some guy came to ask him for 500 dollars because his kids had nothing to eat or because he was in trouble, Kevin gave him the money. If he hadn't left the ghetto, he would be unable to provide for his own family. Berry Gordy lived under this constant pressure and had to face the same kind of dilemmas. He decided to leave for Hollywood in 1972. He wanted to produce movies, but I'm sure the pressure from all those people wanting money made from Motown helped him make that decision. I'm sure of it, because we're under the same pressure.

'Other pressures pushed Gordy to leave Detroit. Motown artists had become stars and they simply wanted a better life in a nicer town with sunny weather. Up until the end of the 60s, Gordy still had full control over his artists by managing them with a rod of iron. But some of them became too famous, they started paying him less attention and started talking about moving to California whether he liked it or not. He couldn't bare the idea of seeing them moving away from him. So he left for California, to produce his movies and keep an eye on his artists. I still have an article on him – that had a big effect on me – in which he says the worst mistake he ever made was leaving for California, because it changed the sound of Motown. It changed the soul of the music. The sound, the sense of urgency and the struggle weren't the same … Maybe if they had gone to Compton, Inglewood or any other place, things would have turned out different. But those idiots, they went to Beverly Hills or some place like that! And there, they lost their mojo. The magic vanished!

'I'm not attached to Detroit like a clam to a rock, but when you go inside the Motown building, you can feel the spirit of the musicians is still alive. There are places in Detroit where you can feel that vibe. I feel like I'm a part of this city. I often say to my boys that you can feel the change in the music when an artist moves away. In the beginning, they're in Detroit, working on their tracks and they have a real sound. Then they travel and start doing other things. They work less in Detroit and they deal with people who think that because they're from Detroit, they must be someone important in techno, so everything they do is great. That's when it goes bad! Then one day, they find themselves back here and realise they lost something on the way.

'I'm not saying everything comes from our surroundings. Other factors influence our music. In my case, one important factor is to save my ass! Some of the best producers I know were very poor. Their inspiration came because they needed money: "Someone told me I could make money making music, so listen to this."

[Mike Banks reinvests all of UR's profits into the community – neighbourhood associations, nurseries, etc. … and into building the label's offices.]

'The construction of the Submerge building was a great learning curve. The people who I thought would be by my side during the work weren't there. The people who rallied round me and supported me were cousins and a few friends. A lot of them had drug problems. Before, I thought they were wasting their lives; it pissed me off. Then one day, I found myself overwhelmed by the work still left to do on the building and I had no more money left. I said to them, "Listen guys, that's it. We can't continue. I don't have a cent left." My cousin Cliff replied, "You think we're here for money? With what you pay us?! What we want is to see this building finished!" They blew me away. Because my problems were nothing compared to what they had been through with drugs. That day, I realised you should never judge people.

'The Submerge building is a tribute to all the people who have bought our records. Every single cent we earned is invested in that building. I want to be able to pass on what I've got to the people around me, to my kids and to my friends' kids. I want them to be able to work here if they want to, instead of working like robots in the factories. At Submerge, everyone has a role to play and can find his or her rightful place. Learn and move on. I want people to say, "My dad worked here 30 years ago, smart-ass, so this is how you should wrap a record! Like my dad showed me." Working for Underground Resistance and Submerge means joining a family business.'

Since 1992, daily life in Detroit has became harder and harder. The techno scene has been marred by rivalry, quarrels and jealousy. The most important artists have deserted Detroit for Europe. Detroit's police invariably break up the rare techno events still held in downtown Detroit.

While Mike Banks and Underground Resistance continued their struggle from Detroit, other American producers and record labels started to become aware of how big the house and techno phenomenon was in Europe. Eager to leave Detroit, certain DJs and producers gave in to easy money and flattery. An American DJ scene developed, satisfying the demands of Europe, which had eyes only for Detroit, New York and Chicago. Whereas the most famous American DJs couldn't hope to be paid more than 500 dollars a night in their own country, some New York DJs were demanding 15,000–20,000 dollars to perform a three-hour set in the UK. Taking advantage of this, other US DJs began asking for indecent amounts of money, and many of the promoters and clubs in Europe agreed to their demands.

This worldwide phenomenon spread to the Holy of Holies: Detroit. The reputation of the Detroit label was soon under siege. For the majority of the artists living there, music was an escape route from their difficult lives; it wasn't a question of money or fame. But when in 1993 promoters in Berlin invited a host of Detroit's DJs to perform at the Love Parade, the DJs understood they had possession of 'a goose that lays a golden egg'. They could sign sub-standard records to labels who were happy just to put the Detroit stamp on the tracks. The artists could have a lot of fun with this newfound wealth. Unsurprisingly, for some, it went straight to their heads. And for quite some time, a minority of these artists fobbed off their shoddiest productions on European record labels and were well paid for it. No European record label was going to refuse a track by an artist from Detroit, even if the music was mediocre. It was a win-win situation. The result was that 80 per cent of tracks signed by Detroit artists to European labels were not great. People in Europe idolised Detroit, but there was no love involved.

MIKE BANKS:

'Our community has no experience when it comes to managing money. Some people lost it when all of a sudden they had some money, because they were scared it wouldn't last and wanted to make the most of it. I get that. In Detroit, if you never go out, you have a very distorted idea of the real world. The news on TV continuously reels off all the bad things going on out there ("somebody has been killed in this place or that"), reiterating the message to the people living out in the white suburbs that they've made the right decision to live away from downtown Detroit because otherwise they might end up with a gun to their heads. They serve up this kind of story, or stories about model citizens handing out soup to the poor. This town is split in two, even in the way an event is relayed. The news on TV gives a biased version of reality. I think that the people who are making techno are trying to get away from this. But I've already talked about the influence this city has on us … Even when we try to escape, a part of the city stays within us.'

Underground Resistance continues to work towards helping music in the city, in keeping with their value system. They look towards the street and to the future, exploring the possibility of other worlds in their music. As Jeff Mills states below, the theme of space, omnipresent in black music (from Sun Ra to Funkadelic, from Coltrane to techno), has always had a significance.

JEFF MILLS:
'It represents freedom. Out of here. Out of this world. Space, the unknown, it can be anything. Even if it's worse than here, it's not here. Space is The Final Frontier. We have a chance that life elsewhere is better than life here, and this is why the outer space theme is so important. It represents hope. Because, in this country, if you're born black, the outlook is bleak. Really!'

A taxi took me back to the airport. I was slumped in the back seat reading the titles of the records in my bag. The words 'future', 'warfare', 'fugitives', 'planet', 'mystic' and 'riot' stood out. Outside, the dreary landscape passed by. In Europe, nobody ever talks about Detroit's real ruin: in terms of culture, Detroit is a failure. Everything has been wiped out, even the memories. The Italian Renaissance-style Michigan Theatre, a remainder of the golden age of the 1950s, has been turned into a parking lot. The same thing has happened to concert venues. You have to go to the Baptist church in Greek Town to find the only bookshop downtown. And there's no music here anymore.

When I got back home, people wanted to pick my brains about the real Detroit. Like most people in Europe, they had pre-conceived ideas about Detroit's so-called techno scene. Fuck that shit! I saw nothing in Detroit that resembled a scene! To have a 'scene', you have to have nightlife, and venues, and clubs, and a network. You also have to have other people who share your aspirations. But in Detroit, everything seemed damaged and fragmented.

Before I set foot in Detroit, I had my own fantasies about the city. I imagined it to be incredibly violent. And that is exactly what it was. But Detroit also had an exciting vision of the future. Yet mistakenly, I thought that because the violence in the city was so intolerable, the bond between the techno producers in Detroit would be stronger. I thought they would all be driven by the same ideals, but I was disappointed to find that some of them were simply interested in making money in Europe from the Detroit name.

That first trip to Detroit wasn't life-changing. I didn't like the music from Detroit more because I had breathed the city air. But what Detroit did teach me was the importance of putting your heart and soul into your music. The reason why Detroit techno strikes a chord with me is because its producers lay bare their souls in their music. They lay bare their sorrows, their resentment, their wounds and their hope. Derrick May's words kept going round inside my head, 'You don't make a record for fun, man.'

If the music of Chicago shoots from the hip, the music of Detroit has always spoken straight to the heart. It can bring tears to my eyes. It produces an intense emotional reaction. Records like World 2 World or Strings Of Life are the soundtracks to my life. I can listen to them time and time again and still feel the hairs on the back of my neck stand on end. This cannot be manufactured. This is real.

vertigo

When I got back from Detroit, I made the decision to get to work on my first solo album. It was something that I had wanted to do for a long time, but up until now I hadn't had the confidence to get on with it. In the past, I had not taken writing music seriously – it had just been something that I did for fun; a good way to spend time with friends (Ian Bland, the Moose Posse, Shazz and Ludovic Navarre). It was simple: we had a laugh, switched on the studio gear, and if we liked the result we released it. But because of these collaborations people began to say, 'Garnier never takes risks. He always relies on Navarre's input and it's only because of him that Garnier makes music at all.' I was determined to make good music on my own, to dispel these rumours, and show how I had evolved musically. My challenge was to produce an album entirely on my own.

I had bought myself the studio gear that every techno producer had: keyboards (DX 100, Juno-106, JD-800, SH-101), a drum machine and a sampler (Akai S1000). On top of this, I had an Atari 1040 computer, a pirated version of the music software Cubase, and a now-legendary TB-303. I had all the basic gear at an affordable price. The great house music classics (Can You Party by Royal House, Altered States by Ron Trent, etc.) had all been produced using extremely basic technology (a 4-track mixer and a cheap keyboard along with another couple of bits and pieces), but the results were there.

At the end of the 80s, in the early days of dance music, musicians would make the most of whatever analogical studio equipment that they could get their hands on. Electronic pop bands such as Tangerine Dream, Human League and Depeche Mode had used the same machines in the 70s and 80s. Then, technological advances meant that sounds evolved, and most of these keyboards and sequencers were consigned to the back of a cupboard. That is, until dance music producers got their hands on them and started experimenting, ignoring the rules and discovering new sounds, often by accident.

I set up my studio in my cramped one-bedroom apartment where I spent all day everyday familiarising myself with the world of htz, mgbts, Midi, Analog, Bts and in-out. I followed my instincts and began to make music in an anarchic, DIY-kind of way. I was happy as long as it sounded raw and techno. I was naïve and impatient. As the days went by, I learned more and more, gently coaxing my machines into producing the sounds I wanted. I tried to work out how to configure a recording studio, how to program sounds, rhythms and melodies and then synchronise them together … it was really one great big confused mess.

I had no real structure to my working methods. I listened to my favourite records from Chicago and Detroit and switched on my machines. Through trial and error I eventually stumbled upon an original idea for a track, then a gimmick, then a bass line, then the strings, then the percussion, then the atmosphere. Within a couple of hours I would have 90 per cent of a track. But then I would go round in circles. I would add layer upon layer of different sounds and end up getting lost. Until the day I realised that the key to good writing is simplicity. The secret is to strip away all that is superfluous and concentrate on the core, the substance that is the music.

I also learned another important lesson: I had to make sure that the music told a story, and, most importantly, learn to write tracks that could stand on their own as well as being an integral part of an album. I didn't just want to write 'tracks' for the dance floor. There was much more to this than I thought…

This went on for months, writing music on my own, in secret. At times, when I found it impossible to translate a musical idea I had in my head onto the keyboard, I felt my complex about not being a trained musician growing inside me. For nights on end, I sat up for hours going round and round in circles, unable to see a way forward. But there were also times when inspiration came effortlessly. I can remember one night in particular when I sat down in my studio and everything just flowed…

Since arriving back from Detroit I'd wanted to write a track that would pay tribute to my time there. I quickly found the theme, a melancholic melody, which struck the same emotional chord inside me as Detroit. I started building a track around this melody. As the grey dawn broke over Paris, I put the finishing touches to Track For Mike and collapsed into bed. A few days later, terrified at the thought that the track might not be as good as I had originally thought, I locked myself in my flat, unplugged the telephone and put Track For Mike on the DAT player. I still liked what I heard so I put it into an envelope, scribbled UR's address on it, wrote a quick note to Mike explaining that the meeting I'd had with him had inspired this track, and that I was not sending it to him to be released on his label but simply to get his opinion, and posted it off. For several weeks I heard nothing. Then one morning, when I got back from a gig, I found a reply on my fax machine. His reply was short: 'I like it. It's cool. Put it out – Peace – Mike.'

Of course, this kind of thing didn't happen every day. My first album was produced with plenty more blood, sweat and tears.

Once I had finished the first few tracks for the album, I played them to Eric Morand. He encouraged me to continue. Hardly any techno albums existed back then, except for those by Kenny Larkin, LFO and Orbital. In 1993, techno producers were focusing their efforts on the dance floor and albums were still very much the domain of rock musicians. The dance music market consisted mainly of 12-inch vinyl. There were a couple of other formats that existed, the double single and the 8-track EP, but the core market was clubs and raves. Eric and I were convinced that releasing an album was a way to reach an international audience. But Fnac Music was in financial difficulty so, for now, everything was on hold.

Eric Morand was at the mercy of Fnac Music's dire financial situation. When things started looking really bad we decided to make the break and set up our own record label. In 1993, only about half a dozen independent record labels existed in France. These included Boucherie Prods, Media 7 and PIAS. Most of these labels had been set up at the end of the 80s to cater for the alternative punk scene. We wanted to associate our new label with an existing infrastructure that would take care of the logistics (distribution, contracts, etc.) and leave us with complete artistic freedom. We set up meetings with Warp and Eye-Q, labels that were distributed by Fnac Dance Division and whose owners were now friends, but we were unable to come to a deal that made everyone happy. Kenny Gates and Michel Lambot, founders of the Belgian independent label PIAS (Play It Again Sam), became aware of our plans. Having worked for a long time with industrial music (Meat Beat Manifesto, Cassandra Complex, Young Gods), they were open to electronic music. PIAS had also been distributing Fnac Dance Division in Holland for several years. So when they showed an interest in a partnership with us we knew they were the right company to work with. A deal was drawn up; it was all very straightforward. In 1994, Eric released a Fnac Dance Division retrospective compilation called *La Collection* before leaving the company.

Not long after, I asked Eric to come with me to a DJ gig at a club called The Eclipse in Coventry, one of the craziest clubs in the UK. My album was finally finished but I still didn't have a title for it. Eric and I had a theory that UK motorways were made out of a substance that was purposefully designed to spray water at you instead of repel it. That night it was chucking it down. As we headed up the motorway to Coventry, there was a moment when we were sandwiched between two lorries that were bombing along at full speed spraying unimaginable quantities of water at us. I couldn't see a thing. 'Shit! We've got to get past them. We've got to overtake them or we've had it!' I slammed my foot on the accelerator and shouted: 'This is a shot in the dark!' The car pulled away from the two thundering lorries just in time, but we still skidded on the wet tarmac. I pulled over onto the hard shoulder to collect myself. For a moment, we lay back on the headrests. Silence. Then Eric said, 'Well, you could call your album Shot in the Dark ...'.

A few hours later, we arrived safely in Coventry. The Eclipse was a three-storey warehouse where anything could happen. One of the club's distinctive features was that the DJ booth was cordoned off from the public by a metal fence. Before my set began, I stood on the top floor watching people down below on the dance floor going mad. The sound of foghorns was so loud it almost drowned out the music. I spotted a guy in the middle of this mass of writhing bodies wearing a t-shirt with a huge letter E. He was completely off his head. He was obviously enjoying himself and was the perfect embodiment of what the UK rave movement had become. This was the antithesis of what we were fighting for.

In fact, there were a significant number of people trying to get the message across that 'no, techno does not just boil down to taking ecstasy'. It was a separate culture. Unbeknown to him, this guy was undermining our efforts. I stood staring at him for a while, and then I turned to Eric, 'We should print t-shirts with the letter F. Because after E comes F. No one will get it, but who cares, at least we'll be distancing ourselves from this shit.' And Eric replied, 'I've got an even better idea. We should call the label F. Because after drugs comes the music. And at the end of the day, all that counts, is the music.'

Let's get things clear, once and for all: drugs and excess have always been part of the nightlife scene. Without LSD the Woodstock generation would never have existed. And we can now say, in hindsight, that without ecstasy dance music would never have taken hold of Europe. I've experimented with drugs, but music has always been my driving force. But back then, most UK clubbers were only interested in how many pills they could take. The music had become a pretext. Like many others, I didn't like the way things were going.

F Communications was created in April 1994 with the slogan 'After E comes F'. The label was the logical progression from what had been achieved at Fnac Dance Division. The major difference now was that we had control of the cheque book.

F Comm arrived at the right moment for the development of dance music in Europe. The really hard work, i.e. getting our music accepted in France, had been done. The success of Fnac music artists such as Lunatic Asylum, Deepside and Shazz, and the labels Eric had licensed, Djax Up, + 8 and Warp, represented 30 per cent of the sales of dance music in France. Since the release of Acid Eiffel on Fragile and Wake Up on Warp, the British and the Americans were starting to take notice of our music. And a series of articles in magazines such as *DJ Mag* and *Mixmag* boosted the image of French dance music in the eyes of the British music industry.

After E, comes Ⓕ

During the first month of F Comm's existence we quickly realised that the challenge we had set ourselves with Fnac had been achieved, and our desire to see French house and techno artists recognised abroad had come true. So what challenge remained? To release the music we wanted without concession, and to keep a watchful eye on the French dance music scene and anticipate the arrival of new trends.

The dance music scene in Paris had been evolving since 1992. Every weekend, the demand for raves got bigger. New promoters appeared – Invaders, Fantome, Tekno Tanz – and their raves were friendly and good-natured. The promoters would often grab the microphone in the middle of the night to thank the ravers for making the effort to come and then would go and join them on the dance floor. Different styles of music – house, techno, hardcore, trance, etc. – co-existed in harmony. The relationship between DJs and promoters was simple. Radio FG played a role as the go-between and DJ's fees were reasonable (the equivalent to about 150–200 euros).

Warehouses, lofts, underground car parks, greenhouses, chalk quarries, the Usine Éphémère in Asnières or the Frigos, an ex-squat at Quai de la Gare in Paris, all hosted this first generation of raves. For the people going to these events, it was something new where everything was different: the music, the concept and the atmosphere. It was refreshing to see people coming together. In the morning, ravers followed each other to after-parties in unusual places such as on houseboats, in the basement of a kebab shop opposite the Palace, in dilapidated nightclubs, or just simply in someone's apartment, as long as the party could continue. These after-parties were a breeding ground for young, upcoming DJs, a sort of school of techno where guys such as Manu Le Malin and Torgull got to know the ropes. They would turn up at 7am with their record bags, observe the DJ at work and quietly wait their turn before playing for an hour, free of charge, as a sort of work experience.

Within a few months the Parisian rave scene had grown exponentially. Each week, news of what was happening in Switzerland, the UK and Germany filtered through to France. New records, artists and labels broke into the French market. The expansion of raves into huge techno gatherings in these neighbouring countries suggested that the same was about to happen in France.

Producers began making techno records with the idea in mind of them being played over huge sound systems in giant warehouses. The music started getting harder, and public demand for this harder sound was growing. As a result, a split took place. Certain DJs refused to adapt their sound to large warehouses and chose instead to go back to the clubs.

The 3615 FG Minitel, which up until then consisted mainly of gay personal ads, became the place to find out about future raves. At that time, FG was still a community radio station and was on the verge of financial collapse. Organising parties seemed to be a lucrative plan for the radio, so they seized the opportunity.

In April 1993, Radio FG joined up with a group of rave promoters and organised an event at the Abbaye du Moncel, near Compiègne. The DJs were Jeff Mills, Liza 'N' Eliaz, Pacman, Sonic and Aquarium. People who were there that night will remember the extraordinary atmosphere inside the chapels and refectories of the Abbey, which had previously been inhabited by monks and was now transformed into one giant dance floor. Different styles of music came together, for example, Jeff Mills' techno smoothly followed on from Jerome Pacman's progressive house. When the amps in the monitors blew, the DJs continued playing. When an hour later the headphone output on the DJ mixer went, they carried on without headphones. The atmosphere in the room was such that the energy from the dance floor enabled the DJs to overcome these problems. Some of the people there were experiencing their first ever rave and were able to experience, first-hand, the great spirit of these events.

The rave at the Moncel Abbey was a great achievement and the perfect showcase for FG. It was deemed their first major success. Taking advantage of their newfound success, FG decided to get more involved in organising raves.

With the help of FG, a bus full of ravers left for Germany and were taken to the Mayday rave on May 1, 1993. The next day they were all taken back to Paris to enjoy an After Mayday rave co-organised by FG in a warehouse in an industrial zone in Villeneuve-Saint-Georges. Under the banner 'The Future of the Universe is in Our Hands', 7,000 people discovered the talents of DJs like Miss Djax from Eindhoven, Damon Wild from New York, Mike Dearborn from Chicago and Olivier Bondzio from Frankfurt. All the ingredients were there to make it a perfect rave: a big sound system, lasers, and thousands of ravers dancing together.

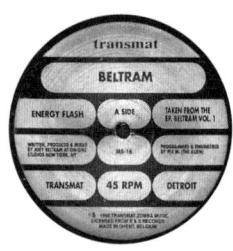

In the morning, the first rays of sunlight pierced through gaps in the corrugated metal roof, revealing a huge cloud of dust suspended above the dance floor. People's faces were showing signs of fatigue. Their eyes were dilated, their skin pallid. Just as a group of ravers stepped out of the hangar looking for the shuttle to take them back to Paris, Energy Flash by Joey Beltram belted out of the speakers, and with it the cries of joy of thousands of ravers. Everyone who was there felt the hairs on the back of their necks stand up on end.

Patrick Rognant was one of the key figures during that golden age.

On his programme, Rave Up, every Saturday night on FG he gave out information on all the weekend's dance music events, whatever the style. He also played all the latest releases and invited various DJs to come and mix on the radio, such as Liza 'N' Eliaz, whom he introduced to FG listeners. The rave movement was getting stronger, and Rave Up became compulsory listening for those who wanted to know what was going on. Patrick Rognant became very influential. He had the power to decide whether an event was a success or a failure, and the power to make or break a DJ.

Flyers advertising raves were distributed in the record shops in Bastille: TSF, USA Import and BPM. And on the Saturday of the event, at 10pm on the dot, Patrick Rognant waved the green flag for the fun to begin. People were told to gather at one of the motorway exits leading out of Paris, and from there they were handed a detailed itinerary of how to find the rave. A large convoy of cars would gather, knowing that they were going to dance, have a good time and feel free.

By 1993, raves were well established in Paris. The atmosphere then was still very relaxed. Many of the rave organisers were simply punters, who became promoters for just one night only, paying an American DJ 4,000 francs (roughly 600 euros) plus expenses, an economy class air ticket, a simple hotel and a taxi to take him to and from the venue.

Yet the arrival of a much harder style of techno would split the Parisian rave scene in two. At the end of 1993, the word 'hardcore' made its way into people's vocabulary. Certain tracks played in raves were considered hardcore because of the dark and sombre tone expressed in the music and in the titles (Mentasm by Joey Beltram, Coldrush 008 by PCP, X101 by UR). Even though these records were in essence techno, they were the soundtrack for the emerging hardcore scene. The music being played in raves was pushed to the very limits, the sound was more and more aggressive. And with this sound, a new crowd began to appear, mostly from a rock or industrial music background that had nothing to do with house music.

With the arrival of hardcore techno, the Parisian rave scene split into two camps. The raves became more extreme and the happy coexistence between different musical tribes disappeared.

'Listen carefully, my little Kim: techno is an art form ... with its genres and sub-genres, its schools and its disciples. Hardcore is the most radical of all the genres, that's all, like cubism was at the time! "Does cubist techno exist?" Kim asks, surprised. She didn't understand my cultural

▶ Playlist
HARDCORE
Mescalinum United
We Are Arrived
(Aphex Twin Remix)

The Horrorist
Flesh Is The Fever

Liza 'N' Eliaz
Stockhausen

Micropoint
Anesthésie
Internationale

D.O.A.
Muthafuckin' New
York Hardcore

Spy
Bloodstrike

Lenny Dee & Sal. C
Fucking Hostile

Laurent Hô
Look For Markine

Dr Macabre
Poltergeist

Protectors Of
Bass & The Mover
Pill Driver

comparison. I was trying to get her to understand that hardcore is Art with a capital A in the same way that in the cubist era Picasso was a painter, with a capital P. Picasso painted a person's profile, yet we could see both of their eyes, that was pictorial hardcore.'
Milan Dargent, Soupe à la Tête de Bouc *(Le Dilettante, 2002)*

Due to all its different styles, hardcore, like its UK equivalent break-beat, became one of the major musical styles of French raves. Different schools of European hardcore became apparent too, whose styles, even though they had their roots in techno, covered a wide spectrum from purist experimentation right through to the most radical, violent sound.

One of this movement's unquestioned leaders was Marc Arcadipane, musician and founder of the label PCP in Frankfurt, whose influence could be felt throughout the European techno scene. Then Rotterdam gave birth to its own style of wild, industrial, upbeat music that really got your heart racing called gabber. In Brooklyn, Lenny Dee created America's first hardcore label, Industrial Strength, and defined a style of hardcore that encompassed techno, breakbeat, rock and hip-hop.

Yet, even though all these styles of music were available from 1993 onwards in the record shops in Paris, there was no one to represent this movement apart from Laurent Hô, one of the hardcore movement's pioneers. So it was not surprising that Liza 'N' Eliaz, a Belgian DJ, became the high priestess of French raves.

Liza had the same impact on the French hardcore scene as Derrick May had on the European techno scene in the 90s. Everything about her was fascinating: she was an androgynous person who had an amazing knowledge of music (having spent years studying classical music). She loved playing with sound and innovating. Her music was extreme and had an intensity that has rarely been equalled. She carefully weaved together tracks of ferociousness, finesse and a dash of humour. There is no doubt, Liza made her mark on an entire generation of French ravers.

Hot on her heels, another true rave child was also making his mark as one of the leading French hardcore DJs, Manu Le Malin. He talked openly about having had a very troubled adolescence and owed his salvation to the amazing wake-up call he felt when he first went to an Invaders event in 1991. Fascinated by the dark sounds he heard, he threw himself into the hard techno sounds of labels such as PCP and Industrial Strength. At the time, the public began to realise that each DJ had their own personality and their own style. Manu le Malin, a charismatic DJ covered from head to toe in tattoos, took his warrior look and his talent to play at all the big European raves.

Soon the majority of raves were hardcore raves. The organisers often invited the masters of Dutch gabber, and promoted Manu Le Malin and Laurent Hô to the rank of chief representatives of the genre. Hardcore had proven itself in France: it had its leaders, its code of conduct, and a devoted following. But it would also become a victim of its own success and prey to unscrupulous promoters.

Within a few months, the spirit of community disintegrated to be replaced by the bigger business interests. There were more and more raves each weekend. The first generation of promoters were superseded. Every Saturday, within a small geographical area, four competing parties took place.

As different factions slowly broke away, people's attitudes and looks became more radical and the drugs became more and more important. By 1994, the majority of French raves were soulless gatherings of thousands of kids who were only interested in hardcore and trance. In the main, they were giant factories of techno, void of energy, imagination and sincerity.

Even though a small group of Parisian promoters tried to maintain a level of quality at their rave events, Paris was slipping into an era of dishonesty. Among the newcomers, some promoters were no more than gangsters, who saw that warehouses packed with several thousand people all having paid 100 francs (around 15 euros) to get in represented a huge money-spinner. They got hold of an empty warehouse, printed flyers with the first name that came into their heads, booked a couple of international DJs, and that was that.

As in the UK, the drugs and easy money to be had from organising raves attracted gangsters. Sometimes the security people were equally as corrupt; they allowed their own dealers into the parties, or demanded money from the organisers. In March 1994, during La Parade, a rave that had limited financial resources but big ambitions, with a line-up that included Jack de Marseille, Manu Le Malin and Guillaume La Tortue, the takings were stolen by two armed men in balaclavas. Shots were fired. The crowd panicked. Several thousand francs disappeared into thin air. The police were nowhere to be seen.

But in spite of these goings-on, the rave scene was still getting bigger and bigger, drawing in over 30,000 people each weekend. The flyers advertising the raves during this period are surprisingly similar: repeatedly one finds similar line-ups, and similar design. The average entry ticket was about 100 francs, and for this the ravers were given very little in return: the decoration was scarce, there was nowhere comfortable to relax, no one bothered to try and achieve good sound quality, there was often only one toilet, but lots of other ways to spend your money. Raves were no longer synonymous with freedom and pleasure, but with big business and easy pickings.

In France, the police – who were put in charge of closing down raves as from 1992 – were unbelievably ignorant of rave culture. Every single raver has witnessed the following scene:

Dawn. A dozen or so gendarmes in uniform cautiously enter a warehouse and come across thousands of smiling weirdos jumping up and down to a type of music that doesn't exist in their training manuals. Organisers and ravers alike converse with the police, who are determined to find the syringes, and the people unconscious on the floor, in short, rock 'n' roll paraphernalia … but to no avail. These interventions by the forces of law and order were the starting point for several amusing stories that the 'elders' still enjoy telling today. During one open-air rave organised inside a private park on the outskirts of Paris, the police raided at dawn. They requested that the music stop immediately. The organiser asked the police captain to make the announcement himself to the ravers. The captain stepped up onto the stage, took hold of the microphone and announced, 'Ladies and gentlemen, the party is over'. The ravers booed. The organisers then begged the police captain to let the guest DJ, Stika from the UK, a friend of Orbital's, play one last record. They promised to close down the party at the end of one more track. So the police captain climbed back up on the stage, as the sun was coming up, and announced over the microphone, 'Ladies and gentlemen, I realise that you have come to listen to an artist from afar. So you can have one more record, but after that, that's it.' As the sun came up, there remained seven minutes for the crowd to get in as much dancing as possible. Good will all round.

Confronted with the rave phenomena, the authorities were faced with a judicial void. For the most part, the parties took place in industrial zones, fields, quarries, far from residential areas so there was no one to complain about the noise. In these circumstances it made it difficult for the police to intervene. But as weeks went by, and under pressure from the head of the local authority, the police changed their tactics and made it their mission to find proof of the illegality of raves.

Lyon was a middle-class city whose nightlife had up until 1991 been limited to a couple of clubs such as L'Ambassade. Then, from 1991 onwards, house and techno were played at the Factory, the Hypnotic, the Fish, the Pyramide and the Zoo. In February 1993, Cosmic Energy, the first official large-scale rave organised in the Rhône-Alpes region, was organised at the Halle Tony Garnier with Cosmic Baby and Hardfloor live and DJs including Kid Paul and Pascal FEOS, attracting almost 8,000 people.

The concert venue Le Transbordeur also regularly hosted techno events. During one party created by the Swiss radio station, Couleur 3, the police raided the dressing rooms in the middle of the event. The police, very confident of what they were doing, ordered the DJs to, 'Empty your pockets, take out all the ecstasy and cocaine!'

Soon, undercover police were posted at every event, and ravers in Lyon had great fun making a point of going up to them and saying, 'Good evening officer, and how are you? Everything alright?' Then followed a series of raves in the idyllic setting of Beaujolais. The police were present at each, and became part and parcel of the event in the same way as the DJs, the psychedelic decor and the sound system …

In the south of France, the atmosphere was becoming more confrontational between the police and ravers. Raves such as Atomix, organised in the warehouses belonging to la Seita in Marseille, or Creative Action in Toulouse, and Spiral Tribe kick-started the rave movement in 1993. After the big rave, Transeruption, in Grenoble in 1993, where the police led a heavy-handed raid, a clamp-down spread throughout the Rhône-Alpes region right down through to the south of France.

Gradually, the police began to break up rave events. Their reason for enforcement: public disturbance. The organisers and police began a long game of cat and mouse, the former devising creative ways to outwit the police. It was at the time of '3615 Rave' on Minitel (France's prehistoric internet system) and the first mobile phones. Like in the UK, both the organisers and the authorities used mobile phones. The organisers used them to avoid police blocks and the police as a source of information. Word got round and the party was moved. When the reserve venues were also discovered by the police, the parties moved out into fields, woods and even car parks. A makeshift sound system was plugged into a generator, hundreds of cars marked out the dance floor, and ravers danced on the bonnets.

I played a lot at the raves in the south of France as well as in the Rhône-Alpes region. I was able to witness first-hand the way things were going and the problems with the authorities. I also had my residency at the Rex with the Wake Up nights, which allowed me to experience the Paris nightlife scene. At the weekends, I DJ-ed at raves in the south of France or in Germany, Switzerland or the UK. In the UK, despite the pressure from the police, Tribal Gathering kept the spirit of the rave scene alive.

I invited a friend, Eric Napora, to come with me to Tribal Gathering. There he witnessed the equivalent to the population of a small town – 25,000 people – peacefully wandering in and out of the six dance tents that made up the site. The line-up was incredible: no less than 40 artists, with a free funfair to boot. In short, here was a vision of a dance music event that was positive, ambitious and authentic. Eric Napora had a mini-revelation and returned to Paris determined to organise the first large-scale dance music event in France. It was baptised oz and intended to be the French Tribal Gathering. We decided to form a partnership and organise the event together.

At the start of 1993, Eric Napora stumbled across an exhibition centre in Amiens. It was a huge empty space with three different rooms with capacities for 3,000, 6,000 and 10,000 people respectively. There was also a large dome and several auditoriums that could be used for projecting films. Just outside was a park that could hold a funfair and a car park with space for several thousand cars. The exhibition centre was situated just next to Amiens' racecourse, far from any residential areas. Amiens had direct train links to Paris, Belgium, the uk and Holland. Basically, it ticked all the right boxes for a large-scale dance music event.

All year round, different events took place at the Amiens exhibition centre, including trade fairs, exhibitions, conferences and concerts. It clearly fulfilled all the necessary health and safety requirements. So talks got underway with the local police and the council and everyone seemed thrilled that such an event was going to take place. In just six months, everything came together. Oz was allocated a budget of 1.2 million francs, which was a considerable amount of money for a French rave. Thirty DJs and ten bands were booked to perform. They included Carl Cox, Rok, Dave Angel, Colin Faver, Daz Saund, Liza 'N' Eliaz, Spiral Tribe live and all the key players in the French dance music scene. Sven Vath was booked to DJ at the after-party, and 200,000 flyers were printed. Yet, in spite of plenty of goodwill and openness on behalf of the organisers, the press did their best to keep the event quiet, and so-called members of Paris' underground techno scene did their best to bad-mouth the event. But the public knew nothing about any of this and were very enthusiastic. Oz sold tickets throughout Europe. The telephone didn't stop ringing; everything looked set for a great event.

At around the same time, Eric Napora decided to organise a party to raise money for a charity, and so a partnership was put in place with the charitable organisation, AIDES. Napora suggested organising a dance music event in the foyer of the Grande Arche de la Défense. He would be in charge of organising the party, all AIDES had to do was hire the venue and all the money raised would go to their charitable organisation. The party was organised in the space of a few weeks in association with the record label Harthouse. Artists like Spacelab, Sven Vath and Hardfloor agreed to play and waive their fees as it was for a good cause.

But on June 15, 1993, a few days before the party at the Arche de la Défense, and only a couple of weeks before Oz, an article was published in the daily newspaper *L'Humanité* that would have a devastating effect. The article was about Celebration, a party organised by Liberation on June 5 at the Grande Halle de la Villette. Under the headline: 'The rave phenomenon, a blend of music, solitude and drugs', the journalist wrote: 'Presented as harmless fun, raves – with their rituals, followers and vocabulary – trivialise drug trafficking – for physical submission is essential to ravers, and bands flaunt neo-Nazi ideologies.'

It was not the first time that this sort of stuff had been written; jazz, rock and punk had all been under attack at one time or another. But this time round, the article triggered a seismic reaction. Beyond the fact that this article stated that 'techno = drugs', it put the cat amongst the pigeons. A volley of articles followed slating dance music, and raves in particular, provoking the authorities to respond with a crackdown. Whereas Eric Napora and his team were trying to build bridges between dance music and charitable organisations, the article in *L'Humanité* read: 'Suddenly it hits you. You think, wait a second, where am I? Is this really Saturday night, at La Villette, in the heart of Paris? There are young people on acid in here, ruining their lives, and nobody's saying anything? Nobody's doing anything? And this is going to happen all over again on June 26 at L'Arche de la Défense and this time the profits will go towards the fight against AIDS? It's absurd!'

And that was when the anti-rave witch-hunt, and our troubles, really began. Horrified by what they had read, AIDES pulled out just two weeks before the event at La Defense. Napora tried to find another charitable organisation to work with but he was running out of time, so he decided to move the event to Mozinor where he had organised raves in the past. A couple of journalists from *France Soir* came to the event and wrote an article basically stating that a DJ's worth could be measured by the quality of the ecstasy pills he sold to the ravers. The climate was becoming intolerable.

With Oz only 10 days away, a journalist from *Le Courier Picard*, a local newspaper, contacted Napora and convinced him that he wanted to do an 'objective' interview. The interview went well. But a week before Oz, the article was published on the back page of the newspaper. And there, to everyone's surprise, the journalist described how hordes of hooligans were preparing to descend on Amiens and that, during Oz, Amiens would become a centre of drug activity. Things were getting worse. A communist MP took advantage of the situation to jump on the bandwagon. But neither the police authorities nor the council did anything. Despite the increasing tension, the party was still due to go ahead.

The day before the event, a 200 kw sound system, last used by Prince for his European tour, was set up in the three rooms within the exhibition centre. The stage and the lights were all ready. The technicians were running through their final checks when, suddenly, two men appeared. They walked across the room towards Eric Napora. They had in their hands a two-page-long Prefectural decree listing the risks to public order: 'This Saturday the Tour de France will be passing through Amiens and the city is unable to ensure security for both the cycle race and a rave party'; 'The policeman's ball will take place this Friday and therefore the police will not be able to guarantee the security for the rave party', etc. It was 10pm, the wheels of bureaucracy had been set in motion and the rave was cancelled.

I was in Cologne when I found out. I was devastated, but I still played my set and then took the first plane back home the next morning. I arrived in Paris feeling stressed and jumped into my ravemobile to go straight to Amiens. It was like a ghost town. The shopkeepers had barricaded their shop windows with wooden panels and three CRS squadrons were stationed in the city centre. At around midday, the first ravers began to arrive by train, car and coach from all over Europe, unaware of the disappointment awaiting them. Meanwhile, in Paris, FG radio organised a live debate and talk show about Oz being cancelled.

A spontaneous, peaceful demonstration took place at Trocadero, under the watchful eye of the CRS. Then the 6,000 ravers marched to the Ile de Cygne, a small island on the Seine, opposite Radio France's headquarters. But when night fell someone had to do something about the thousands of ravers scattered between Paris and Amiens. Several promoters scrambled to organise last-minute events. They all charged an entry fee. In Amiens, some of ravers from Oz discovered the Spiral Tribe sound system, a posse from England who had become persona non grata in their own country following the Criminal Justice Bill and a raid on one of their illegal raves at Castle Morton. Having taken refuge in France, Spiral Tribe were supposed to play at Oz. When they learnt that the event had been cancelled they set up their sound system in a field not far from Amiens and held an improvised rave. This would be the first ever Teknival in France – i.e. an illegal rave without any official organisation or structure behind it.

Unfortunately, this wasn't the end of Eric Napora and his team's troubles: TSF, their record shop, closed down, their dance music magazine *Coda* went under after only two issues as all the pre-sale tickets from Oz had to be refunded, Mozinor was closed down ... In the midst of all of this was one sign of humanity; a few days after Oz was cancelled, a guy walked into TSF record shop: 'Hi, I'd like to buy a ticket for Oz'. Silence. 'I am really disappointed that Oz was cancelled, I know you are in the shit, so really, I would like to buy a ticket from you.'

French authorities had sacrificed Oz as an example to others.

In the months that followed, French rave organisers decided to structure themselves as legitimate companies so as to protect themselves from the law. However, with a helping hand from the press, the climate around dance music continued to darken.

The press had a field day with the 'raves = drugs' comparison that they drew. The French Press Agency published a dispatch on June 29, 1993 that largely contributed to spreading the fear of techno across the national press. The dispatch read: 'It is 1am on the dance floor and the master of ceremonies has arrived. Dressed from head to toe in black, she raises her hand to give the signal. People on the dance floor are hypnotised, hanging on her every word. They go mad to the metallic, violent music that blasts out of the speakers at 20,000 watts, speeding up your heartbeat. This violent music is supposed to accompany the effects of the drug ecstasy and gives it the name acid music.' Further on it reads: 'Two hours later, after the first wave, people start collapsing onto the ground in a corner of the room. Their eyes are dazed, their bodies weak. They slide down the walls like zombies. Others stumble out of the venue, their pupils dilated, a look of fear on their faces.'

The bosses of Radio FG and Radio Nova, the two major media supporters of house music culture, were summoned to the Paris police authority. There, Jean-François Bizot and Henri Maurel were cordially asked not to promote the rave culture on their radio stations.

A circular issued by the MILDT (Mission interministérielle de la lutte contre la drogue et la toxicomanie – Interministerial mission in the fight against drugs and addictions) entitled 'Rave parties, high-risk events' was distributed to all police headquarters. The circular took as its starting point the UK's Criminal Justice Bill. It gave a detailed description of raves, from taking ecstasy to the music that was played. The circular was interpreted to the letter by French gendarmes. This was when things began to get out of hand.

In 1994, Les Pingouins, a student collective from Montpellier, organised their third dance music event called Borealis (the first two had attracted 11,000 people to the Arènes de Nîmes). The anti-rave hysteria was at its peak, so Montpellier council refused to allow them access to Espace Gramont, a large stretch of land on the outskirts of the city. Les Pingouins decided to organise a winter version of Borealis called Polaris in Lyon. But since the boom in the number of raves in the

Rhône-Alpes region, Lyon's nightclub union was concerned about the number of young people deserting clubs at the weekends. They put pressure on the local authorities urging them to set an example. So, on the eve of Polaris, it was decreed that the rave could only go on until midnight! As a result of yet another dance music event being disbanded, Technopol came into being. Technopol was set up as an organisation to fight against the crackdown that was targeting the French rave scene.

The prize for the most ridiculous reason of all for disallowing a rave goes to the mayor of a town in the suburbs of Toulouse who banned a rave that risked endangering public decency because the flyer stated: 'live performance by Scan X' and the mayor believed this to be a live 'sex' act on stage!

Among the many raves raided by the police in France between 1993 and 1996, some turned nasty. During an event organised by the Parisian sound system Teknokrat in memory of one of their friends, recently deceased, squadrons of CRS appeared at dawn. They challenged 4,000 ravers, sprayed them with tear gas and smashed up their equipment. This resulted in fighting, people being chased, and several arrests.

In the south of France, as in the Lyon area, police tirelessly tracked down raves, often treating the organisers and DJs as though they were criminals. During this time, several Parisian DJs' telephones were tapped and some even had dawn raids from the drug squad wanting to search their apartments.

The motive behind these tactics, the intimidation and police harassment was, of course, drugs. Drugs could be found at parties, but were generally sold by well-organised networks of crooks. These people are in part responsible for destroying the rave scene, and discrediting the first generation of DJs, ravers and promoters.

But there was also another reason behind this crackdown: money. Apart from Oz and a few other raves, none of these parties ever paid any taxes to the state. Yet every weekend, thousands of people were going to raves and paying between 100 and 200 francs to get in. Not to mention the drinks that were being sold without licence. The organisers were raking in colossal amounts of money … Which makes it easier to understand why the local authorities had no qualms about mounting larger-scale police raids.

Whatever the reasons, the wheels were in motion to try and ban raves for good.

By 1994, it had become almost impossible to obtain the necessary permits to organise a rave. While some organisers persevered and invited the authorities to sit round a table and talk, others turned their backs and got involved in more underground events, known as free parties. The free party scene in France was a reaction to what was happening on the rave scene. Their motto? Rather than paying 200 francs to go to a rave in a legal venue with proper organisation and DJs, free party organisers would turn up with their sound system and squat somewhere, without a second thought for security or toilets. A concept imported from the UK, these parties were another type of techno event. With the arrival of free parties, a tribal spirit appeared on the French rave scene. Groups of travellers and members of marginal communities joined together in a radical form of techno, travelling up and down the country holding spontaneous outdoor parties from the back of their old lorries. French sound systems also began to appear – Psychiatrik, for example – organising free parties in the same spirit as their UK elders, Spiral Tribe. But soon the free party movement also began to fall apart. For some, the warehouses were becoming more and more dilapidated and the atmosphere unbearable, the music was no longer a pleasure, and the only value that seemed to hold true was, 'We don't pay'. For others, the spirit of community and the quality of the music played was what was important.

The witch-hunt was on, and the rave scene was disintegrating, but a beacon appeared right in the centre of Paris that stuck its finger up to the authorities. Throughout 1994, the Tolbiac bridge provided a home for the most spectacular after-parties in the capital. On a deserted bank of the Seine, bang opposite the National Library of France (BNF), Manu Le Malin and a promoter named Rakam were in charge.

Paris' after-parties are a well-guarded secret. Le Ruby, a narrow boat, was one legendary Parisian after-party venue. Other after-parties took place in nightclubs, or, as in the case of the Apocalypse rave after-party in 1994, in a room below the Montparnasse Tower, measuring several thousand square feet and belonging to France Telecom.

From 8am onwards, French techno fans came together under Tolbiac bridge. The majority of Paris' DJs played there, whatever their style of music, and the people who came were from all areas of dance music: hardcore, techno, free parties, trance. Clubbers straight out of the Folies Pigalle would head there, whereas others would go home to rest first before going to Tolbiac bridge. This after-party became the Sunday hangout for the Paris rave scene, but soon closed after it had become a victim of its own success.

Several months later, a second Apocalypse rave was organised. Manu Le Malin and Rakam decided to throw one more after-party at Tolbiac bridge for old time's sake. Black and white posters emblazoned with

'Sunday, Tolbiac bridge, like old times' were put up in all the dance music record shops in Bastille. That Sunday morning, 800 ravers came and danced on the banks of the Seine in the centre of Paris in the sunshine.

At 2pm, the CRS descended upon Tolbiac bridge. Identity checks, frisks, arrests. Word spread among the ravers, 'No one is the organiser, everyone keep their mouths shut'. Manu Le Malin was behind the turntables. A police officer walked up to him and told him to switch off the music. Manu played one last record to annoy the police and was struck with a baton. All around, even on the bridge, people took photographs.

The atmosphere that pervaded the French rave scene had become intolerable. Ravers, DJs and organisers didn't identify with the more radical aspects of the culture, and so some moved back to smaller-scale events. Soon, as had happened in the UK, house and techno would find salvation by returning to the clubs.

Thanks to the Temple parties (organised by Pierre Herman and Thierry Vincent), Trance Body Express and Wake Up, the Rex had become the leading dance music club in Paris. It was a landmark on the world clubbing map and hosted international artists that opened the public's ears to the latest trends in dance music. The Rex had successfully made the move over to dance music, renewing its spirit and its public between 1992 and 1994. From a strictly commercial point of view, this music had become profitable.

In 1995, the Rex had reached the natural end of its relationship with rock music. Its public had aged and had not renewed itself and Christian Paulet made a radical decision: the Rex should be reborn and be dedicated to electronic music. As I've said before, a club that doesn't take risks is a club that dies. There was no other club in Paris where you could listen to house and techno every night of the week. The Rex took that risk. The design of the club was changed: the DJ booth was moved and put where the stage had been. The dance floor was lowered to allow more headroom. The lights were changed. New furniture was designed. The walls were painted bright orange and electric blue. And last but not least, a brand new sound system (a Turbo Sound – the Rolls Royce of sound systems at the time) was installed.

The Rex Club, with its new electronic music identity, reopened in September 1995. This was the dawning of the age of glory. Over the next 10 years, Number 5 boulevard Poissonnière would welcome with open arms the most important techno artists from all over the world. But behind the scenes the reopening of the Rex Club took place in a difficult climate. The club was under the continual and watchful eye of the authorities due to the belief in the 'techno = drugs' equation. Different elements of the Parisian techno scene could all be found at the Rex Club. Some of these were promoters who were fed up with the deteriorating rave scene and were keen to work within a legal structure from here on in. Watched by the police, Christian Paulet's authority was immediately challenged by the drug problem. His position was very clear. Drugs were not to pass through the doors of the Rex Club and the promoters organising parties at the Rex Club must all adhere to this. We were here to listen to house and techno and to dance.

Shot In The Dark, my first album, was released on F Communications in 1994. Early in 1995, Ludovic Navarre released *Boulevard* under the name Saint Germain, and catapulted F Comm into the limelight when sales of his album reached 200,000 copies.

A sign of the times saw the French media go back on their previous allegations and start considering the techno movement as a movement with which they were going to have to come to terms. The first positive articles mixed up house music and gogo dancers, raves and foam parties, techno and drag queens. Who cares? It was a step in the right direction. Soon it would be the French house and techno scene itself that would break into the international music business.

beyond the dance

Things were shifting again. Techno was facing yet more

changes. In the UK (one of the many countries I still travelled to regularly), techno was living through some of its darkest moments. Gangs and drugs were gnawing away at the positive attitude that had once been so strong. The press' anti-techno campaign had worked to demonise the rave culture. The government, under pressure from public opinion, made the eradication of these events a priority. They refused licences, and any illegal gatherings were systematically raided and the organisers brought to justice.

The war against raves was costing the state thousands of pounds in both logistics and police time. In order to recoup some of this money, the fee for a rave licence was set at £75,000. This was to cover the costs of policing traffic during the event, or so they said. However, this sum soon rose to £80,000 and then £100,000 with no explanation. The majority of promoters were unable to meet these demands and decided either to throw in the towel, or, as in the case of Paul Shurry, to go into exile in order to avoid police harassment and possible bankruptcy. Universe moved Tribal Gathering to Germany, and reappeared at Love Parade.

At the end of 1994, the British parliament passed the Criminal Justice Bill, making it illegal for gatherings of 20 or more people in the open-air or in a building with the intention of listening to music. The definition of music was 'sounds wholly or predominantly characterised by the emission of repetitive beats'. The definition of the type of music was particularly pertinent as its intention was to target dance music. But Ravel's Bolero or James Brown's Funky Drummer could equally have fallen into this definition. For those daring to break the law by organising an illegal rave, the punishment was severe: a £20,000 fine and six months' imprisonment. Legal parties could go ahead, but the organisers had to respect a long list of requirements, most often to do with safety and security, in order to obtain their entertainment licence. For example, these demands required a certain number of square feet per person under the marquees in case of rain, and a large number of toilets. Organising a rave had become the equivalent of building a small town.

Enforcement of the Criminal Justice Bill resulted in a wave of arrests being made throughout the country. Within just a week of the bill being passed, 836 ravers were arrested at a warehouse near Leeds. The DJ Rob Tissera was also arrested that night and sentenced to three months in prison for inciting the crowd to block police access. Demonstrations calling for the right to party were organised all over the country, mainly by the Freedom to Party movement created by Tony Colston-Hayter. Several influential rave scene artists, such as KLF and Orbital, as well as a few magazines such as *NME*, also joined the protest against the Criminal Justice Bill. However, as the house and techno scene in Europe had never been political, the wave of opposition soon ran out of steam. Those sound systems that could no longer bear the police's systematic repression, such as Spiral Tribe, fled the UK and took exile in France.

The British tabloid newspapers, who had been against raves from the outset, proudly reported 'Ecstasy: the party is over'.

Concert promoters quickly spotted the opportunity to cash in on a public that now had nowhere to party, and took control of the rave scene under the approving eye of the authorities. These promoters were used to working within the law and fully cooperating with the police. They had both the logistical and financial power to be able to fulfil all the legal requirements. But the raves that they organised were commercially led, sponsored by every brand imaginable, and, at the end of the day, just carbon copies of rock festivals.

In the midst of this, several DJs were propelled into dance music stardom: Carl Cox, Paul Oakenfold and Sasha were treated in a way that was previously reserved for rock stars. Their faces were all over the press and their names on the line-up became moneymaking guarantees. Quick off the mark, the British music industry began to develop dance music based upon the same business model as pop music. As most DJs were not musicians, CD mix compilations began to flood the record shops in order to satisfy an ever-growing demand: *Journeys By DJ*, *Mixmag*, *X-Mix*, etc.

The money was now flowing freely, and a commercial music market was well established with the DJ at its centre. The DJ had become a precious commodity. His/her place was now on stage, facing the crowd. DJs' names were more important than the music, and the fees they earned reflected their reputation. In 1992, the budget for a rave such as Tribal Gathering was evenly divided between production costs and artists' fees; by 1994, 70 per cent of the budget was attributed to artists' fees. As the line-up of DJs grew, so the price of an entrance ticket rose.

Because of DJs reaching pop star status, the face of dance music changed in Britain. While the line-ups at raves kept getting bigger and bigger, a new generation of super-clubs was born: Cream in Liverpool, Renaissance in Nottingham and Gatecrasher in Sheffield. The promoters of these clubs didn't hesitate to pay huge amounts in order to attract DJs who were guaranteed to fill their venue. These huge clubs, known as corporate clubs, were all about image. It didn't matter what kind of music the DJ played, as long as he was a big name. The biggest DJs from America, David Morales, Todd Terry and Frankie Knuckles, were booked and received star treatment. Soon, many UK rave DJs who had previously been happy to be paid a reasonable fee, as long as their names appeared on the flyer, turned their backs on raves and turned to the clubs. The appearance of clubs had changed. Each venue had been redesigned to direct all eyes towards the DJ booth. DJ booths were designed like airline cockpits, brimming with the latest technology: three turntables, CD players, a mixer with extra effects, a frequency modifier and a DAT recorder. There were no longer any microphones or records in sight. Just two empty black boxes ready to house each DJ's own records.

People flocked to these new venues, where the DJ was now centre-stage. Super-clubs and super-DJs had arrived in the UK, and *Mixmag*, *DJ Mag* and *Muzik* were the monthly magazines that related what was going on.

In this system based on overload, reputations were made and all people wanted was the novelty element – like in pop music. So it was not surprising that the resident DJ became something of the past, making way for the guest DJs, who often played two or three different gigs on the same night, sometimes playing half a dozen gigs over a weekend.

Soon, the time that the DJ had to play was adapted to fit in with this agenda. While, during the 80s, it was commonplace for a DJ to play all night long in a club, flyers were now stamped with 'Two-hour set' next to the DJ's name. The variety of music played was also considerably reduced. The DJs who fought to play a little longer were few and far between. Most were working less but earning much more. A couple of promoters in London decided to fight back against this 'new' way of doing things, and founded Club UK and The End. Both of these clubs had a mission to bring back the true underground spirit of techno and give the DJs time to express themselves.

But money and stardom were now engrained in the heart of UK nightlife. There was no more room for any magic.

If it wasn't the Criminal Justice Bill, or big business eating away at the dance music scene, it was the press or gang culture having a go at it. For years now, the Haçienda had been living a nightmare of gang violence and police harassment. Yet the club still fought to recreate the same energy that had existed during the second Summer of Love by booking a new generation of record labels and DJs from Manchester (e.g. Grand Central Records or the DJ Elliot Eastwick) … and introducing new concepts.

Paul Cons launched Flesh, a monthly gay night, which was the first event to create the same energy and atmosphere as in the early days of the Haçienda. It became very popular. Then in 1995, Paul Cons asked Dave Haslam to take up a residency in the newly refurbished, 1,000-capacity basement room. And so, every Saturday night, an eclectic mix of funk, hip-hop and rock was played, and the new weekend format at the Haçienda quickly became a huge success. In May 1997, when the Haçienda celebrated its 15th birthday in great style, people began to believe that the Haçienda was finally experiencing something of a revival.

But the underlying problems with violence were still there. And business wasn't great. For Tony Wilson, founder of the Haçienda and director of Factory Records, the reason was clear: when people take ecstasy they do not buy drinks from the bar. The Haçienda swallowed up all of Factory Records' profits. On June 28, 1997, the club closed its doors for the very last time.

Over in Germany, the harmonious collaboration between rave organisers and the authorities had enabled a huge industry to develop around raves. Raves were now for the masses and had become gigantic events. Mayday, for example, was not a rave but an extravaganza. It was the German way of doing dance music in the 90s. In Dortmund's immense indoor stadium, over 40 DJs played 30-minute sets, one after the other, dazzled by a sea of lasers and 3D images. While Mayday produced the event, their record label Low Spirit released the official anthem. As for the sponsors, they could not have fought harder to be associated with the event. The spontaneous nature of raves had been overrun by a desire for big business. Within a few years, this would result in the death of the rave scene in Germany. Love Parade in Berlin would also go down the same path, as it too was organised by the same promoters (Low Spirit and Frontpage).

On July 24, 1994, the Love Parade was at the height of its success. The most influential American DJs and producers could be seen on every float. And while the rest of the world was watching the World Cup football semi-final on television, over 200,000 ravers were making their way down the Ku Damm, dancing to the sounds of over 30 sound systems. Yet, in spite of the positive slogans ('the spirit makes you move'), the Love Parade was showing the first signs of outright commercialism. The organisers charged about 3,000 marks (about 1,600 euros) to enter a float in the parade. Gema (the German music rights association) also charged the same amount again (no one really knew how this money would be fairly distributed between the artists). Every year, more and more clauses were added to the contracts, and security requirements got stricter, with every float having to employ security guards. By 1996, the average cost of a float was estimated at 11,000 euros. Approximately 3,000 people were working directly or indirectly for Love Parade. It was an industry. DJs and musicians received contracts stipulating that they were not allowed to perform anywhere else in Germany three months prior to or after the event. Labels were forbidden to sign contracts with any unofficial sponsors to fund their floats. During the event, advertising banners were visible all over the city and inside the clubs. The music had become an appendage to this huge moneymaking machine. But, this aside, DJs had the amazing privilege of performing in front of a crowd of half a million people.

In 1996, Love Parade attracted a crowd of 750,000 people, under the banner 'We are one family'. It was not long before they reached the one million mark. But, by then, what had once been one of the most amazing celebrations of dance music in the world had now become a soulless commercial venture.

A victim of its own making, the German rave scene began to decline. When, in 1997, Sven Vath closed his record label, Harthouse, it marked the end of a chapter in European dance music history.

In the meantime, Switzerland was modelling itself on its German neighbour. Arnold Meyer, a local promoter, had witnessed both Love Parade and Mayday. He ran with the idea and created a similar event in Zurich called Energy. The first event took place in an abandoned warehouse and was a great success. Other promoters followed Meyer's example, organising parties in warehouses and industrial buildings. In 1993, Energy took place in the Hallenstadium, an indoor stadium with a capacity of 20,000 people, on the outskirts of Zurich. I was asked to DJ and was surprised to find an exact replica of what the Germans had set in motion with Love Parade. First, there was a parade through the streets of Zurich ('Street Parade'), and once the local council had swept away the litter, a huge rave was organised inside the sports stadium. The leading artists from the world of techno were there, playing on one of many stages: Aphex Twin, Jam & Spoon, Joey Beltram, etc., even though their set time was reduced to a minimum. Thousands of ravers packed out the venue. The main room had at least 20 lasers and boasted an incredible sound system. The backstage area was buzzing with international DJs, having a drink and a laugh, swapping records and chatting. We were paid handsomely, and our work environment was more than satisfactory. No one was complaining.

Like Germany, the golden age of raves in Switzerland lasted until 1996, and established Zurich as one of the international capitals of techno. That same year, electronic music also made its way into the prestigious Montreux Jazz Festival, with a night dedicated to the record label Harthouse. Simultaneously, Couleur 3, an avant-garde national radio station, began to include what they called 'music for your feet' in their programme Les Metissages, reflecting the growth of dance music in French-speaking Switzerland too. Swiss raves gradually became big commercial events, attracting a younger and younger crowd who were less interested in the music. In contrast, the city of Lausanne became a centre for Swiss clubbing with venues such as the Loft and the D! in the same part of town as the MAD.

In Europe, techno now had its own one-night festivals, mega raves, club circuits and everything else that went with it. However, there was nothing yet that resembled an annual get-together for the electronic music culture. Not just to celebrate music but also the imagery, technology, and media that went with it. The answer came from Spain, a country that up until then had shown little interest in electronic music. Spain should not be confused with Ibiza, whose island club music had not yet filtered across to the mainland.

F Communications was contacted by a group of promoters in Barcelona to take part in the first ever Sonar. Apart from Baccalau, a hideously commercial style of techno from Valencia, we had no idea what was happening in Spain. We were always looking for new territories to explore, so of course we accepted the invitation. We went to Barcelona and met three people passionate about music: Ricard Robles, a journalist and clubbing connoisseur, Enric Palau, a musician, and Sergi Caballero, who was involved in contemporary art and theatre. These three people were sure of one thing: that electronic music would become a global affair and would embrace culture and media.

The first Sonar festival took place over three nights. The English DJ Mixmaster Morris, Sven Vath and myself played at the Apollo, an incredible venue for 500 people in the historic centre of Barcelona. It was there that I heard the expression 'la puta madre' for the very first time. It seemed to punctuate every phrase. During the first hour of my set, the public looked at me strangely, wondering who this strange man was playing strange music. During the second hour I played Follow Me by Jam & Spoon and something happened. There was a sudden change in energy in the room and the crowd went crazy. At the end of my set, people came up to me shouting 'Gracias!' over and over. It was mad! I thought to myself, these Catalans seemed to have really enjoyed themselves. They definitely need more techno! The next day, I left my hotel with an almighty hangover and went to check out the record shops in Barcelona. I came across a gold mine. I found hundreds of rare re-editions and second-hand records. There was everything: rock, euro dance and industrial pop by the shedload, but not one techno record. Techno simply didn't exist in Spain. Open-air parties were nothing new in Spain, which is probably one of the reasons that raves never took off. Ibiza remained an exception.

In 1994, the idea of inviting a DJ to play at a festival in Spain was revolutionary. Sonar went even further than this by scheduling concerts as well as multimedia, contemporary art and design exhibitions and conferences, all based on electronic music. Sonar prided itself on being completely independent and made its ambitions known from the outset: to be the annual meeting place for the dance music community. The festival took place inside Barcelona's Centre for Contemporary Culture, as if to say loud and clear that this event was nothing to do with raves and ecstasy. While it would have been inconceivable to create such an event in France or the UK, Sonar managed to persuade the Spanish authorities that electronic music was an important aspect of contemporary art.

The Sonar festival liberated techno culture in Spain. The first event resulted in the appearance of a flurry of Catalan DJs, including Angel Molina, who would become one of their leading lights. Within a couple of years, Sonar was at the centre of international electronic music culture, and gave a platform to the most important players on the electronic music scene, whether they be famous or unheard of, avant-garde artists, or future pop stars. They managed to create a perfect balance between underground music and the Spanish sense of fiesta.

Sonar remained the exception. Every other country was focused on big business and bigger events. A global network was now in place consisting of DJs, bookers, promoters, clubs, magazines and sponsors. DJ-ing was now a full-time career for many, and the demand was still growing. In order to deal with the increasing number of bookings, DJs began to hire agents to act as go-betweens between themselves and the clubs. Together, they would plan a schedule and choose events to play at, and then the agent would be in charge of dealing with fees and contracts, enabling the DJs to concentrate on their work. The first generation of agents developed close ties with their artists and managed to build up impressive pools of international DJs. Nick was one example. She was quite eccentric but she was mad about music. She was the agent for several DJs, including Carl Cox, Josh Wink, Richie Hawtin and myself. She became a close friend to all of us and loved to call us her 'babies'. Working with her was a real pleasure. She was professional, generous and a party-harder. She was a good friend as well as an agent and remains the best example of that first wave.

Then, a new generation of agents began to appear on the scene. Their working methods were similar to those of rock concert promoters and bankers. Everything was about money and ego. Their way of doing business was simple: 'How many tickets are on sale? How much is a ticket?

Give me a minute so I can find my calculator. Okay, so you are making this much. So if you want my artist to play you have to pay this much. Plus my 15 per cent.' This practice gradually became the norm, and if a DJ refused to be part of it, he would be told, 'The less money you ask for, the less people will respect you.'

By 1996, most international DJs had a team of managers, lawyers and accountants working for them, managing their careers like micro businesses. This dramatically changed the nature of our jobs as DJs. DJs playing on the international circuit were faced with a dilemma; play the money game, or risk seeing your career stagnate. We all had to make the choice: accept the situation and take the money, or refuse and stay loyal to certain values at the risk of being pushed aside.

My position has always been extremely clear. I have never been interested in the money. What is important for me and what has kept me DJ-ing is the relationship I have built up with the public. The relationship that I have with the dance floor over the years is so strong that it is like a drug I can't say no to. Whenever I play records for people, whether in a club, at a festival or at a private party, it's like an exclusive moment with the people I am playing music to. Not being able to do this would be like stopping speaking or stopping having sex. I have been lucky in that I have had a very loyal following over the years. But, this relationship didn't just happen, it has developed gradually; record by record, gig by gig. Money has absolutely nothing to do with this.

Why follow an artist? Why trust in him and dance to his music? Because there is a real connection, a real relationship. A DJ's job, wherever he is playing and however much he is being paid, is to make people dance – even if it is 7am and the last few people left on the dance floor are in a terrible state, and he only has one record left in his record box. It's my duty to make them dance and enjoy themselves. To be able to do this, and this is by far the hardest part of our job, you have to establish a connection, and understand them. You have to be able to read what they want and satisfy their desires. You also have to be able to take them with you into unexplored territories, by force, if necessary. You have to surprise them, seduce them, and at the end of the day give them what they came for, i.e. a good time. What does a DJ get in return? An extraordinary feeling of power, even control. I have felt this many times – for example, when playing in a small club with a packed dance floor. You can really feel the energy rising from right under people's feet up through to the roof. And people come up to you asking, 'One more, one more!!'

What makes us want to be packed inside a hot, sweaty club? For reasons of instinct that date back over centuries. The night has always been synonymous with danger. When we go inside a club we are simply repeating the age-old instinct of self-protection. When we come out of the dark into the light and find human warmth and join together in a rhythmic beat, we feel protected. When we dance together in a group, the energy is such that we let go of our fears, our anxieties and our most basic emotions. Dancing enables us to exorcise our demons and rise above.

As a DJ and someone who loves to dance, I have experienced moments of pure joy when I felt I would have been happy to die there in that moment. Like the perfect orgasm, you would want the experience to last forever. I believe in energies. And I truly believe that the DJ channels this energy through the record needle and filters it through the speakers onto the dance floor. I believe in an invisible thread that links the DJ to the people on the dance floor, and that when they connect there is an exchange of energy between the two.

One night, at the DJ David Holmes' club in Belfast, I remember feeling that I knew what was going to happen within the first few minutes of my set. I was instinctively playing exactly the right tracks at exactly the right moment, whereas some nights I have to struggle for a bit before getting the crowd to follow me. During the whole four hours of my set that night, I can confidently say that I had the crowd on my side from beginning to end. I had them eating out of my hand without making any concessions. A girl came up to me at the end of the night and said, 'Tonight was really strange. You controlled us.' It was true, that night I had a strong connection with the dance floor and was very much in charge. The crowd took my cues and danced; they went crazy. When I think back to that night, I can still remember the feeling. The vibes you get on a night like that leave their mark. That's how it goes. Our bodies are transistors; they give out and pick up vibrations. The American hip-hop artist Saul Williams raps that we are made up of sounds, and goes as far as to say that the Latin root of the word 'persona' literally means 'to sound through', and therefore sounds are part of our makeup. This theory may leave many people cold. But, it's like the mystery of dance. Where does the deep-felt need to dance come from? Why do we instinctively tap our feet or move to a four-by-four beat? Because we have this inside us, it is part of our being, it is eternal.

After years spent DJ-ing all over the world, I have learned that no crowd response should be taken for granted. Ever since the beginning, I have always built my DJ sets with the crowd and I always place my wristwatch on the mixer, so I can respect people in the club's natural body clock. DJ-ing is all about timing, listening and watching. Over the years, I have come to realise that observation is one of the most important factors in building my sets. You have to be able to read the grooves on each record to be able to anticipate any breaks or silences. But, most importantly, you have to be able to look into the crowd's eyes to read what they want. People on the dance floor aren't just a pair of feet. Having said that, I know my way of thinking is very different from most DJs around.

Promoters will tell you that most DJs leave clubs straight after their set to go back to their hotel, as though it's just another day's work. I know DJs who never dance because they don't enjoy it, not even behind the decks in the privacy of the DJ booth. I find it strange that you can be a DJ and not like dancing; it's a contradiction in terms. How can you communicate passion if you don't feel it yourself? Just watch Jeff Mills DJ. He's completely entranced by the music he plays, his whole body moves, you can see he feels the music in every pore of his skin. If a DJ is incapable of feeling the vibes that make people dance, he cannot feel the energy that the crowd is sending back to him. The rules of the game are merciless: you give nothing, you get nothing in return. I also know DJs who only keep DJ-ing for the money. Others do it just to travel or to meet girls. Others do it for the celebrity status. Fortunately, there still remains a significant number of DJs who do it for the love of music.

One night in Berlin, I was booked to play at a club night organised by Miss Kittin, a rare and vibrant DJ and producer who is passionate about music. Miss Kittin was originally from Grenoble but was by then living in Berlin. When I entered the club, the walls draped in red, the sound system was amazing, the crowd were there to enjoy themselves and I immediately picked up on an energy that I hadn't felt in a long time. It was around midnight, which is early by club standards. Miss Kittin was playing the warm-up set. I went and stood in the middle of the dance floor and closed my eyes and listened to the music for a while. A huge feeling of wellbeing bubbled up inside me. I went over to the DJ booth to get my records ready. When I put on the first record, I felt like I was floating above the crowd. There was such a good vibe that night that I played for seven hours non-stop. I played techno, deep house, drum 'n' bass, hip-hop, electro and rock – everything! At seven in the morning there were still about 200 people in the club. They may have been exhausted, but they weren't ready to go home quite yet. The only record I had left to play in my boxes was the album *Kid A* by Radiohead. So I played it – an avant-garde pop record with mad saxophones, a saturated bass line, and Thom Yorke's eerie voice filling the club – to say 'thank you and goodnight'.

People stood on the dance floor, their arms in the air, their heads hanging back with huge smiles on their faces. It was a magical moment.

The needle got to the end of the record and then there was silence. Nobody moved from the dance floor, as if they were caught up in an overwhelming emotion and were afraid that the spell might be broken.

Not everyone is as open-minded as they are in Berlin, and sometimes people find it difficult if you stray from the confines of techno. One night in Frankfurt, I was playing in a techno club and decided to break up my set with a hip-hop track. A guy came and stood in front of me and shouted, 'What the fuck is this shit?' I told him to go and have a drink, as this track was a way for me to bring things down for a bit. But he carried on, 'What is this shit?' So I asked him, 'What are you doing here?' – 'I'm here because you're Laurent Garnier.' – I couldn't believe what I was hearing. 'Exactly. So what did you think I was going to do? I'm not a jukebox. I'm here to make you discover new things, to open your ears to new sounds!'

He stormed off in a fury and the night continued.

The following night I was playing at a club in Mannheim. The same guy turned up at about 5am, just as I was playing Love To Love You Baby by Donna Summer. Poor guy obviously had the flair for turning up just when I was slowing things down a little. He came up to the DJ booth looking rather sheepish. I clenched my jaw thinking, oh God he's going to do my head in again. But instead he smiled and said, 'It's great!'; I asked him, 'What are you doing here this time?'. He hesitated before replying, 'Well, I thought about what you said and maybe you were right.'

During that time, every DJ was faced with an increasing inability to connect with younger audiences who found it difficult to embrace any other kind of music than what they had come to hear. Many of us were getting tired of this and were hungry for new experiences and new audiences.

In 1995, Europe was no longer the place to explore uncharted territory. It was time to take our music to new places. I began to travel further afield, embarking on international tours that took me away for several months at a time to places such as Mexico, Hong Kong, Brazil and Australia … Most of these countries were just discovering dance music, so going there to DJ was a way of spicing things up and served to remind us, if we needed reminding, why we had chosen this career.

During a four-date tour of Brazil, I saw first-hand the deep-rooted cultural rivalry that existed between Rio and São Paulo. In a nutshell, Rio's laid-back way of life was in stark contrast to São Paulo's energy. In terms of clubbing, these differences expressed themselves in Rio's preference for house music and São Paulo's taste for techno. A dance music scene existed in Brazil, led by the DJs Mau Mau and Marky.

After two crazy gigs in São Paulo, the promoters came up to me and said, 'You haven't seen anything yet! Wait until you see Hell's Club on Sunday, it's even crazier!'. Hell's Club was legendary on the underground scene. It was an after-hours club that opened at 5am and was the rendezvous for thrill-seekers. The crowd was very young. Appearances reflected the violence of the city: piercings, tattoos and scarification. I remember, in particular, one striking-looking girl who had a shaved head and was covered in tattoos. Hell's Club was a big venue, spread out over two floors. The club harboured a colourful mix of transvestites, bad boys, clubbers and gang members. In the dark alcoves, you could make out the shapes of transvestites performing lewd acts on local bad boys. The DJ booth was up on the first floor and only had a narrow slit through which you could look down at the dance floor.

As the party got going, a strange charade began. Several groups of transvestites piled into the DJ booth to have their photo taken with me. They seemed really pleased to be able to have their photo taken with a DJ from Europe. There was something really exciting about this place. When I started playing some Chicago booty-house, the whole place went wild. Transvestites, gang members and people covered in body piercings got down on the dance floor. The transvestites were making a big show of things on the dance floor while all sorts of stuff was going on in the alcoves. With each new record I played I could feel from right up in the DJ booth an intense vibe of pure pleasure building in the club. It was caliente! In fact, even the madness at Quadrant Park seemed like child's play by comparison. I finally left Hell's Club late that afternoon. I walked out exhausted, happy and arm in arm with a couple of transvestites, while two bad boys covered from head to toe in tattoos insisted on carrying my record boxes for me and a couple of drag-queens argued about who was going to show me back to my hotel.

It's these kind of extraordinary encounters that make me want to continue travelling the world. Experiencing these kinds of adventures makes you realise how futile the whole agent/manager/promoter charade is. Yes, they are a necessary part of a DJ's career, but when a DJ is on the other side of the world, standing in a DJ booth, facing the crowd, ready to play for them, the DJ is on his own.

On the downside, every DJ experiences the same feeling of solitude every Sunday while waiting at the airport. Sundays are not good days for DJs. Having spent the past few nights in a club, tiredness sets in just as the long struggle to get home begins – taxi, check-in, airport lounge, flight, and then the same ritual in reverse order at the other end. And there are others…

After years of DJ-ing, stroboscopes have played havoc with my eyes. My ears have been subjected to torture. Cigarette smoke, smoke machines and dust have polluted my lungs. And like every DJ, I have back trouble thanks to endless nights spent hunched over a pair of turn-tables and lugging around record boxes that weigh a ton, only stopping to put them down at a taxi rank or in an airport lounge where we don't ever take our eyes off them for fear of losing them. Losing a record box is the ultimate nightmare for any DJ. These are records that have been collected over many years and are cherished for their magic or their rarity. These collections are priceless. It might not seem like much, but the 50 or so records that are stored in one record box are part of a DJ's identity. When the rumour spread that an organised gang was stealing records at Madrid airport, somewhere between the aircraft and luggage reclaim, several international DJs refused to go there. I even know some DJs who have the same recurring nightmare: they arrive at a party, go inside the club that is heaving with excitement, get behind the decks, go to take out a record and their records have gone!

However, none of this is of great importance compared with other factors that threaten both a DJ's longevity and integrity. The environment in which we work poses its own set of problems. Partying is at the centre of our business, so DJs are constantly exposed to temptation: alcohol, drugs, casual sex. And it's so easy to give in to temptation. I know dozens of DJs who have ruined their careers by partying too hard, and some who have completely lost touch with the meaning of our job – giving pleasure to others. Yet, to do this you have to have both feet on the ground, respect the public and be constantly aware that we are part of their lives for one night only. That's what's important. It's a question of respect. I have always had the same attitude ever since the beginning, and it has never taken away any of the intensity or pleasure that I get out of my job.

There are other constraints, too, that are directly linked to the status of an international DJ. Travelling to the other side of the globe means accepting the risks that go with it. A gig on the other side of the world can be booked, but even when the contracts are signed and an advance has been paid up front, something can go wrong once you arrive in an unknown city or an unknown club. Like the true story of two European DJs who went to play in Russia. They arrived at the airport and were kidnapped by rival promoters. They were forced to play in their club until closing time. They were then escorted back to their hotel two hours before their flight, were paid double what they were supposed to earn and politely thanked. It is not uncommon for things like this to happen when you are touring internationally. Sometimes it's less dramatic, sometimes more.

Every international DJ has experienced this slow learning curve of adventures and nightmare situations, like arriving at an airport in a foreign city and there's no one there to meet you. At times like these, your ability to problem-solve and to adapt is put to the test. Many a time I've found myself waiting for hours before finally managing to get hold of the promoter to then be told to fend for myself; I've spent hours on the phone desperate for someone to answer the other end; I've experienced the cold glare of Russian customs officers who suspected me of carrying God knows what, and held me in a room for hours on end waiting for an interpreter to turn up.

A couple of other stories also come to mind. Like when I went to Sweden for the first time back in 1991. I landed at a small regional airport with my 40 kg record boxes and no return ticket. I scanned the arrivals hall for somebody holding a sign with 'Garnier', but there was no one to be seen. I waited and waited and then finally managed to get through to the promoter on the phone. He told me in English in a gravelly voice, 'I can't come and pick you up. Get a taxi.' I spent a good two hours trying to find a bank that would change my money, then looking for a taxi and finally repeating the address several times over to be sure the driver understood me. When I eventually arrived at my destination with no money left, I was surprised to find a group of 18-year-olds waiting for me. 'We've got some bad news, the party's been cancelled,' they announced. I tried to contain my anger as I explained to them that I was hundreds of miles from home, I had no money to get back to France, and on top of that it was my birthday and I was in the shit! Silence. Then one of them piped up, 'Don't worry, we'll find a solution.' I wasn't sure whether to trust him but I mumbled an 'okay'. That night I found myself DJ-ing in a school classroom where they had set up a rented sound system. They had managed to get together about 200 people. A small entrance fee was asked at the door; every last cent was to go towards paying for my ticket home. At 2am, one of the organisers stopped the music and took hold of the microphone. I didn't understand a word he said but all of a sudden that whole room began to sing 'Happy Birthday'. I was really touched. At dawn, they dropped me back at the airport and handed me the entire night's takings. As I carried my records onto the tarmac I could hear them shouting, 'Bon voyage!' as they drove off in the car.

This is a nice story because it ends well. But I have also come across promoters without such big hearts who will happily leave you standing on the deserted pavement outside the club at the end of the night saying, 'Make your own way back to the hotel. I'm off to bed. I'm knackered.' Or others who disappear before the end 'forgetting' to pay you. I have experienced the stress of losing my records on a connecting flight. I have flown for hours only to end up playing in an empty club on the outskirts of town. I've stayed in the seediest and noisiest hotels in the middle of nowhere where you are literally thrown out of your room first thing in the morning because supposedly it's check-out time.

But these are only minor setbacks. On the heavier side, I've known promoters who've refused to pay me and laid a gun on the table when I insisted. I've known promoters who didn't have money, so they offered to pay me in ecstasy pills instead. How many times have I known parties being cancelled, or being raided by the police. I've had a gun pointed at me by police officers – twice! In Mexico City and in Grenoble. And probably one of the most extraordinary things that happened to me was when someone threatened to kill me because I played a drum 'n' bass record in a techno club …

… I was playing at the Orbit Club in Leeds with Richie Hawtin. The club had a reputation for being about hard techno. But I did warn the promoter beforehand, 'I don't want to play banging techno all night long, I want to be able to bring it down a bit too, with some more melodic stuff.' The promoter was fine with this, 'I want to change the music policy here a bit anyway so do what you want. Trust me, it'll be fine.' Richie played banging techno for about two hours to a crowd who clearly loved it. Then it was my turn to take to the decks. After about half an hour into my set I decided to break up the pace and play a drum 'n' bass record. People on the dance floor looked surprised. I decided to reiterate my choice of music by playing a second drum 'n' bass record, when all of a sudden a guy appeared over the barrier that separated the DJ booth from the dance floor. He was armed with a broken bottle and launched himself at me, ready to cut my throat. Two of the bouncers managed to grab hold of him just in time. They dragged him off into a dark corner and gave him a going over.

More stories like these?

Ok, here's another.

As part of an American tour, I went to do a party in Detroit. I learned that Kenny Larkin, who had been the first person to invite me to Motor City, had left town. Why? Because a couple of guys had knocked on his door one day, and when he opened it they shot him several times in the stomach. Once he had recovered, he moved to California. The promoter came to get me at the airport to take me to the venue. As usual, I went to get into the passenger seat, but he stopped me and asked me to get into the back of the car. 'We're gonna be driving through some bad neighbourhoods, so you'd better get in the back.' He told me these were the kind of neighbourhoods where a white guy like me needed to be low-key.

The party was being held in a building in the centre of a run-down neighbourhood. As we walked inside, the first thing I noticed was the metal fenced windows. Mad Mike was waiting for me inside. He warned me, 'There's a weird vibe tonight, watch your back.' I learned that a gang that ran the neighbourhood had had a run in with a rival gang, who were in charge of security that night. I was playing in the downstairs room with Stacey Pullen. The party got underway and a friendly crowd started to fill the dance floor. Everything was going well until one of the bouncers stormed into the room and told me, 'Stop the music right now. Get your records and leave.' He seemed scared; people in the room began to panic. Stacey and I quickly put our records away and ran up the stairs towards the exit. There was a girl just in front of us. When she got out onto the pavement, a car slowed down and stopped in front of her. The passenger window wound down and a gun appeared, pointing at the girl. A shot was fired. The bouncers ran out to the girl who was lying in a pool of blood on the pavement. Once they had carried the girl back inside, one of the bouncers grabbed my record boxes, shouting, 'Quickly, get back inside!' Once inside, someone shouted, 'Get down!' The 20 or so people still left inside the venue lay face down on the floor. The girl, who had been shot in the shoulder, was lying on her back covered with a blanket. We lay there in the dark for what seemed like hours, but was probably only about 15 minutes, listening to the cars going back and forth along the road in front of the building. Then there was silence outside and in. Except for a few people whispering, 'Fuck, man,' and the injured girl who was whimpering in pain. It took the police over 15 minutes to arrive. When they burst into to the club, their faces covered by masks, they found a group of terrified people, lying on the floor in the dark.

The following day, I found out that one of the gang members in charge of security at the party was shot and killed in the car park that night by a rival gang. His body had been dumped in a rubbish bin. We were lucky; it could have been a bloodbath.

All these experiences have helped me to mature and have strengthened my resolve. There were also new things I wanted to do. Firstly, for F Communications, as the label was expanding, it was time to go and win over new audiences, and secondly for me, as a musician. *Shot In The Dark* had opened new doors for my career and had enabled me to experience a new pleasure: making music on my own. I was secretly harbouring plans for a second album and decided to take the time to make it happen. However, for now I went back to France, where in the south preparations were being made for a very special wedding that would join together two citizens of the house nation.

can you feel it

Techno had been around for about seven years and was entering a new phase: its so-called 'age of reason'. And with this, dance music experienced its first wedding and its first funeral. On December 22, 1994, one crazy night in Cannes, Carl Cox tied the knot with the drag queen and respected DJ, Lady B. A few months later, the musician and journalist, Lee Newman, aka Technohead, lost his battle with cancer.

At around that time, F Communications was looking to expand into countries where dance music had yet to make a name for itself. Among the markets F Communications wanted to break into was Eastern Europe. Eric Morand and I had been very surprised by what we had seen in both Moscow and East Berlin. So, after an unforgettable first birthday party at La Locomotive, we left Paris to do an F Comm night in Belgrade. Up until then, Eastern Europe had been spared the dance music invasion. This was especially the case for former Yugoslavia, which was still recovering from a war that had lasted several years. The buildings in the city centre were in ruins; the atmosphere on the street tense. Soon after we arrived, a demonstration was taking place under the watchful eye of army tanks. The shouts of the demonstrators could be heard in the reception rooms of Belgrade's town hall, where we were attending a reception in our honour. Every promoter in Belgrade was there. The mayor wanted to give the city's nightlife a kick-start. We were the object of an official presentation, and at the end of his speech, the mayor handed us the keys to the city as a gesture of goodwill. It was all very formal and we felt slightly awkward, as we were not quite sure why we were being honoured in this way – until someone explained that we were the first European artists to set foot in Belgrade since the end of the conflict, and that our presence was symbolic in that it was a breath of fresh air for the young people of the city. Through the window we could see tanks rolling across the square in front of the town hall, as we were handed a charter to sign in the fight against drugs. The contrast was surreal.

We were then taken by the promoters to a warehouse in the city centre. Inside, old railway tracks were stacked up on huge shelves. There was also a big sound system that the technicians were testing with a copy of Pink Floyd's album *Dark Side Of The Moon*. A group of Romany children were running around and dancing to the music that they had never heard before, especially so loud. It was such an amazing sight to see these gorgeous children, with their scruffy clothes and muddy faces, leaping around to the sounds of Money.

The party got underway. We were apprehensive about playing in front of an audience who knew nothing about dance music, but we found ourselves playing to a crowd of enthusiastic young people who looked like they had just stepped out of a German rave. The promoters had purpose-fully lit the railway stock, which gave a very techno feel to the venue.

When Aurora Borealis (Shazz's trance project) began playing, the crowd went wild. The atmosphere was electric. People seemed genuinely happy to be taking part in the rebirth of nightlife in their war-torn city. Drunk guys climbed up onto the stage to hand us packs of beer or bottles of strange-looking alcohol. Someone got hold of Eric Morand and intro-duced him to the local custom: drink, drink and drink … The next day, on the plane back to France, we all felt the worse for wear.

Three days later I was on my way to Japan. I had gigs booked in Tokyo, Kyoto and Osaka. The minute I found out that I was going to Japan, friends of mine began telling me with a glint in their eyes about how exciting it was to DJ in Japan. I enjoyed listening to all their stories and asked them to repeat the bits about the crowds going crazy and the Japanese people's total adoration of music. I spent three days off in Paris without switching on my machines. I was focusing on my trip to Japan, as I knew it was going to be special. In fact, I spent the entire three days preparing my records. I unplugged the phone as I needed to concentrate. I listened to every single record in my boxes, trying to memorise them all. Then I listened to hundreds of new records that I had accumulated over the past few weeks and began to make piles of them. The ritual of choosing my records has remained the same for years. Out of a hun-dred records I listen to (i.e. what I get through in the post in one week), I only select about 20. Then, once I have completed my selection, I note them in my own special way: 'Dog's Bollocks!' (when it's a real blast), 'Ffffwwwaaarrrhhh!' (great!), 'Deep', 'Techno', a wriggling bottom drawn on to the centre label which means booty-house, etc. Then I arrange the records in my record boxes according to the intensity of each track: from the softest to the hardest. Almost as an afterthought, I also picked out a few other records for my DJ sets in Japan: a few reggae records, a couple of Brazilian samba tracks and one or two funk and soul classics. On day three, my records were finally ready.

I left for Japan feeling nervous with anticipation. By the 11th hour of my flight I was pulling my hair out, I would have done anything just to get there. Finally, we landed in Tokyo. I was met at the airport by Alex Prat, a.k.a. Alex From Tokyo, a French DJ who grew up in Japan and who had been, for the last few years, the main contact in Japan for the French house scene.

I had a few hours to acclimatise myself before my set. I was so excited that I quickly forgot how tired I was. Alex took me straight to the buzzing

streets of the trendy Shibuya district. We went to the most incredible record shops, where records I had been searching for for years were right there, neatly lined up on shelves. I took out my credit card and went mad – each record was outrageously expensive – but I couldn't stop myself until I had to beg Alex to get me out of there.

Inside every DJ there lies an obsessive collector with the desire to accumulate more and more records and build the ultimate collection. The quest for a rare or exclusive record is just what we do. For a DJ, vinyl is not only a working tool, it is also a treasured object. It is this obsession that drives us to rifle through the record bins in record shops the world over looking for the 'Holy Grail'. And for the vinylmaniacs that we all are, Japan is the Promised Land.

My first DJ gig in Japan was at Yellow, a legendary dance music club in Tokyo and regular port of call for international DJs. An incredibly well-dressed clientele stood inside a large, barely lit room, inspired by the clubs in New York. A huge disco ball hung from the ceiling. There was no bar, no tables, no chairs. The Japanese came here to dance to the huge sound system that belted out an inescapable torrent of thunderous bass lines. When I set foot inside the DJ booth, the public looked at me shyly and smiled politely. A DJ from Tokyo was coming to the end of his set. As he didn't speak any English, he used his hands to gesture that he was handing over the decks to me. I was just about to refuse – there was no rush, I was supposed to be starting my set half an hour later – when Alex whispered to me, 'He's being polite, and showing you respect. You mustn't refuse.' I started getting my records ready – I could feel lots of pairs of eyes staring at me – I swallowed hard and played my first record … from then on, I was completely overwhelmed by what I witnessed on the dance floor. The crowd literally went mad. With every record I played it was as if the level of excitement stepped up a notch. I went from feeling very unsure of what was going on ('What's got into them? Are they mad?'), to a feeling of pure elation. This fever spread right across the dance floor. I glanced up at the kids who were pressed up against the DJ booth, they were all grinning at me. The stories I had been told about the Japanese clubgoers came flooding back … These people were passionate, their tastes were sophisticated, they were true music lovers.

Whichever record I played, at least one person would come up to me, singing along with the track, and look straight at me, their fingers spread out in a fan to mean: Great! Whether it was an obscure funk record, a brand new techno track, or one of the latest UK drum 'n' bass hits, the Tokyo crowd enjoyed each and every minute. They pushed me to take them further, to surprise them and have fun with them. Whatever I chose

▶ Playlist

JAPANESE HOUSE / TECHNO

Ken Ishii
Garden On The Palm

Flare
Reference To Difference

Fumiya Tanaka
Micro EP

Susumu Yokota
Acid Mt Fuji LP

Mato
Drifting

Calm
Shadow Of The Earth

DJ Kudo
Tiny Loops

to play, they accepted with absolute pleasure and devotion. It was exhilarating. Unnerving. A wonderful surprise. I went on to play in Osaka, where I experienced the same, then to Kyoto. I finally left Japan feeling amazing and bursting with positive energy. Just like new.

A lot of DJs who have been lucky enough to play all over the world also felt this same energy in Japan. By 1994, the global dance music scene was entering a new phase. The line-ups – whether in clubs or raves – now brought together DJs from very different backgrounds, and mixing things up like this was a breath of fresh air. This was how I found myself playing in Australia alongside Judge Jules, forerunner of the UK commercial house scene, or in Japan alongside LTJ Bukem, the drum 'n' bass maestro. These gigs on the other side of the world produced a multitude of unexpected musical collaborations that would have been unheard of a few months earlier. For example, the electro track made by Westbam and Afrika Bambaataa, or the hardcore track I did with Lenny Dee for his label Industrial Strength, when I was staying in Brooklyn.

Simultaneously, another type of line-up was starting to appear: the all-star DJ line-up. Jeff Mills, Carl Cox, Richie Hawtin, Sven Vath and I were booked on tours lasting several weeks. But what was initially a group of friends having fun together soon reached its limits. The promoters saw these tours as a way to increase ticket prices whereas we found ourselves playing in front of crowds who were already fans of techno so there was no real challenge. It was then that I decided to stop playing at raves and corporate clubs and to stop playing in all-star DJ line-ups where there was no room to surprise or touch the audience. I wanted to go back to playing in smaller clubs. I was fed up with my sets being drastically reduced to fit a time slot. By going back to smaller clubs I could extend my sets again to four or five hours. I concentrated my efforts on the UK, extolling the virtues of techno to a public that really only wanted to listen to trance or drum 'n' bass (a new style of breakbeat – a concentrate of bass and rhythms) that had recently become huge.

1996 ended on a happy note – I was voted Best International DJ by *Muzik* magazine – and also on a sad note. On December 17, the legendary Chicago producer, Armando, lost his fight against leukaemia. For the second time, the dance music community experienced the loss of one of their shining stars. Armando was a master. His music influenced every house music producer working at that time. His death left a big void.

In 1996, house and techno started exploring different genres of music – jazz, dub and even rock – soaking up the colours, sounds and language, digesting them and fusing them with electronic sounds.

Three years after *Shot In The Dark*, I felt ready to start work on a second album. I was almost 30 years old. I had evolved musically, had dipped into the mysterious world of jazz, and had become more open and interested in an even broader range of music. I had recently moved into a house in the southern suburbs of Paris. My studio/sanctuary, brimming with records and machines, was on the top floor of the house. It was there that I started work on my new album.

Within the first few days of getting to work, new ideas began to bubble up to the surface. For this album I wanted to create different moods. I wanted there to be an introduction, a couple of down-tempo tracks, some dance floor tracks; contrasting moods that would better reflect my personality. Up until then I had worked alone, but now I was facing a big problem as I didn't have the technical know-how to master my machines. Previously, I had been able to get round this. For *Shot In The Dark*, I had stumbled around, spending hours at a time trying to work out how to reproduce a sound or a melody. I often came across sounds by chance that I hadn't been looking for at first, and let myself go with the flow. But for this second album I wanted precision. I wanted to establish myself as a producer and tell a story.

I was both conscious of my technical limitations and put off by the hefty instruction manuals that accompanied each piece of studio equipment. So I asked Stephane Dri, a.k.a. Scan X, to teach me the fundamentals. Scan X was one of the leading artists on F Communications and was passionate about sound. He earned his stripes playing live at French raves, where he developed a raw techno sound, affirming himself as one of the major players on the French dance music scene. Scan X is a discoverer, an explorer of the infinite capacities of machines, as well as being a great teacher. Every morning for a month, he came to teach me the theory of the mixing desk, the sampler, the effects, the compressors – basically all the technical know-how that I had ignored for so many years.

One morning, he showed me an effect that reversed the compression, giving the sound an uneven texture. Later that day, when Stephane had left, I locked myself in my studio and decided to take my machines for a spin. I had a minimal dance floor track in mind that I wanted to be rough, sexy, angry and funky. On my JD-800 keyboards I found a bass line and put it in a loop. Then I added a kick drum and high hats before compressing the sound as much as I could. I went out for some fresh air and to give my ears a break. When I came back I listened to the track again. I liked it but I felt that there was still something missing. I copied the track onto a DAT tape and plugged in my MS-20 (a patchable semi-modular monophonic synthesizer which modulates sound). I pressed on a note on the keyboard while twisting and turning the buttons on the modulator to add a saturated texture to the track. I decided to leave it there. I could imagine playing it in the middle of the night to blow away the dance floor. On the DAT box I wrote the words 'Crispy Bacon'.

A week later, Jeff Mills was in Paris. I invited him over. As soon as he arrived I played him Crispy Bacon. He listened, in silence, with a smile on his face. When the track ended, he offered to do a remix. I took it as a good sign … However, he did question my choice of title: 'Why did you pick such a stupid name?' I tried to explain to him that when I listened to the track the first thing that came into my head was bacon sizzling in a pan. He smiled, 'But, crispy bacon is already cooked! You should have called it sizzling bacon!'. There was a moment's silence. 'Are you sure?' – 'I'm telling you, it should have been sizzling bacon'. We both laughed. I thought it was quite a funny mistake but still decided to stick with the title.

Apart from the track Flashback that was a tribute to Armando, the other tracks on the album were more personal and took a step back from dance floor techno. There was, for example, Theme From Larry's Dub, a dub track featuring the flautist Magik Malik; For Max, a downtempo track that I wrote for a friend's newborn son; and The Voyage de Simone (after Simone Garnier), featuring the female vocalist Lauren Garnier who I had met through Remy Kolpa-Kopoul from Radio Nova (and who had been receiving phone calls and letters addressed to me for years).

The recording of this album came together very organically. But once I had finished all the tracks, I was faced with a big problem: how to mix the sound. In 1996 techno had a bigger and better sound. A lot was at stake, and groups such as Autechre, on the experimental label Warp Records, represented a new school of artists that was constantly pushing sound to its limits. I was still a great believer in the DIY school of music-making and had been determined to produce this album entirely on my own, using my instinct. But I had skipped over some of the basics: I had absolutely no notion of frequencies and I didn't understand a thing about wavelengths. Yet I refused to work with a sound engineer. In hindsight, even though I love the compositions, the album as a whole was amateurishly mixed and lacking in depth.

Apart from Eric Morand, the first person I played my album to was Jack de Marseille, my friend and opposite number in the south of France. We were in my car. I slipped a tape into the cassette player and my album began to play over the speakers. When it was over Jack said, 'I don't like everything in it but I think it's very mature.' It was then that I knew what the title of the album should be: 30. I was at an age when I was asking myself a lot of serious questions about life. I had a lot of doubts. This album seemed to sum up all of the big changes going on in my life at the time: my wedding, my dreams, my anxieties, and my ambition to establish myself as a musician. I decided to release 30 as it was, with all its naïve imperfections and youthful mistakes. I hoped people would appreciate it for what it was: a desire for eclecticism and a baring of my soul.

Everything happened very quickly after that. I began thinking about the visuals that would accompany the album. I wanted the graphics to be different from clichéd techno visuals: fractal images, psychedelic colours, digital imagery. Eric and I met the artist Marc Anselmi. He put forward an idea for the album cover that was refreshingly sober. The cover would be black and white with my face appearing through a scratched image that seemed to rip apart the cover.

The videos for Crispy Bacon and Flashback (the second single) were written and directed by Quentin Dupieux, a musician and filmmaker who had made several short films. Instead of a pop video, Quentin suggested for Crispy Bacon that we make an off-the-wall short film called *Nightmare Sandwiches*. The result was very original, extremely weird and very funny. The album 30 came out in record shops in December 1996, receiving mixed reviews. For some, it was 'pretentious' and 'all over the place', whereas for others it was 'mature' and 'ambitious'.

By now, the earlier government and media hostility to the French techno scene was dissipating. In the provinces, several ambitious projects went ahead: a big rave took place in the city of Carcassonne; the Guy L'Eclair festival in Nantes played host to the first techno parade in France; the Transmusicales festival closed with Planet, a huge techno gathering at the Rennes' exhibition centre; in Grenoble the Futuria parties were in full swing, and in Concarneau the Astropolis festival showcased the full spectrum of electronic music and invited the leading international names in electronic music to play in what can only be described as a fairy tale castle. In the south of France, from Cannes to Nice, from Aix-en-Provence to Montpellier, under the guise of DJs like Jack de Marseille, techno really took hold.

Yet, nightlife in the south of France still had a poor reputation. In the clubs, corruption was widespread. I remember one particular night at the club La Nitro in Montpellier with Manu Le Malin. One of the organisers was secretly recording my DJ set with a tape recorder that was hidden behind a pile of jackets in the DJ booth. At that time there was a thriving black market for DJ mixtapes throughout Europe. As soon as I realised, I ripped the tape out of the machine and stuffed it into my pocket without telling anyone. At the end of the night the security guards bounded over: 'It's simple, unless we get that tape back, you're not leaving.' It was then that a friend of Manu Le Malin's took the tape, threw it on the floor and stamped on it. 'Go on. Take it. You can have it!' Not the best of atmospheres.

Raves had been organised in the south of France since early 1992, but it was the Borealis festival that really put it on the European techno map. In 1997, for the fifth Borealis festival, an entire village was created to host the rave within the Espace Grammont in Montpellier. The day before the festival officially opened, the organisers put on a series of exhibitions, concerts and parties in Montpellier's city centre. The programme included Jeff Mills performing with a contemporary ballet and Stephanovitch DJ-ing in the Place de la Comédie. That year, on five different stages, Borealis brought together DJs such as François Kevorkian, Manu Le Malin and The End sound system, as well as concerts from Daft Punk and the Chemical Brothers. Sixteen thousand people attended.

I began my set at 6am. The music on the other stages had come to an end. The DJ booth was down in front of the stage, about five feet off the ground. It was close-up to the crowd. It felt like I was playing in a club to 100 people, even though there were thousands in front of me. As I began my set, the sun came up. With the first rays of sunlight all I could see was a huge cloud of dust that hung above the crowd. The previous week, when I had been playing in Hong Kong, I had met the French-Chinese duo Technasia, who gave me a copy of their first single Theme From A Neon City. What an amazing track. Throughout my set I kept this record to one side, waiting for the right moment to play it. When the sun finally seemed to settle into place just above our heads I played Theme From A Neon City. Thousands of arms thrust up into the air and the cloud of dust appeared to get even thicker. The record was like a bomb going off. I dived back into my record box to dig out one of my favourite records ever, World 2 World by Underground Resistance. I put the needle on the record and ... this was one of the best moments of my whole career.

By 1997, techno was on the verge of becoming respectable. Politicians and the press were finally realising that dance music could benefit them, both in terms of its cultural image and the economy. Jack Lang, former minister of culture, announced that he would be attending Borealis and the Love Parade in Berlin that year. Now the national press had among its ranks some of the leading writers and journalists in electronic music: Alexis Bernier (*Libération*) and Stephane Davet (*Le Monde*). *Trax*, a monthly magazine devoted entirely to dance music, was available in every corner shop in the country. But it was a group of French producers that really put French house and techno in the spotlight. This phenomenon had a name, not a very original one, the 'French Touch'.

A few months earlier, the UK music magazine *Muzik* voted the album *Pansoul* by Motorbass (Philippe Zdar and Etienne de Crécy) 'album of the month'. As a result, the rest of the UK music press began to write about the French Touch and the wave of new producers from Paris making house music. The term French Touch (which had already been used in the early 80s to describe Metal Urbain on the label Rough Trade as well as the Stinky Toys on the cover of NME) was then picked up by the European press. In fact, the French Touch boiled down to a group of friends who made music together and hung out at Rough Trade records in Bastille. People like Philippe Zdar, Alex Gopher, Thomas Bangalter, Boombass, Etienne de Crécy and Dimitri from Paris.

In the beginning, the term French Touch designated a certain sound: a type of filtered house music that leant towards disco and ghetto house. Paris had forged a link with the house masters of Chicago. They used the Chicago sound as inspiration and added a hint of pop. The first tracks labelled French Touch had in common a raw and funky sound along the same lines as the productions of their American counterparts, Romanthony and DJ Sneak. But, soon enough, every Parisian house music producer was labelled with the term French Touch.

The role of the majors was crucial in the explosion of this movement. There is no doubt that it was the majors, helped along by the press, that created the French Touch out of nothing. In the first half of the 90s, a smattering of independent record labels cleared the way for electronic music till it was ripe for export. So when Emmanuel de Buretel, the head of Virgin France, signed Daft Punk in 1996, he had all he needed to prepare for the international release of a French house music artist as well as a solid international distribution network and huge financial backing at his disposal. When Daft Punk's first album *Homework* was released, everything was in place for it to thrive internationally.

The French press embraced the French Touch, as it offered a presentable and more commercial face of dance music. While the Goa trance, hardcore and techno scenes continued to grow stronger, with great artists emerging in Lyon, Grenoble or Bordeaux, the press chose to focus on a small number of people who represented the new Parisian house music scene. National radio followed suit. They began to include tracks from the French Touch even though dance music had never previously figured in their playlists. Soon, each major label was on the hunt for their own Daft Punk. Within the next few months a whole new group of producers appeared on the electronic music scene under the banner French Touch: Kojak (the only real group on the French house scene); I:Cube (discovered by the DJ Gilb'R and released on his label Versatile);

▸ Playlist

FRENCH TOUCH

Stardust
*Music Sounds
Better With You*

Daft Punk
Around The World

Da Funk

Kojak
Hold Me

Superdiscount
*Le Patron Est
DevenuFou*

Motorbass
Fabulous

Cheek
*Venus (Sunshine
People)*

Mojo
Lady

Cassius
1999

Bob Sinclair; and Air, whose sophisticated music was light years away from house.

Hundreds of independent labels sprung up in 1997. International sales of anything labelled French Touch went through the roof. Record labels willing to exploit the successful formula for filtered house could almost guarantee selling 5,000 copies in Europe and Japan. It was a licence to print money.

The press, thrilled at the idea of an international success story for French artists, branded anything and everything that resembled dance music the French Touch. All of a sudden, DJs became heroes. DJ culture had a huge impact on French teenagers. Young kids began asking for record decks for Christmas and swapped playing football at the weekends for staying in their bedrooms to learn how to mix. In Paris, Radio Nova handed over the airwaves to DJ culture every weekend. Loïk Dury and DJ Gilb'R came up with the idea for 'Novamix' from 8pm on Friday till 1am Sunday. The finest representatives of urban and dance music took it in turns to mix on Nova: Dee Nasty, Lord Zeljko, Eric Rug, Loïk, Gilb'R, DJ Volta, Morpheus, DJ Clyde and Joey Starr, Cut Killer, Ivan Smagghe, Jean Croc, Ariel Wizman. I joined the 'Novamix' crew in September 1997. It was a unique radio experience. There was no musical censorship and a large panorama of DJ culture was on offer. It was also home to Nova's British friends (Gilles Peterson, Ninja Tune and Grand Central). Journalists, artists, filmmakers and writers were all welcome to come on air to discuss current topics. This was a new concept for music radio.

In 1998, Thomas Bangalter, Alan Braxe and Benjamin Diamond released the track Music Sounds Better With You, under the pseudonym Stardust (on Daft Punk's label Roulé Records). The track went straight onto the playlists of the majority of French radio stations. The video was heavily aired on all the music channels and several million copies were sold worldwide. With Stardust, the French Touch reached another level. It went from being a fashionable phenomenon to a tidal wave. A few months later, when Cassius' album was released, the excitement of French Touch was at its peak. But whereas Daft Punk were very careful to remain anonymous, other French Touch protégés were more than pleased to take up the mantel of pop stars.

The whole world was desperate to get their hands on French Touch artists. Producers, publishers, distributors and record labels were raking it in. The movement was at the height of its powers and, thanks to this, dance music was finally making its way into people's homes. Dance music was everywhere: in clubs, on the radio, in the press, on TV, in the cinema, etc.; advertising companies used it to sell scent, trainers and shampoo. It was the music of adverts and fashion shows. Even politicians started using it: during a right-wing political party congress, the politicians made their entrance to a French Touch artist's music.

With the French Touch came recognition for French producers. But the French house and techno scene still had to persuade people that these artists were real musicians even though everything was generated by computer. We tried over and over to explain that a computer is nothing more than an instrument like any other, and that you need a musician to compose melodies in order for machines to be able to play them. These preconceived ideas were hard to change. The only way that we were going to get the general public to understand was by taking our music out of the studio and playing live. LFO and Orbital had paved the way in the early 90s, followed by Underworld, the Prodigy, Chemical Brothers, and, nearer to home, Daft Punk who performed amazing live shows. As far as I was concerned a real ground shift in attitude would only come through live performance.

It was a big risk to take and the idea of going on stage was terrifying. Even though I dreamt of being a musician, there was a huge discrepancy between my abilities to make music in a studio and playing in front of a live audience. Going from being on my own to working with other musicians was also a big step. Eric Morand encouraged me to face my fears and look beyond.

At around that time I met the drummer Daniel Bechet, Sidney Bechet's son. We met quite regularly and began working together. But within a couple of weeks I began to see a problem: I needed to make room for the musicians in my tracks. I spent the next six months reworking my album to get it ready to go live. I sent the newly adapted version of my tracks to Daniel Bechet and to a young classical violinist from Bordeaux, Karine Laborde. For the next three months, the three of us worked together.

In the meantime, I asked Christian Paulet from the Rex Club to be my manager. He introduced me to my first sound engineer, Didier Lubin, a.k.a. Lulu. Lulu was well known in the rock scene and was also responsible for designing the sound system for the Rex Club. Not long after this, I hired Ulrich and KKO, the two founders of Les Nuits Blanches, a dance troupe from Montpellier. Two other people were hired for production purposes: Fred Quiquemelle, ex-stage manager from the Rex whose job was to be in charge of lighting, and Laurent Deflores, a roadie. Thanks to Karine's connections, we were lent the 400, a concert venue in Bordeaux, to rehearse in for three days. The conditions were ideal to get a feeling for the show in a proper venue. It was the first time we were all together as a group.

We began an 18-month tour that took us to several European festivals, before touring France with dates in Lyon, Marseille, Bordeaux, Rouen, Lille and Dijon. My main job on stage was to play the rhythm sections, made up of short loops and sequences. I controlled this from my mixing desk, building each track carefully, and each night letting new structures unfold and taking the tracks in new directions. I told the other musicians what to do and decided which parts of each track they should play on. All in all, our concerts were well received and sometimes when we were on the road it felt like being on a school trip – great fun.

We had only been touring for six months when Eric Morand told me that my album 30 had been nominated for a Victoire de la Musique award in the newly created dance music category. I had never imagined that one day I would be part of a prestigious ceremony such as that. Eric had put 30 forward for the award without my knowing (he knew we would have time to prepare if it was nominated)... and it was.

The awards ceremony was to be conducted in a formal way: all five nominees of the dance music category were required to prepare a track to play live. They also needed to set up their gear, attend a sound rehearsal, and rehearse the day before the awards ceremony at the Olympia. I chose to play Acid Eiffel. On February 19, 1998, I arrived at the Olympia early afternoon with Karine and Daniel. We had been told that there would be a philharmonic orchestra available to accompany us should we so wish and if we had the written music parts for them.

Once we had settled ourselves in we went looking for the stage manager. Several people laughed at us: 'Oh yeah you're those techno guys. Your music really is a load of rubbish!'. My wife arrived via the main entrance at the same time. She quietly sat in the front of house and overheard several technicians moaning about us, 'Techno at the Olympia, it's outrageous!'. We witnessed the same kind of welcome backstage but kept our heads down.

Then Lulu arrived. He was a well-respected figure. Some of the technicians went to greet him, 'What are you doing here, Lulu?'. He replied, 'I'm Garnier's sound engineer'. You could have heard a pin drop. The technicians then went to greet Daniel Bechet and asked him the same question. 'I'm with Garnier,' he replied. They could not believe what they were hearing. 'What?! You play that shit?' Daniel smiled, 'You're joking! I love it. We're playing in venues to 6,000 people!'

It was our turn to do the sound check. The technicians were watching us. The atmosphere was slightly frosty as we began setting up. Karine handed out the sheet music to the orchestra with the string parts for Acid Eiffel. The musicians smirked, 'Is that all we have to play?' Yet, even though it was simple, the string section proved incapable of playing in time. Karine had to show them and they had to follow her movements. And got lost again. We stopped the music. Karine stood in front of the orchestra and said, 'Well! I thought this was supposed to be too easy! You have to begin playing on the off-beat …'

In some ways, I could understand why the people working at the Olympia, who only knew about techno from what they had read in the press, might be shocked to see techno being performed inside the spiritual home of French music that had welcomed artists such as Edith Piaf and Jacques Brel in the past. Once we had finished rehearsing we politely thanked all of the technicians and left.

Now the story steps up a gear. The following day, I put on a suit and headed back to the Olympia. I told the organisers that I was playing later that night at the I Love Techno festival in Ghent. They agreed to move the award for dance music forward. My album 30 won; I dedicated the award to the entire dance music scene. We played Acid Eiffel. Straight after the show I jumped into my technomobile and headed for Belgium. A police car was waiting for me at the border. I was pulled over and the police explained that Peter Decuypere, the I Love Techno promoter, had asked them to escort me all the way to the festival. With their blue lights flashing, the police car took me right to the backstage entrance of the festival. I was greeted with bottles of champagne and plenty of congratulations. This was their way of saying, 'We're so pleased for you'. When I got up on stage to start my DJ set I realised that the crowd were aware that I had won the award too. They seemed very pleased and let out rapturous applause. It was very touching. I started mixing and it was there, in Belgium, wearing a suit, in front of a crowd of six thousand people, that I celebrated my Victoire de la Musique award.

The Victoire de la Musique award introduced F Communications to people from the music industry and culture who had nothing to do with dance music. It also made me into non-official spokesperson for techno. The press were no longer interested in interviewing me about my work, all they were interested in was my opinion on 'techno = drugs' or about the French Touch, even though neither myself nor F Communications were really involved in it. It became completely pointless. In the meantime, I was also victim of plenty of bad-mouthing. How many times did I hear, 'Garnier has sold out!' So we decided to release my next single Dangerous Drive but only press 300 copies and sell it through the F Comm offices. We wanted to do the opposite of what would have made commercial sense – i.e. pressing 10,000 copies with a big fat 'Victoires de la Musique' award-winner sticker in the centre.

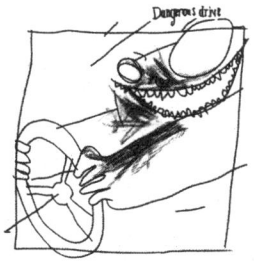

We continued our live tour right through till the end of 1998, with dates in the UK, Germany, Ireland, Spain, Holland, Scandinavia and Switzerland. During the summer of that year we were invited to perform at the Montreux Jazz festival. I couldn't see myself playing there without at least one jazz track in my repertoire. While we were rehearsing before a gig in Ireland, I found a gimmick that I temporarily named 'Jazzy Track'. Two days previously I had met a saxophonist called Finn Martin. We took advantage of a break in schedule before Montreux to work on this track that we would then improvise during the concert.

While I was on tour, the French Touch phenomenon was gaining ground. In September 1998, Paris hosted its first ever Techno Parade. If I had to name one date that epitomised the explosion of dance music in France and the crowning of the French Touch movement it would have to be this. Technopol, an association set up to defend dance music, was behind the Techno Parade. From 1997 onwards, they had the support of Jack Lang, who had seen the Love Parade in Berlin and had declared to the press that he felt it was high time that Paris had its own event on that scale. The people involved in Technopol jumped at the chance to go to the authorities with their project. They also contacted all those involved in the dance music scene, including F Comm.

The project for a Techno Parade in Paris began to take shape. Meetings were organised with the Home Office, the police commission, senior police officers, representatives from the drugs squad, and representatives for the Minister of Culture. All of these meetings were held to inform all of the different bodies involved about the reality of techno, the notion of coming together, the true spirit of raves, etc. At the same time, Technopol also held meetings with the Sacem (Société des auteurs, compositeurs et éditeurs de musique) to explain that DJs were artists in their own right and deserved to be recognised as such. But things were not really moving forward.

It was then that a meeting was held with Jack Lang, an important ally of the techno cause. Under his endorsement, the Police Commission agreed to cooperate on the project for a techno parade. But it soon became clear that the authorities were speaking a different language. In public they declared, 'Techno is great, it's the music of today's youth', whereas when it came to organising the parade the police commission ignored our advice as well as our demands for logistical support. But who cares, the parade was going to happen.

While dance music was being played on the radio and in people's homes, techno was taking to the streets … and even entering museums via the Rendez-Vous Electroniques, a series of exhibitions organised around the Techno Parade, including two exhibitions at the Centre Pompidou: Sonic Process and Global Techno.

Paris' first ever Techno Parade took place on September 19, 1998. For the first time, all those involved in dance music in France came together as a family. Promoters from all over France joined in the parade with brightly decorated floats, while every DJ imaginable came to spin records. The vibrant, colourful procession went from the Place Denfert Rochereau all the way to Place de la Nation. It was a sunny Saturday afternoon. A perfect day. F Communications joined forces with the Rex Club to create the Explorers float. The float was covered in tropical plants. All the floats made their way through the streets of Paris; everywhere we looked people were smiling and cheering. We watched as families danced on their balconies, and children waved at us. When we arrived at the Place de la Bastille I couldn't contain myself any longer. I grabbed hold of the microphone and shouted,

'Techno has taken the Bastille!'

Everyone was happy. This parade was the result of 10 years spent fighting and trying to get our music accepted in France. We finally got to the Place de la Nation late afternoon, where a huge stage and enormous sound system were waiting for us. It had been agreed with the local authorities that the party would end at midnight. Carl Cox, Manu Le Malin, Jack de Marseille and the band Kojak (for one of their first ever concerts) took it in turns to perform on the big stage. In the crowd were many onlookers and couples with their children amidst the thousands of ravers.

But as night fell problems started. A couple of hundred troublemakers who were there just to cause trouble began insulting people and starting fights around the Place de la Nation. It went from bad to worse. From where I was playing on stage I could see sporadic fighting. Realising that things were getting out of hand, the organisers decided to cut my set short. I saw gangs of boys violently setting upon innocent members of the crowd. Even members of the Red Cross were being attacked as they tried to evacuate the injured. People were running all over the place, trying to get away. It was crazy! Two hundred idiots had succeeded in terrorising 5,000 people. During the Love Parade in Berlin there were 1 million people in the streets and not the slightest sign of violence. Unfortunately, the first ever Techno Parade, which had long been imagined as a model of pacifism, turned sour.

By the time I had gathered up my records and was ready to leave the stage, I realised that all the staff had abandoned ship. There were only seven of us left backstage, including Lenny Dee. We were stuck, trapped behind the fence with our record cases that weighed 40 kilos. There was no way that we could run carrying such a weight. Wherever we looked we saw groups of people smashing windscreens of parked cars and ripping the speakers from the stage before throwing them to the ground. One of the guys stuck with us backstage risked running out to get his car. We waited for him for an hour and a half, freaking out. When he finally appeared we all piled into his car and prayed that we would get out of the Place de la Nation. I was gutted.

Despite the violence at the end that left a nasty taste, the Techno Parade marked the beginning of a new era. In the space of two years, dance music in France had gone from being a musical underground trend into a mainstream cultural phenomenon. It now had unlimited potential, mainly thanks to the record sales from the French Touch. The general public finally realised that there was no longer any need to demonise techno; it was now an emblem for young, dynamic people. But, as always in these situations, commercial interest threatened it. I, too, was quite tempted to step into the ring and give in to the lure of easy money (the majors all had their cheque books at the ready), and I can understand why many artists did, but I made the decision to stay on the edge and focus on other goals.

chaotic harmony

Ever since I began touring, it had been Christian Paulet's dream that we do a concert at the Olympia. He said, 'We're going to move mountains to get a booking there. If we get a date, then whatever happens, we'll learn from the experience.' As for me, I felt terrified at the very thought of it.

For anyone involved in dance music, the Olympia seemed like an unachievable dream: a legendary venue that played host to the best of French and international singers and songwriters. The Olympia had never booked a dance music artist. Dance music was not considered highbrow enough. Yet, when my album 30 won an award at the Victoires de la Musique ceremony, attitudes changed. As if by magic, the doors to the Olympia opened up to us. The week that followed the Victoires de la Musique awards, Christian Paulet sent a request to the Olympia to book it for a concert. He was offered a date and confirmed it without even asking me. On September 17, 1998 (just a couple of days before the first ever Techno Parade), and on the legendary singer Annie Cordy's day off, I was booked to perform there.

This concert was very poignant for two reasons. Firstly, I was to take techno into a legendary venue. Secondly, I was to perform in a venue I remember from my childhood when my parents took me to see Annie Cordy (the very same one!) and Gerard Lenormand in concert. Later, I learnt that James Brown, Jimi Hendrix, Kraftwerk and Nina Simone had all performed there. For the band, the Olympia was *the* venue. It was every musician's dream and a mecca for music lovers. Just the idea of adding my name to the long list of artists who had performed there felt like the highpoint of my career.

We were determined to create an elaborate and unforgettable show aimed at a dance music crowd. Most of them had never set foot inside the Olympia before. During the six months leading up to the concert, we worked hard at putting together a show. We had to work out the scenography: the stage was wide and deep enough to house up to 60 musicians. We thought hard about the decor and the lights, as well as the technical aspects that were necessary to ensure the smooth running of the event. Technical riders detailing the band's needs were sent to the Olympia's stage manager so that everything would be ready on the day.

But our hopes were dashed when we were confronted with the financial realities of organising a concert such as ours in a venue like this. All the extras we needed: overtime, catering, seats that needed to be taken out before the concert, and then put back again afterwards, etc., cost more. Even putting the artist's name up in the traditional bright red letters on the façade was not included in the cost of hiring the venue. But

I refused to play my only concert at the Olympia with Annie Cordy's name on the façade.

So we kept writing the cheques. To make our dream concert happen we had to ask all the people involved to work for less. This included the musicians and the dancers, who all agreed to be paid a minimum; my brother, who organised all the catering with one of our neighbours; and my brother-in-law, who was in charge of the decor and managed to borrow huge panels of wood and rolls of fabric.

On the morning of September 17, 1998, four huge rust-coloured panels were put at the back of the stage. They were pierced with hundreds of little holes that let the light filter through. On either side of the stage stood two large panels of semi-transparent fabric lit from behind for the dancers to dance behind on raised platforms in a shadow play. In the centre of the stage, just behind my machines, a long cylinder of the same material stood bathed in light projected from an angle. That is where the singer Lauren Garnier would stand.

My machines took centre stage. In the middle I had my Yamaha 03D mixing desk, to the right of me there was a rack with my sampler and my computer, and to my left a row of keyboards. The saxophonist would be at the front of the stage. Daniel Bechet would be next to me with an electronic drum kit. And our violinist would lead a string quartet seated on a raised platform, just behind the other musicians.

Throughout the day, each member of the group was concentrating hard during rehearsals. We all felt the extraordinary atmosphere in the Olympia. It was as if the vibration, the echo of thousands of nights, where thousands of people had experienced intense musical emotions, was all around us.

Everything was ready by 6pm. It felt like slow, dull torture as the hour of the concert approached and our nerves got worse. I stepped outside onto the Boulevard des Italiens with Christian and Eric. We crossed the road and stood opposite the Olympia staring at the bright red letters that hung above the entrance: 'Tuba Productions in association with F Communications presents Laurent Garnier Live.' We all felt very emotional. I could see tears in Christian's eyes. Eric stood staring at the words not moving, in case he broke the spell. I had very mixed feelings – I was very happy but at the same time terrified. We stood there for a while in silence until the sound of a mobile phone ringing brought us back to reality. It was our sound engineer, 'What are you doing?! It's 7pm!'

It was time to go.

We walked back to the artists' entrance, which stood only a few feet away from the entrance of what was once Le Boy club. I stopped for a second to look at the walled-up entrance. As the memories of crazy nights came flooding back, someone grabbed me by the arm and dragged me into the backstage entrance of the Olympia. The violinists were putting on their make-up and adjusting the jewellery lent to them by the designer Odette Bombardier, and tuning their electric violins that had been hired specially for the occasion. Lauren Garnier was getting dressed in silence. Ulrich and KKO and the other dancers from Les Nuits Blanches were warming up over in the corner. Further along, an African dancer from Frederic Galliano's band was getting ready. While all this was going on, the musicians prepared their instruments. I walked into my dressing room. It was filled with flowers, kind notes of encouragement and several bottles of champagne. I stood there for a couple of minutes, enjoying a quiet moment alone before the big event.

Then someone knocked at my door. It was Daniel Bechet. He sat down with me looking serious as he took his father's clarinet out of its case. 'Forty years ago, during one of my father's concert here, the audience smashed the place up. Tonight, we're going to smash the place up too!'

It was time to go. Ariel Wizman introduced the concert. In the first row of the balcony sat my parents, Jack Lang, Pierre Henry, my mother-in-law, Catherine Trautman the Minister of Culture, Richie Hawtin, Jean-François Bizot and Jeff Mills.

The lights went down, the crowd began cheering and Lauren's silhouette appeared inside the tube of fabric bathed in light. She sang Voyage de Simone. At the end of her song, I walked onto the stage with the rest of the band. I went and stood behind my machines. The saxophonist began playing. Daniel joined in on the electronic drums and slowly the concert began. My nerves disappeared as soon as I saw people in the first few rows nodding their heads in appreciation of the music.

The concert reached 'cruising speed' after about 30 minutes. The rest of the band left the stage and I was alone with the audience. Ulrich and KKO walked onto the stage on stilts, in suits covered in hundreds of diodes that emitted red lasers. They took their positions in the middle of the stage, swamped in smoke from the smoke machines. The audience could only see shapes moving in a luminous red halo of light and smoke. But I was clearly able to make out the audience as they thrust their arms into the air as I played the opening bass line to Crispy Bacon. I could hear their cheers as the kick drum kicked in and could feel their anticipation as the long break set in that announced the final explosion. I could feel right down to my core the wave of energy and excitement that rushed from the dress circle down into the auditorium and right up to the stage. The group all came back on stage for the final leg of the concert. The first notes of Dance To The Music played out. During the final track, Flashback, I signalled to the Nuits Blanches to get ready. When they appeared on stage they no longer had their light suits on but were spinning balls of fire.

We exited the stage, then came back and did two encores, which I really enjoyed as that is something a DJ never normally gets to do. Suddenly, it was all over. The band and I bowed and waved goodbye to the audience and the house lights were turned up. I will never forget seeing 3,000 people clapping, cheering and smiling. For weeks, the thought of this concert had given me sleepless nights, and now it was over I felt strange. It went by so fast, it was as if we had only been on stage for a few minutes, as if once on stage we had slipped into a different time zone where with each note time speeded up.

When we went backstage everyone was waiting for us. This concert was the culmination of the work of a team of people who, for months, had laboured tirelessly to ensure its success. We had all become very close. Everyone was happy, laughing and joking.

An after-party had been planned at the Rex Cub with Jeff Mills DJ-ing. Everyone who had bought a ticket for the Olympia could get in free. Once we had come back down to earth, we gathered together our friends, family and the whole crew. As we got to the club and walked down the stairs towards the DJ booth, there were people everywhere waiting to say thank you and congratulate us. I was on cloud nine. I went to join Jeff in the DJ booth and had to sit down for a few minutes to take stock. I watched him moving behind the decks, like a cat. I could see hundreds of people glued to the window of the DJ booth sticking their thumbs up in thanks, and it was then I realised what a long way I had come. I was happy… As for the rest of the night, my memories are rather hazy… all I remember was that it was one hell of a party.

We continued touring for two months after our night at the Olympia, playing some great gigs and some not-so-great ones. Then the saxophonist Philippe Nadaud joined the group. We finished the year playing a New Year's Eve gig on December 31, 1998 in London alongside New Order and Underworld.

With the tour finished, I found myself back at home feeling a bit lost without a project. Being the hyperactive person that I am, I found it difficult to spend weeks on end in my studio only broken by my weekends spent DJ-ing. I have a demon inside me that needs constantly pacifying, but this time round I couldn't manage it. I was at home pacing up and down, having a battle inside my own head; on tour, I had been working with people who knew nothing about the likes of Derrick May but who talked to me about Sun Ra, Coltrane and the Art Ensemble. Through them I had discovered jazz. I began listening to rock again and became increasingly interested in contemporary composers. My musical horizons had broadened and my attitude towards making music had evolved. In brief, the tour had changed me. I had changed.

Somewhere deep inside, I still had feelings of frustration about the mistakes I had made with my album 30. Although many of the tracks had got a positive reaction, this body of work still left me dissatisfied. I had suffered because of mistakes made on this record and felt the need to start making music again. But now I was more considered in my approach and less impulsive. I had been working with musicians for two years now and, even though I still had hang-ups, I was ready to accept a different role, that of bandleader. When making music, I didn't want to feel the frustration of not being able to get exactly what I wanted from my machines. Working on my own didn't suit me. Nor did the language of machines. It did my head in!

I began touring again as a DJ. One afternoon, in my hotel room in Argentina, I was watching CNN on TV. It was during the war in Kosovo. Civilians were dying of starvation, the country was ravaged by war, yet these American journalists were obsessing about the loss of a military jet that was worth hundreds of thousands of dollars. It was obscene. It drove me mad. For several months now I had been in a state of turmoil. I was 33 years old, and had travelled the world over, but didn't like what I was seeing.

A strange period followed during which I questioned the way house and techno were going. I was challenging myself about the future of our music and the meaning of my career. I needed to find new motivation. As the call to make music kept getting stronger, I decided that maybe it was time to start writing tracks for a new album. I dug out the demos I had done while on tour and that I had been playing live for a year. But this time I wanted to stack the odds in my favour and produce an album that corresponded exactly with what I wanted. I didn't want a repeat experience of 30, so I decided to employ the skills of a sound engineer.

I called Laurent Collat, who really knew his stuff when it came to studio equipment and was an artist in his own right; he had an album out on F Communications under the name Elegia. I asked him if he would like to record and mix my third album.

One of the first tracks I wanted to work on was Jazzy Track. This track had originally been written to be performed live, and even though it worked well on stage, the idea of including a saxophone track on my album worried me. Laurent Collat and Philippe Nadaud came over to my studio. I programmed a loop and explained to Philippe that I wanted a sax solo that would suddenly take off in the middle of the track. Philippe put on a pair of headphones and began playing. For about 15 minutes or so, Philippe played around with different techniques, from bee-bop to free jazz. It wasn't working. Philippe was unable to let go. I knew him quite well by now, having spent several months on the road with him. He's the kind of musician who needs to be pushed in order to let rip. So I took the microphone next to my mixing desk and started shouting, 'It's rubbish', 'We might as well bin it all', 'Philippe, you're not getting it.'

Philippe remained calm at first but soon began to get annoyed. And then, suddenly, he started playing like a man possessed. 'That's it, that's great! We've got what we need. Thank you.' He stood there bright red in the face, pouring with sweat, his headphones still on and the mouthpiece of his sax still between his lips, staring at me. I looked at him and said, 'You know what Philippe? I've just found the name of the track: Man With The Red Face!'

The next night I was DJ-ing in Nice. I got to work editing the track on my own and decided that I would take a rough version to the club with me. I played The Man With The Red Face in the middle of my set and stood back to see how the dance floor reacted. It worked! I decided to play it a second time a couple of hours later and got the same reaction. As soon as I got back to Paris I called Laurent Collat. 'You've got to help me mix this track!' The Man With The Red Face was the first track I made for what was to be my third album.

Next I wrote Downfall, a sombre track that was intended to reflect what I had felt in that hotel room watching CNN. I had this image inside my head of a man wandering around a city, ravaged by war. In the middle of Downfall I wanted to create a flashback, as if the track had rewound before carrying on and then I wanted it to end in destruction. Other tracks followed. There was Greed, which was a reaction to the flood of free music now available on MP3 and The Sound Of Big Babou, the first single from the album, a big track that got its name from my Radio Nova nickname.

As soon as the album – which I decided to call *Unreasonable Behaviour* – was completed, I wanted to put together a band and take it on tour, even though I had no idea what kind of a response the album was going to get. We had films made that were to be projected on screens on stage, and I put together a new band: Marc Chalosse on keyboards, Philippe Nadaud on saxophone and two young contemporary dancers.

Christian Paulet got to work on an 18-month world tour. The tour began on March 23, 2000 in Cambridge in the UK, and travelled across

Europe throughout the summer. The music critics praised *Unreasonable Behaviour*, calling it an 'album of maturity'. Meanwhile, we were on the road playing in big festivals such as Roskilde in Denmark, Iceland, Spain and France at the Eurockeenes de Belfort and the Route du Rock, stopping off on the way for a date in Paris at the legendary rock venue, the Elysée-Montmartre.

Christian joined forces with an American tour agent, as *Unreasonable Behaviour* was to be released in the US on the label Nova Mute. A tour was planned in the US and Canada in Autumn 2000. I was very excited about the idea of a North American tour, even though my DJ-ing experiences there had been mixed. Nobody was really interested in house and techno in the US. For years, you heard international DJs coming to the same conclusion: the problem wasn't finding gigs there, but finding good gigs. I felt that America was a different planet. The nightlife was very different to ours, and the club scene was divided into very distinct scenes: the black gay scene, the kids who only went out to listen to trance, and an underground scene that had been losing momentum and was struggling to exist. So it was no surprise that techno remained underground. In any case, it would seem that in most big cities in the US, the music takes second place. Take New York, for example, the city of dreams for many DJs because of its legendary nightlife. The clubbers there go out to dance (this must be the only place in the world where kids go to listen to techno and break dance). Music is just the pretext for clubs to exist.

On November 3, 2000, we began our tour in Hollywood, in a small club with a 500-person capacity. We then went on to San Francisco, Chicago, Detroit, New York, Washington, Boston and then Canada for two concerts, one in Montreal and the other in Toronto. We arrived in LA the day before the concert, but when the club opened its doors we still hadn't received our gear. It finally turned up an hour before our concert was supposed to begin. We had to rush through the club and set up on stage while the crowd looked on and a DJ played the warm-up session. As fast as we could, we plugged in our machines and did a quick sound check with our headphones on. As soon as we were ready the concert began and we sweated like pigs during the first four tracks as we tried to get all the effects and the levels right. The club was half empty. The crowd was made up of regulars and people who had come to see us out of curiosity. But they started to get into it and we managed to avert disaster.

When we left the club, the tour bus that was to take us from one city to the next was outside waiting for us. It looked like something from the 70s, from the Eagles' last tour. We were to spend the next few weeks living in this bus as we crossed the States and covered over 6,000 kilometres. The next morning we left for San Francisco and the morning after for Chicago. While we were driving towards the state of Illinois, not far from Salt Lake City, we were caught in a snowstorm. In less than three days, we had gone from the swimming pools of California to the freezing Mid-West and when we finally arrived in Chicago, it was pouring with rain.

I had begged Christian to sort out a gig for us in Chicago; it was something I had always dreamt of doing. But I soon realised that I had been in love with a picture postcard image of the city. Even though the legend of Frankie Knuckles' Warehouse club was etched in my mind, house music in Chicago had been dead for some time.

There was nothing in place in Chicago to ensure the survival of house music: no real scene, no real house clubs, except perhaps for a few underground ones in the ghettos. In the second half of the 90s, the rebirth of house music in Chicago was attributed to the DJ, Green Velvet. A handful of record labels such as Relief, Casual and Guidance had been started. But what remained of this now? Not much. Green Velvet was known in Europe, as were the few labels and DJs that existed in Chicago, but there didn't appear to be anyone left in Chicago still fighting for house music.

We received a lukewarm welcome. When the concert started, all the elements were there to make it a shit night: there were only about 30 people inside the venue, the atmosphere was downbeat, but we played our set in spite of all this. At the end of our concert, which felt more like a mistake than anything else, I went to speak to the promoter, 'We've just spent three days travelling on a bus for hundreds of miles to get here, and there are only 30 people in the club. What's the problem?' The explanation was, 'Well it's only Wednesday and on Wednesdays there's never anyone. And it's raining too, and when it rains …'

We left Chicago, keen to put that terrible night behind us. But just round the corner was what I now consider to have been one of the best dates we had on that tour: Montreal, and an amazing crowd. Then there was Toronto. Then from Toronto we crossed over to Melbourne and ended the year in Australia.

A new tour started in 2001. In the summer, the programmers of Torhout-Werchter, the most important rock festival in Belgium, got in touch with us. They had really enjoyed our concert there the previous year and wanted to know if we could stand in for Guns N' Roses (who had pulled out) on the main stage. At first I said no. I thought it would be suicidal to play in front of 70,000 people who had come to hear a legendary rock band. But the festival organisers insisted and told us to trust them. I finally relented and we packed our bags for Torhout-Werchter. As soon as we arrived I was overwhelmed by anxiety: the stage that we were playing on was huge and we were playing half an hour after Sting. How about that for a change in direction! I was feeling more and more nervous. As I stood backstage while the technicians finished off installing our gear, I could see the people in the first few rows. They were all wearing t-shirts with heavy metal bands emblazoned across the front: Slayer, Metallica, Guns N' Roses, Sepultura … I was convinced that we did not have a chance in hell. We were going to be booed off stage by thousands of people who had come to listen to rock music and nothing else.

Just as I was about to fall to pieces backstage, the stage manager came to find me. We were on. We got up on stage, and after a brief introduction by the master of ceremonies, we banged out one after the other of our most pumping tracks: *Flashback, Man With The Red Face, Crispy Bacon.* I kept glancing at Marc Chalosse who was on keyboards just next to me. I could see from his facial expression that he was saying, 'Fuck, they like it!' He smiled at me nodding his head towards the crowd of 70,000 people who were smiling, dancing, jumping up and down and shouting, as after each long break a heavy techno bass drum blasted them like a cannonball. We kept this up for a whole hour, track after track, with no let up. We did not take the pressure off, we had the crowd eating out of our hands … we'd let the dogs out.

That concert was one of the most intense experiences in my career. It was dangerous and electric. As I left the stage, the festival promoter jumped on me and said, 'So, what did you think?' I collapsed into his arms and gave a breathless, 'Thank you'. I could have gone on to tell him that the Belgians were one of the best crowds in the world; one of the most open and enthusiastic. I could have told them that of all the parties I had played in the world, none had the same intoxicating atmosphere that I found every time I came to play in Belgium. Whether at the Fuse, in Ghent, at the I Love Techno Festival or during the Ten Days of Techno. But that was what I meant to say in that one 'thank you'.

After that, I went on to do a couple of DJ gigs on my own in the US. My tour ended with a live gig in Detroit as part of the second edition of DEMF (Detroit Electronic Music Festival), the first electronic music festival to have ever been organised in Motor City. My band would be joining me there.

The festival was the brainchild of one of the most talented producers in Detroit, Carl Craig. He had been on the techno scene since the end of the 80s. Carl had started out with the likes of Derrick May and made some of the most memorable techno tracks. A prolific producer, founder of the Planet E label, a charismatic figure in the international techno scene,

Carl Craig is one of the few producers who has managed to be successful as both a DJ and a producer. In 1994, during the international explosion of US techno, where many an American producer tried playing at being a DJ, Carl made the move into DJ-ing too, but successfully. Later on, he played live concerts and made a foray into jazz. He was living in an apartment in a rundown neighbourhood in Detroit; Carl has always remained loyal to his city. In 2000, he created the first ever electronic music festival in Detroit, the DEMF, which took place on Hart Plaza, in front of Lake Michigan. The first DEMF was a real success and achieved its aims: to give credibility to techno within the city where this music was born.

When I arrived in Detroit for the second DEMF, I learnt that the sponsors, for reasons that were unclear, had put pressure on the Detroit city council to fire Carl Craig from his own festival. Yet, the DEMF was still taking place right there in the centre of Hart Plaza. Thousands of people were there in front of the different stages to hear artists such as Carl Cox, Autechre, John Acquaviva, Moodyman, Gary Martin (the only white techno musician living in downtown Detroit), as well as the godfathers Derrick May and Juan Atkins.

What appeared really interesting on paper turned out to be one of the most badly organised festivals I have ever been to. As soon as we arrived I went to introduce myself to the stage manager, who instead of a hello barked, 'You're playing in an hour. Get your gear ready.' Not one thing that we had requested on our technical rider was there. But we managed to work with what we had and, an hour later, we were ready to play. John Acquaviva was just playing his last record when the guys from De La Soul appeared on the stage.

One of them came over to us and shouted, 'It's our turn to play now! Get off the stage!' The stage manager was witness to this but said nothing. So we had to hurriedly unplug all our machines. A bit later, when De La Soul had left the stage, we were told to plug in our machines again and to hurry and play our set. It then began to pour with rain. There were only 300 people who stayed in the rain to watch our set. I was really gutted. We played, but our hearts were not really in it, and then the rain really started bucketing down, the electrics on stage began to pack up, so we decided it was time to stop.

Later on, I was wandering through the stands in the festival, where several local labels, who for the most part had only released about three records in the last five years, were there selling their label t-shirts for 20 dollars a piece. I saw red! I spoke to one of the guys and said, 'What is this? Is this Detroit's future? T-shirts??'

I had to get out of there. I wandered off to check out what was going on on the other stages and realised the sound everywhere was terrible. No effort had been made to achieve quality. Yet more and more people were arriving.

In among the crowd I saw quite a few people wearing t-shirts stating, 'I support Carl Craig'. They obviously knew about his demise. I also met quite a few people who had driven for over 10 hours to get to the festival. Someone was seriously taking them for a ride. We were surrounded by advertising banners brandishing the merits of this brand of beer, or that brand of soft drink. There were endless stands, too. I met a group of French people. We chatted for a moment and I could not believe it when I heard them saying, 'This festival is great!' If the same festival had been organised like this in Paris they would have been furious. But because they were in 'Detroooiiittt', it was far cooler! I do not dare imagine what they told their friends back home.

I was feeling really down when I bumped into Carl Craig. He was gutted at the way things had turned out and told me that he was organising a party in a warehouse downtown and that if I wanted to go and DJ with him there, I was welcome. That night, I went down to his party that was organised inside a two-storey building. The place was full of a really nice-looking, happy people. I joined Carl down on the ground floor, where Kenny Dixon Junior, a.k.a. Moodyman, one of the best house music producers of the new generation, was performing along with the singer and saxophonist Norma Jean Bell.

I was still angry from what I had been through that afternoon: our disastrous concert, seeing a festival that had been imagined by its founder as an authentic experience going the way it had, and the absence of judgement in the kids who were there with regards to the mediocrity of what they were experiencing, and the attitude of some of the labels that were unable to see any further than marketing their image … all of that made me cross, so I took the opportunity that night to get it off my chest. I gave all the energy I had to the crowd that night. There it was, the real Detroit underground scene, full of energy and life.

That is precisely what is contradictory about Detroit. You can only count on one or two amazing nights in the whole year. Yes, they might be unforgettable. But once the excitement surrounding the DEMF has subsided, there is nothing else going on. No one seems to want to get involved in the nightlife there anymore, perhaps because they consider it too dangerous.

The next day I met up with Mike Banks. He had just finished dealing with what turned out to be one of the most outrageous scandals in the history of techno …

In 1999, Underground Resistance released a single by the DJ Rolando, under the pseudonym the Aztec Mystic. The EP was called Knights Of The Jaguar. The record was amazing. It had a timeless quality and brought together all the aspects of real Detroit techno: groove, experience, speed, emotion and a certain magic. Jaguar immediately became a classic, as had Strings Of Life or No UFOs in the past. The record had the perfect balance between house and techno. It brought down the barriers between the two different schools, making its way into the sets of DJs as diverse as Joe Claussell, Gilles Peterson and Jeff Mills.

A few weeks after the release of Jaguar, Sony Music contacted Mike Banks and asked him if they could include this track on a compilation. Mike refused, and that's where the story should end. But a few months later, Underground Resistance began to be flooded with emails full of insults, accusing them of being 'sell-outs'. Some of the emails even came from European artists, who up until then had always been on very friendly terms with the label. Mike could not understand it. He did some research and found out that Sony had released a cover version of Jaguar, without his permission. Even though this practice is very ugly, it remains legal. Anyone is allowed to do a cover version of a record as long as royalties are paid to the composer. This sent a wave of panic across the techno scene. Underground Resistance, the legendary bastion that embodied integrity, had been tricked and crushed by a major.

Using the internet as their only line of defence, UR declared war.

The gut and determination of the underground versus the greed of the major label management at Sony.

MIKE BANKS:

'Our community has deep-rooted musical traditions that survived slavery: voodoo, the power of rhythm and a certain magic. Sometimes these things find a place in the real world through music and records. That's what Knights Of The Jaguar was all about. The spiritual versus the material. The name Aztec Mystic comes from those Mexican restaurants that we liked to go to with Rolando. There were always drawings of relics on the walls to represent the Aztec culture. One night we were in one of those restaurants with Rolando and we were trying to imagine what the music and the melodies would have sounded like in Aztec music at the height of their civilisation. We wondered how much mystery was hidden in their music. How it must have sounded. And that's how the idea for Jaguar came about.

'When those guys from the majors did a cover version of Jaguar, I was really upset. They had absolutely no idea of the reasons why that track was made. They had no idea of its spiritual meaning. What shocked me the most was their ignorance. It was weird seeing those people acting as if that track was theirs and watching them turn it into a commercial pop track. I know that in the music world we are used to sampling, that's not a problem, it's part of our culture. But stealing a track, that hurt! The fact that this cover of Jaguar came out on Sony is one thing, but the name of the person who wrote the track was not even mentioned (which is criminal)! They even used the image of an ecstasy tablet for the record sleeve!

'Our guerrillas got things moving on the internet. When we first found out about what was going on we tried to get in touch with the people from Sony, but they never returned our calls. So a massive flood of protest emails was sent to Sony management. It was only then that they finally decided to change tactics and to call us. All of a sudden they wanted to make a deal. My answer was very simple, "No deal. Take that record off the shelves." There was not going to be any kind of deal with those guys! I think Sony learnt a lesson from this: the internet can be a powerful weapon. Then they tried to fool us. They stopped selling the record in Europe but they kept on selling it in South America. That was dirty!

'Aside from the legal aspect, as far as we were concerned this was a spiritual violation. I pray for the souls of the people who did that. Because what they did was like defiling an angel.'

Rolando's record became a symbol of resistance in underground dance music. To defend this record, an entire community stood up to the cynicism of the majors. It is said that the cyber harassment carried out by those defending UR's cause was such that the voicemail and email inboxes of Sony and BMG (who licenced the cover version) were clogged up with messages of protest. Neither of these record companies had ever been the target of such a large-scale attack. In some ways, Jaguar became a way to remind us, symbolically, that the soul of this music is not for sale and that there are no deals possible in the face of attack and the underhand tactics of music business gangsters.

UR's response was to release a record called The Revenge Of The Jaguar, with remixes by Derrick May and Jeff Mills. One of the tracks on the record is simply the rhythm section and harmonies (the chords that make this track so amazing) carefully isolated as if to say, 'This is the essence of the track, go ahead and sample it, if you want'. On the record sleeve there are words of warning to the circling vultures at the majors: 'Your faulty system will be overturned by electronic music and wiped off the face of the earth.'

cycle 30

12

When I returned from my tour, it took me a while to get back into my everyday life. All of a sudden there was no longer a group of 30-something-year-old guys on a tour bus to share a stupid joke. It was difficult making the adjustment.

Having spent 15 years exposed to high levels of sound almost every night, my ears were seriously beginning to suffer. An ear specialist explained to me in a very clinical manner, 'You have lost part of your hearing at 4,000 hertz'. Up until then, I had never allowed myself time off. Now I could see that my body was showing signs of fatigue and that it was time to take a break; I had to slow down a bit, take longer breaks between my gigs, go on shorter tours. It was time to come back down to earth.

I did not have any choice but to do something that I had been putting off for years: take a break, get some rest and accept the worrying that goes with taking time out.

I went back to work at Radio Nova for a while and renewed my contact with the French dance music scene that was going through a time of upheaval.

On February 19, 2001, Liza 'N' Eliaz died. In the 1990s she had represented everything good about the French rave scene. Now there really was nothing left of that golden age. Big French techno events were long gone. Raves no longer existed and had been replaced by free-parties. As for the French Touch, this movement had run out of steam and evaporated.

Nevertheless, a spirit of revival was evident. Some fantastic record labels, managed by true artists, came into being. A new dance music scene was in the making, with artists such as John Thomas, The Hacker, Miss Kittin, Avril, Blackstrobe and Dima. A couple of new venues were breathing new life into Paris' nightlife scene: The Pulp, for example, a lesbian club that had become an important venue for electro, and the Batofar, situated a few feet from the Pont de Tolbiac, a new place to discover cutting-edge music.

Dance music had become universal and its influence was everywhere in pop music. By 2000, international pop stars were calling on dance music producers to revive their careers. Madonna and Kylie Minogue are both good examples, and the result was positive, as they both went straight to the top of the charts and at the same time gained credibility with the people in the know. Dance music was no longer just reserved for the few – it had joined the mainstream. The new generation of American R&B producers (Timbaland and the Neptunes), as well as the upcoming stars of the new rock movement from New York (the Raptures, LCD Soundsystem), began to include sounds in their productions traditionally used by electronic music artists. Acid bass lines from the TB-303, techno beats and the powerful strings from the Prophet 5 synthesizer enhanced their music. These were all sounds that fans of electronic music had already heard on records from artists ranging from Daft Punk to PCP. There was a huge sense of achievement. In 10 years, electronic music had made its mark on the world music map.

With the arrival of the year 2000, the dance music phenomenon hit fever pitch. DJ fees sharply increased as the millennium eve approached. Big clubs throughout the world were up against each other to secure headlining international DJs, as this one night was guaranteed to generate huge amounts of money. The fees being offered to DJs were obscene. I know stories of DJs who earned 500,000 euros that New Year's Eve, playing in three different places on the same night. I also heard the story of an English DJ who was offered an exorbitant fee by the son of a press magnate to play at a private party. But I also know of DJs who asked for too much, or refused to play for what they considered too little, and ended up not playing at all that night.

I was offered huge sums of money to play that night. One promoter went as far as offering me 30,000 euros to DJ; he thought that I was refusing to play for him because his offer was not considerable enough. But my answer remained the same, 'No, I am not available.' He insisted, 'Why can't you play for me, have you got another gig?' So I finally told him my reason for refusing the booking: 'No, I'm organising a fancy dress party at my house in the countryside for a few friends.' There was a long silence on the other end of the telephone, and then, 'You're what?!'

On the eve of the year 2000, promoters were buying DJs like they were buying packets of washing powder, and for the dance music industry it became a point of no return. It symbolised the insatiable greed of a system that had become purely commercial, in which music had taken a back seat. And, even if by 2003 the dance music scene was still producing good music, it appeared that a certain spontaneity had been lost forever.

That is probably just the way things go. Dance music was undoubtedly the last music revolution of the 20th century, but as with all cycles, it came to an end and ceased to be the music of the future. In order to find a new lease of life it had to open up its musical horizons, find new perspectives and reinvent itself. The problem is that most young people that have grown up listening to dance music are unaware of its roots, and are determined to keep the different genres of dance music separate.

Yet who or what was capable of finding these new perspectives? The media ceased to be pioneers. Radio and TV's sole concern was audience figures. The exceptions were public service radio (France Inter and

France Culture) and local radio, who continued to try to open up the airwaves for new styles of music and culture. Festivals in their own way also had a role in discovering and broadcasting new talent. For a long time they relied heavily on a blend of rock, pop and jazz, but now successfully managed to open up their musical programme and mix things up. So, for example, festivals such at Les Vieilles Charrues had Enrico Macias and St Germain in their line-up. Les Eurockeens de Belfort booked bands such as Radiohead alongside Dionysos and Toots and the Maytals. Les Transmusicales de Rennes scheduled a night of Mauritian music followed by artists such as LCD Soundsystem and the hip-hop band La Rumeur. As for Sonar, which over the years became the best (if not the only) electronic music festival in the world, you could find Björk, Underworld, Aphex Twin and Gilles Peterson playing on the same bill, as well as contemporary art exhibitions and a true party spirit. Their programme was very experimental, but they also encouraged artists to let themselves go on stage. Sonar was an oasis of creativity and opportunity, a place where DJs could play Ain't No Sunshine by Bill Withers at 4am, and then play a track from the German minimalist label Kompackt. It was the ultimate place for open-mindedness and free expression.

In 2003, the music scene not only suffered from an identity crisis, but it also had to deal with an unprecedented economic crisis. The euphoria experienced by independent record labels during the 90s was over, and most were struggling financially. The few that were left were having a hard time of it. It was vital for the music industry to reinvent itself. The arrival of the internet suggested that the worst was yet to come, with predictions that, one by one, all the protagonists within the music industry would disappear: labels, distributors, musicians and even the records themselves.

The death of vinyl was announced in 1985 with the arrival of the CD, the preferred medium of the music industry, one reason being that it was less costly. However, the arrival of the DJ culture saved vinyl from a premature death. Even though DJ booths all over the world equipped themselves with the new CD-format players being created for DJs (CD players specifically for mixing, mixers with incorporated effects, needles that were more and more sophisticated, etc.), up until that point vinyl had been relatively untouched by technological advances. DJs continued to travel with their record boxes and made only slight concessions by burning MP3s onto recordable CDs to allow them to reduce the weight of their record boxes and test their own latest productions.

But the arrival of Final Scratch in 2001 was to change the DJ's working methods. Final Scratch was a computer program that enabled a DJ to mix (and even scratch) music on MP3 files in exactly the same way as vinyl. Whereas a traditional record box could only hold about 90 records, the DJ now had a way to have 20 times the number of tracks at their disposal. This technological invention was a mini revolution at the heart of DJ-ing. Nevertheless, technology has never led creativity. Could Final Scratch and other computer programs for DJs encourage them to be more eclectic, to renew themselves?

Some envisaged a future where, as a result of new computer programs, the DJ wouldn't really need to do anything once inside the club. The DJ would simply program his set in advance, and probably not even have to set foot inside the club as he could deliver his mix upfront. (A logical follow-on to what we have already seen – for example, Carl Cox played in London and a web cam filmed him, enabling his set to be broadcast via a giant screen at a rave in Paris).

It was thought that clubs throughout the world would be equipped with Final Scratch, and most would be able to broadcast over the internet. The DJ's job would be to download MP3s, and their record collection would become unlimited. They would be requested to play tracks by the public, on demand, just like jukeboxes. It would be the end of an era and the death knell of this form of artistry.

However, neither the advances in technology nor the greed of certain individuals are enough to explain the identity crisis that techno was experiencing. By 2003, techno as we know it had come to the end of a cycle.

In 1994, Jeff Mills released a record on his Axis label called *Cycle 30*. The record consisted of a series of techno loops engraved into the vinyl on one groove so that the needle read the same groove over again. The track on the B-side, The Man From Tomorrow, was a variation of notes on top of a minimal melody that aimed to illustrate that, even if the form changes, the foundation remains the same. *Cycle 30* was a reference to the cycle of the sun's revolution every 30 years. This cycle is reflected in each generation that generate their own cultural upheavals; house and techno are just one of the many permutations.

One night, in 2003, when Jeff Mills was booked to play at the Rex Club, I took advantage of the fact that he was in France and invited him to my studio. The following are excerpts from the conversation we had about his vision of the future of techno at that time.

JEFF MILLS:
'A few years back I did a record called *Cycle 30*. If we go back 30 years, we can see that things repeat themselves. Today we are in exactly the

same place as 30 years ago. In the early 70s music had become so sophisticated that it had become boring. The most popular bands at the time were making tracks to order. Technology had enabled productions to be so clean that they had lost their soul, as near-perfection had been achieved in terms of their production. Now, 30 years on, we are here again. Technology has made so much progress that music has become almost perfect. Every week, I receive demos from young artists, and they are all practically perfect. But when you listen a little closer, the music is void of emotion. Perfection neither gives meaning nor feeling to a record. Nowadays kids are making music without any creative input, the computer does it all. That is what is going to kill techno music. Technology is the guilty party in all of this because all the rough edges and mishaps that make music what it is have been ironed out. There will be change, a backlash. Exactly the same as back in 1971 and 1972. If we look at how the music changed over those couple of years, it became more and more funky, and more and more experimental.

'The problem we have nowadays is that there are more and more people making a living from techno who are not putting anything back into it to bring about change. It is now more about an unscrupulous group of people out to make money. Most people are just making music to sell records. They worry less about composing music and more about releasing a record. That is not how it should be! They are not musicians they are record manufacturers! Unfortunately, they do sell records. I receive hundreds of demos from people like that. I usually reply to them, "Make 100 records and send me the 101st. You will learn a lot from the first 100 tracks and the 101st will be the fruit of your apprenticeship." But the market is flooded by those first 100 tracks. When you listen to them, all you hear is yet another kid who has bought himself a new machine. He has pressed on the first button he comes across and makes a track that he sends to a label that go ahead and release it. That is what is killing our industry. I think that in the next three to five years techno is going to run out of steam and most of us will disappear.'

The energy that had previously been so abundant had now faded. The plan we had in the early 90s for a house nation that would unite all genres of electronic music under one banner was still a pipe dream. Yet proof of the amazing adventure that we were part of lies in some of the most beautiful records ever made and hundreds of wonderful memories. We also had a lot to be proud of, having overcome the mistrust of the authorities, having (finally) installed a club culture in France, having profoundly changed the record industry and installed a new vision of travel and design. Above all, we had made techno one of the predominant genres of music of the 20th century.

Yet, by the early 2000s, techno had come to the end of the road. You only had to witness the nostalgia expressed by those who experienced techno's golden age. A revival of acid-house was followed by Michael Winterbottom's film *24 Hour Party People*, which told the story of Tony Wilson's Factory label and recalled wild nights at the Haçienda as if retracing a long-forgotten past. Fifteen years before, techno had been the result of a desire to shake things up and open up people's minds. In the early 2000s, we needed to reconnect with the hunger for the new and the different and go back to being eclectic if this music was to have a future.

Change in order to exist. Change, again. Begin a new cycle.

The next generation would see house from Chicago and techno from Detroit as retro music from their parent's generation. Books would be published about those crazy years; compilations released to celebrate the memory of techno as we do for punk or 70s rock. Maybe a technologically enhanced version of Jeff Mills' album *Waveform* would be re-released, like the re-mastered version of Pink Floyd's album *Dark Side Of The Moon*, as a relic of the past?

Techno would be relegated to the history of modern music, classified and stored for future generations. The Summer of Love would be regarded as a time when a group of young people had some fun, similar to the image we have of Woodstock in the 60s, and any idea we might have of something being revolutionary or subversive would be forgotten. There would be films made that would feed on our nostalgia, showing the mayhem of raves in the 90s; sets built in film studios and thousands of extras hired to recreate Berlin's incredible Love Parade. Hollywood would film a kitsch version of the life and times of Tony Colston-Hayter. Someone else would make a film about the trials and tribulations of a techno DJ in the 90s; the soundtrack, jammed with rave anthems, would be sold cheaply in supermarkets the world over.

Would the record industry still try to make money from the remnants of house and techno, as they did with punk? And, when everyone had run out of stories, would the industry market souvenirs? As with 70s funk and soul, would kids head out to second-hand record shops to buy their parents' music, looking for the last remaining Chicago house records that weren't swept away during the digital revolution?

Perhaps the future would be behind us, but we would still have that special feeling of having been part of musical history and of having left our mark.

Would the Rex Club survive the decline of techno or would it be abandoned and left to rot, like the Palace? Would we tell future generations about the Rex, and the magic that took place inside its four walls? A place where we immersed ourselves in music and pleasure, cut off from the outside world. A place where the history of house and techno in France was created with true passion and devotion?

In the winter of 2002, Christian Paulet, the heart and soul of the Rex Club, and myself worked out that dance music had been played inside that club for almost 15 years. I knew that the regular crowd had become a little blasé about the club, they knew it so well. They were not only blasé about the DJs but they took for granted what the club represented within the Paris nightlife scene, that is to say, an institution. We decided to celebrate the 15th anniversary with a festival. We scheduled 10 consecutive nights of music with the aim of creating a retrospective of the key moments of the last 15 years.

In May 2003, the festival 'Are You Rexperienced?' opened with a rock night, to remind people that, for years, the Rex had been one of Paris' leading rock venues, and that a significant number of DJs had come from this genre of music. We also wanted the public to revisit the history of house music. And so the following night was an acid-house event with Mike Pickering and Dave Haslam, the two legendary residents at Manchester's Haçienda. The crowd were surprised to discover that, in England, an acid-house night could also include rock, and that the DJs could play The Passenger by Iggy Pop or Kinky Afro by the Happy Mondays as well as The Party by Craze and DJ Pierre's strictly acid tracks. It was an amazing night, and was faithful to the spirit of the first Summer of Love, with moments of pure magic and exaltation. Overnight, the regular Rex crowd rediscovered a certain energy that had not been felt for a long time inside a Paris nightclub. There was a true sense of excitement. It was amazing. Someone came to tell me that even the journalists were dancing – a rare event, as generally they never left the bar! A couple of others also came to complain: 'Iggy Pop isn't acid!' I was overjoyed at the fact that the public were reacting. Fifteen years on from the first acid-house night at the Rex, the same emotions had taken hold of the club and were shaking up the crowd.

Over those 10 days, the Rex had a new lease of life. The sound system belted out French Kiss by Lil Louis, Fight The Power by Public Enemy, Casa by Jeff Mills, I Wanna Be Your Dog by the Stooges, Code Breaker by Underground Resistance, Can You Feel It? by Larry Heard, and tracks from Nina Simone. The Rex was telling its own story and illustrating how this club had become legendary and had contributed to installing house and techno in France's capital city with innovative, uplifting live music back in the 90s; a lifetime ago.

Out of those 10 nights, there is one night in particular that I would like to recall. It was the night Detroit gave a priceless gift to Paris: Underground Resistance, who never play in public, came to play at the Rex. That night was worth a thousand others, the music was sublime. In the days leading up to the event, we were hearing the most unbelievable stories. We learnt that people were coming from all over France, from England, from Ireland and even from as far as Brazil to be there. In the afternoon, as the musicians from Underground Resistance did their sound check in the empty club, my hair stood on end and I was nervous.

That night, the DJ booth at the Rex was blacked out. Mike Banks played keyboards while Juan Atkins, James Pennington and Buzz Goree took it in turn to DJ. Many people in the crowd experienced something new, as they had always thought of UR as defenders of pure techno. Yet the UR DJs did not only play techno, but they also played house, disco, electro and old rave anthems. Mike Banks took to the microphone to thank the crowd for their support and went on to play the organ over tracks such as Don't You Want It and Electric Soul, adding a previously unheard gospel element to these records.

At about 4am, as the club was rammed, a few of the staff made their way around the club holding up signs stating: 'The Rex loves You'. Jeff Mills got up on stage to play World 2 World. Everyone stopped dancing and stood listening in silence, their heads bowed. This was the kind of energy that words could not describe. It was a feeling that hits one person and then sweeps across the whole dance floor. It was alive. It cut through your body and went straight to the soul. It had the power to make you cry and to make you truly happy.

Then followed a very special Sunday afternoon at the Rex. It was pouring with rain outside. Hundreds of children, ranging from the ages of 5 to 15, slowly made their way in. The majority had never heard house or techno before and had definitely never seen a dance floor. They all stared at the huge Englishman standing up on the stage behind the decks. The giant's name was Carl Cox.

Carl was there to play techno for the children. He knew that the only way to do it was to make it as energetic as possible. He was very direct and sincere and his enthusiasm soon spread. He played The Bells by Jeff Mills, a radical, racing, techno track and there, in this venue, which had experienced so much, something amazing happened. Little five-year-olds ran around shrieking with joy, other kids danced like crazy.

Others stood still and stared at the giant, then went up to him to ask for a kiss. Parents stood with tears in their eyes watching their children dancing like lunatics. It did not matter that these children did not really understand what was going on, the important thing was that they were enjoying every minute of this new experience.

Music, dancing, sweat, communion, bright lights, freedom.

All those years of hard work, of giving everything to techno to exist, took on a new dimension that day. What goes around comes around. Here was a new generation enjoying our music. A new generation to whom we could pass on our energy. And, in exchange, we marvelled at their smiles, their dance moves and their shrieks of joy.

Energy never dies, and the magic that was felt that afternoon will remain forever within the Rex. It has seeped into its foundations and has found a place inside the soul of every person who frequents that club. This magic will be passed on and on, and will continue its journey.

In 2002, at the beginning of the year, a journalist, David Brun-Lambert, and his editor both came to see me to talk about a project for a book. They were by no means strangers; I had known them both for years. We quickly agreed upon the tack we wanted to take. Our aim was not to recount the history of techno, but to try to bring to life the essence of what had happened over the past 15 years, through my own experiences.

Over a period of 18 months the book took shape, sometimes taking an unexpected direction. It was a year and a half of interviewing, travelling, researching, going over memories, digging out old records, and asking questions that we had never asked ourselves in order to build up the chronology of events that had shaken the house nation.

We met many influential people who all shared the same fascination for the emotions that music instils, who all believed in the same thing, and who were conscious of the magic contained within the dance floor. These encounters made us realise how much techno has changed the lives of the protagonists of this movement and how beautiful, painful and complex the story of techno really is.

This book was also a kind of therapy for me. I was forced to question what had made me want to make my parents dance in my bedroom when I was a boy, and what continues to make me want to travel the world over and play music to a crowd of people. As the book progressed it even began to influence my work, both my DJ sets and the choices I made. Because of this book, re-visiting places such as Detroit and Manchester again took on new meaning. It was probably also to do with the fact that there were now two of us, me and David Brun-Lambert, walking through the streets, breathing in the air, hanging out at the Heidelberg Project or in front of the Haçienda.

In April 2003, I agreed to play at a night called Electric Chair in Manchester (organised by the DJs from Unabomber). David Brun-Lambert met me at the airport, as he had done in Detroit. It was late afternoon, and we got into a cab that took us through the suburbs of Manchester into the city centre. We left our bags at the hotel and walked to Oldham Street. We went into several record shops, but did not stay long as it was almost closing time in preparation for the big Saturday night out. As the shops emptied I began walking back towards our hotel, but David wanted to explore and see what had become of the Haçienda. It was on the other side of town. We decided not to take a taxi but to walk through the streets of Manchester. We passed restaurants where I had once known the owners, and on past what had previously been nightclubs but were now either supermarkets or shops selling luxury items. We walked past pubs, decaying bridges, and the remains of what had once been textile factories. Then, from a distance, we saw the colourful banners of a huge new building development that enveloped Whitworth Street.

Whereas only a few years back this had been a rundown area on a polluted canal, it had now become fashionable and was full of bars with outdoor seating, smart restaurants, and cafés built in under the arches. Even the colour of the area had changed. The red brick walls, so common in the north of England, seemed to have all been cleaned up. Tall glass buildings had popped up everywhere and in the soft spring light, this neighbourhood now appeared to be carefree.

The building which had once been home to the Haçienda stood covered in scaffolding and was hidden behind huge tarpaulin banners. We saw one banner stretching across the entire building emblazoned with the words: 'THE HAÇIENDA. THE PARTY IS OVER'. On the pavement opposite stood a sales office displaying an architect's vision of the apartments that were soon to be built on the site.

I couldn't believe it. The place that had meant everything to me during my time in the UK was now in the hands of property developers. Tony Wilson explained that developers had bought the Haçienda name a few years back, and that he had not earned a penny from the deal. For years, people had lived for this club; many experienced some of the best moments of their lives in there. Yet the name had been sold and the developers had got to work pulling it apart, erasing an entire chapter in Manchester's history for the sake of profit. 'The party is over'. Make way for business.

As I stare at these words, film-like images begin to race through my mind. Slowly at first, a silhouette appears of someone on stage, standing in front of a crowd, a sea of hands, slowly being engulfed in smoke pumped out by smoke machines. Then the images begin to speed up: an aeroplane landing in an airport in Japan that suddenly starts going backwards. It retraces its flight-path wiping out endless hours of travel in just a few seconds. Inside a studio somebody is putting the final touches to a track; the music is so fast I cannot seem to put my finger on it, but it sounds like The Man With The Red Face. More images flood in, so fast they are hard to fathom: the Rex Club, Hell's, the Fuse, the End. Inside a radio studio. A huge float covered in greenery making its way through the streets of Paris, crossing the Place de la Bastille where thousands of people are dancing in the streets. Dust-covered bodies at Borealis in the first morning light. The inside of a stark hotel bedroom. Somebody waiting in the bright white light of an airport. Inside the back of a taxi racing through the streets, I can almost smell the stale cigarette smoke on the leatherette seats. The images keep coming, faster and faster; now it is Detroit, inside a primary school, a class full of people dancing. Detroit, a warning: 'Do not allow yourself to be programmed'. The kind face of an urban soldier whose face occupies the whole space and then disappears into the shadows. Another face: it's Armando, he is smiling and then he fades. Faster, faster. Bright, colourful lights illuminate hundreds of bodies. An aerial view of the Love Parade in Berlin, with people's cries getting louder and longer. In and out of a huge warehouse, packed with thousands of people dancing. A rapid succession of club nights, where I can make out the walls of the Rex, first orange, then grey. An image flashes up of the inside of the MAD club, the DJ booth at La Luna, the entrance to La Loco. Now the images slow down and I am somewhere in the countryside, all is dark except for a halo of green light, and I can see the shadows of hundreds of people dancing in the middle of nothing. Then I arrive in a deserted industrial town and my journey finally comes to an end on the rain-soaked pavements of Whitworth Street. Now the images are in slow motion. The face of a young boy appears. He is going inside a club for the first time. As he passes through the door, the barely legible brass sign next to the door reads, 'The Haçienda'. The boy walks across the room, flooded with light. He stops on the edge of the dance floor and then steps forward. He puts himself in the middle of the dance floor, throws his arms up in the air and lets himself be blown away by the music.

The party goes on.

side

two

Laurent Garnier

David Brun-Lambert

the warning

[preface to 2nd edition]

Friday October 26, 2012.

The Rex Club is heaving. From inside the DJ booth I stare out at the packed dance floor. I have lived this moment a hundred times over, but this time it's different. Tonight is special. As I look at the crowd, I see people in their forties, people in their thirties, people in their twenties, people in their late teens and they are all having fun dancing on the same dance floor. The energy is amazing. Intoxicating. But the energy's not coming from the music, it's coming from the 800 people here inside the club; 800 people dancing, going wild, shouting with joy, waving their arms, stamping their feet, releasing pent-up energy. There's no 'hey-look-at-me' going on, just people having fun. They are drunk, sweaty and have a burning, almost primal desire to follow me on this very special night. For 10 whole hours, I'm here to celebrate my 25 years as a DJ in the very club that has played such an important part in my career.

So, as I said, it's October 26, 2012. I've been preparing for this night for weeks, thinking about it all day every day. I had knots in my stomach counting down the hours to the doors opening. And now this is it. Here I am. The first few people start to appear on the dance floor. My stress levels are peaking. Soon, there are a few hundred people, and then the club is packed. A quick look around. Everyone is here: family, friends, fans and people I work with now and have worked with in the past. And I see the same look on everyone's faces. With each hug, each pat on the back, each kiss hello, I feel the same warmth. I interpret each hand pressed against the glass of the DJ booth as a sign of support, thanks and affection. Every now and again, over the Rex's powerful sound system, I hear shouts of joy coming from the dance floor. In the darkness I see people smiling among the sea of waving arms. The energy in the room is now even more intense, more potent, more focussed; it cuts right through the Rex and gives me an almighty punch in the gut. As the night progresses, I sink deeper and deeper into an almost dream-like state. I'm engulfed by powerful waves of happiness that leave me breathless and threaten to drown me.

One track after another: Ten City's That's The Way Love Is sits alongside Ame and Dixon, Steve Poindexter's Work That Mother Fucker fades into Alarm by French Fries, Aguila by Mystic Aztec intermixes with Forever Untold by Ian O'Donovan. I had imagined this night as the coming together of three generations of clubbers to share two decades of dance music. I watch them enjoying dance music past and present: notions of pigeonholing thrown out of the window. All I see are hundreds of feverish bodies abandoning themselves to the music. I watch them jumping, grooving, gyrating. They all seem set on putting their lives on hold for a few hours to dance.

▶ Playlist

BIG TUNES FOR 25TH ANNIVERSARY AT THE REX

Tom Middleton
Penrose Steps

Oliver S
Doin' Ya Thang

Kolsh
Der Alte

Fundamental Harmonics
Network Inhibition

Ian O'Donovan
Forever Untold (Satoshi F. Remix)

Electric Rescue
The Rave Child

Douglas Greed
When A Man Sings

Laurent Garnier
Jacques In The Box

Guy Gerber
Timing

Tim Deluxe
Transformation

Tonight is not just the celebration of my long career, it's a starting point and the beginning of a new era for me as an artist, as well as new beginnings with my relationship with the crowd, 25 years after I first started out as a DJ.

Now comes the moment to play the first few bars of Jacques In The Box. What time is it? I have no idea; I lost all track of time ages ago. Something very special is happening. It's not like something changes abruptly from one minute to the next, but more like there's a low, steady uprising. It is coming from the earth's core and from within the club's walls. What happens feels like a tidal wave that sweeps up each and every person in its path. It's as if all the memories and energy of thousands of past nights held within these walls are released all at once. People shout, cry out, thrust their fists into the air, stomp their feet in the near-primal urgency of the moment. This is joy in its purest form; a release, an orgasm. Or perhaps a wake-up call? This happens when I play Jacques In The Box, and the exact same thing happens when I play The Man With The Red Face and Crispy Bacon, too. It happens when I play classic house or techno anthems but also when I play more obscure, lesser-known tracks. Then it just happens again and again and again, until it's time to put an end to this night, to the amazing, indescribable chaos, with people shouting and screaming and celebrating being alive.

A young guy comes up to me just as the club is about to close. He couldn't have been more than 18. His brother had told him, 'Go and see Garnier, it's Tangerine Dream "with beats"!' All night long he had been glued to the speakers. He was one of the 800 people who had made the Rex's heart beat for those 10 hours. At 5am, when Scan X came to join me to do a live set, this young guy heard Acid Eiffel for the very first time. At 9am, he was still there; a bit dazed after the roller coaster ride he had just been on. As I was on my way out, completely exhausted, he came up to me very naturally and smiled, 'That was the most beautiful journey of my whole life!' Then he turned and walked away. I watched him cross the road outside the Rex and felt deeply moved. This young kid had just put into words why I still keep on going as a DJ; to reach out and touch people, to channel powerful emotions to people on the dance floor and to change the way some people think about music, maybe to even have a slight impact on the course of their lives. That's what I am always in search of. That is my job.

For the last 25 years…

It's easy to work out. The first time I stepped foot inside the Rex I was 21. I'm now 47. I left Paris seven years ago to live in the south of France. Since I became a father, my family is my priority. Over the past

10 years, my artistic ambitions have gradually moved in other directions, making soundtracks for films and documentaries, working with contemporary dance choreographers, performing live … many times over! And, of course, there have been albums, several EPs, and DJ gigs all over the world, including in places that I had never been to before.

My record bag now weighs less than 1 kilo; before, it weighed 20. All I need to DJ these days is a laptop, a pair of headphones and six memory sticks, which contain the equivalent to 24 record boxes!

All around me the musical landscape has undergone a seismic change. In the space of 10 years, digital has taken over. MP3 has become the standard format for listening to and sharing music. A new generation has appeared. Spoon-fed by the internet, they have established new codes that have turned the notion of rights and property on its head, and as a result, have completely undermined the music industry as a whole. Record sales have collapsed. Hundreds of record shops and record labels have closed and, since then, others have been born.

On the flip side, music has benefited from the seemingly endless opportunities the internet has to offer to reach audiences far and wide. New trends have appeared, revealing a plethora of new, young and exciting talent that has taken dance music into remarkable new unexplored territories. Yet the internet has also revealed other malevolent characters whose ambitions are other than musical excellence, upsetting the delicate balance upon which electronic music is based.

Faced with these changes, the DJs and producers who did their growing up between the first Summer of Love in the UK and the new millennium were forced to adapt or die. That is when the question, 'how to last?' became crucial for the artists of my generation.

Ten years after *Electrochoc* was first published, David Brun-Lambert and I decided it was time to re-visit and analyse the last 10 years. To do this, we decided to follow the same path as *Electrochoc,* i.e. retrace the trajectory of dance music across the globe through the prism of my experience. Our aim was to offer a true-to-life panoramic view of all of the new sub-genres, venues, events and people who have been at the centre of the dance music scene for the last 10 years. Whether that be the emergence and subsequent triumph of dubstep, the exemplary trajectory of festivals such as Time Warp or the Nuits Sonores, the insanity of the club Berghain and the artistic innovation that Berlin has experienced in the past decade. Then there is the technological revolution and the explosion of social networking sites, as well as the influence of people such as Pedro Winter and David Guetta, the king of the EDM (Electronic Dance Music) movement in the US.

Once again, as in 2003, David and I travelled together, met up with other artists, carried out hundreds of hours of interviews, spent night after night observing people, talking to them, noting things down… but above all listening to music and dancing.

Exactly 10 years ago, our story began with the words 'Where do I begin?' This time, the answer is simple, with the release of *Electrochoc* in October 2003.

last tribute from
the 20th century

We didn't expect the book to be such a success. Nobody did in fact. We were hoping that *Electrochoc* would be well received, but for it to do so well in France and then go on to be translated into nine different languages, with a cinema adaptation in the pipeline … well!! Since the release of my first EP, I was used to critics. They always get to me, of course they do, but they no longer give me sleepless nights like they did in the past. Well, saying that … When our plan to write *Electrochoc* went public a year before publication, some people on the electronic music scene didn't hide their scepticism, 'Why the hell is he writing his autobiography when he isn't even 40?' I just ignored them. David and I concentrated on writing the story as it happened, struggling to find the right words. And then *Electrochoc* was published. Funnily enough, the critics were (almost) unanimously positive in their response … Even now, not a month goes by without someone coming up to me and saying, 'What you said in your book was exactly what happened!' or, 'I never read, but I read your book from cover to cover!' or, 'I gave a copy of *Electrochoc* to my parents so they could understand my passion for techno!'

Wow!

I admit that I came out of the *Electrochoc* experience exhausted. Exhausted from having to go back over my past, week after week for almost a year and a half, and answer the very difficult question, 'Who am I?' To help me find the answers, David really tested me. He was merciless! Those months of intense interrogation and introspection were like being in therapy; pushing myself to re-examine where I came from, to examine the musical tastes and influences I'd held since childhood and explore why. Above all, *Electrochoc* forced me to think about the deep-rooted reasons why I had pursued my music career for so many years, and understand why I was still there while others had quit.

Thanks to *Electrochoc* I came to the realisation that my curiosity and love of music, all types of music, was my strength. It also helped me to identify what had become my musical hallmark: a constant shifting between a darker and a more melodic side. I also learned to see certain traits: my fear of being pigeonholed into one genre, of being labelled, or being identified with just one group. By forcing me to consider my career to date, *Electrochoc* made me realise that, without really consciously thinking about it, I had followed a route without ever making concessions either to the music business or to the public. I had also followed my instincts, keeping well away from concepts and commercial strategies. Once *Electrochoc* was finished, I arrived at a conclusion: my risk-taking, my fastidious nature (not always very easy to deal with for the people working with me) and my determination to follow my own path were finally paying off…

The publication of *Electrochoc* coincided with a new arrival in the commercial musical landscape. What was known as electroclash – the coming together of rock music with a techno beat – was rapidly gaining ground. Represented by artists such as DJ Hell, Tiga, Justice, Vitalic, Miss Kittin & The Hacker, Jacques Lu Cont and Boys Noize, the genre was heavily influenced by artists such as the Chemical Brothers, Underworld, the Prodigy and, of course, Daft Punk. Let us not forget that before the release of Daft Punk's album *Homework* in 1997, rock and house were eyeballing each other, ready to battle it out. The former were concerned that their domination of the international music scene was under threat from the moronic 'boom boom' of house music, and the latter believed that guitars were the ultimate symbol of old-school, conservative pop. Then, with a brilliant first album, Thomas Bangalter and Guy-Manuel de Homem-Christo, a.k.a. Daft Punk, managed a superb turnaround and united rock fans and techno kids on the same dance floor. The rock fans went wild for the tough beats in the classic tracks Rollin' & Scratchin' or Da Funk, and the techno kids lapped up the rock 'n' roll energy.

With the two enemy sides finally united, the conditions were right for the crossover between rock and dance music to move up into the big league. And while pure rock 'n' roll was making a big comeback in the States (the Strokes, etc.) and in the UK (the Libertines, etc.), a mutant form was also developing, with producers giving guitars the treatment that, up until now, had been reserved for dance music. There was the Rapture and their huge hit, House of Jealous Lovers, TV On The Radio with their album *OK Calculator*, Radiohead with *Hail To The Thief*, and the incredible James Murphy with his disco-punk battleship LCD Soundsystem.

Popular bands of the time such as Franz Ferdinand or Bloc Party were spawning huge indie hits (Take Me Out and Banquet respectively) built around a disco beat, and all of a sudden it was normal to hear Nirvana or Blur in a DJ set. Ten years earlier, taking a risk like that would have been deemed suicidal. But during this period, the future of dance music wasn't bright. Even though super-clubs, such as The End or Fabric, were packing in the crowds every weekend, musically things were going round in circles; there were few new horizons. A cycle of creativity was coming to an end. Less than a decade after the explosion of raves had engendered a witch-hunt in the UK and France, dance music was now accepted by the general public and the media – 'ravers' were a term of reference in articles about the May bank holiday free parties …

In the UK, the musical genres that had kept the underground scene so vibrant and alive over the past decade had also run out of steam – drum 'n' bass, for example. Struggling to reinvigorate itself, drum 'n' bass had lost the sense of innovation that had been at its heart. It had to move over to make room for an influx of new hybrid musical tendencies like Grime, a sort of 'gangsta rave' from the tough suburbs of South London, which took its inspiration from US hip-hop and moody techno sounds. While the musical landscape was changing so radically from London to Tokyo, with musical genres that had only recently been so prevalent crumbling to ashes as if suddenly rendered obsolete by the wearing out of the genre, the birth of new styles of music and the mixing of all of these sounds new and old together had become the rule. I thrived on this confusion and took full advantage during my DJ sets, mixing all different styles of music, no holds barred. There was another reason for this: if writing *Electrochoc* had freed me from old demons, the release of the compilation *Excess Luggage* went one step further and freed all of my inhibitions.

From the outset, I imagined *Excess Luggage* as a five-CD mix compilation and as both the soundtrack to *Electrochoc* and a true reflection of who I was. When played one after the other, these six hours of music said, 'There you have it! I stand for all of this!' I am a DJ who can easily play house classics at the Sonar festival, moody techno in a small club in Detroit, edgy electro at the Rex, or more challenging experimental music on a radio show for the BBC. The compilation box set ended on a more introspective mix which was resoundingly cinematographic, and included tracks such as the soundtrack to Christophe Honoré's film *Seventeen Times Cecile Cassard*, the Tindersticks' heart-wrenching A Night In, and Alain Bashung's mesmerising Madame Rêve.

I was going through a big 'Bashung' phase at the time. Ever since I was a teenager, I have often had long periods of being obsessed with one artist or one style of music. For example, the American psychedelic music of the sixties, UK garage rock, be-bop, the Doors, or even Herbie Hancock's mad electronic jazz in Sextant. I'm also obsessed with the blues. Whether it is the blues from deepest Louisiana in the music of Slim Harpo, or the blues from the basements of the UK in the 60s. This raw, intense, sometimes brutal music literally hypnotises me. But, in 2003, it was Bashung who had my full attention. His album, *L'Imprudence* came out when we were working on *Electrochoc*. I listened to it over and over again, at home, as well as other albums of his such as *Fantaisie Militaire* and *Osez Josephine*. So it was no surprise that I wanted Madame Rêve for *Excess Luggage*. At first, Bashung's record company said 'no', but I wasn't prepared to give up that easily. I wanted that track! Madame Rêve wasn't just the manifestation of Bashung's musical greatness; it was the centrepiece of my 'night-time' mix. But the problem was,

▶ Playlist
BLUES

Fleetwood Mac
Love That Burns

Cassandra Wilson
Vietnam Blues

John Lee Hooker
No Shoe

Amos Milburn
Please Mr. Johnson

Van Morrison
T.B. Sheets

Dinah Washington
Big Long Slidin' Thing

Chuck E. Weiss
Extremely Cool

Slim Harpo
I'm A King Bee

Jimi Hendrix
Catfish Blues

Blue Cheer
Rock Me Baby

Arthur 'Big Boy' Crudup
I'm In The Mood

The Black Keys
Grown So Ugly

Big Sexy Noise
Bad For Bobby

the record company who looked after his licensing didn't want to know. Even though I kept on and on at them, the answer remained the same, 'No fucking way!'

Then, one day, my manager Christian Paulet rang me, 'I've got two passes for Alain Bashung's concert at the Zenith tonight. We can go and see him after the concert.' I couldn't believe my luck. Once the concert was over, we passed security to go backstage. I felt as nervous as a kid on his first day at school. And then there we were; I met my hero. How long did I spend with him? Probably only about 10 minutes. But 10 very special minutes all the same, during which this man, at the height of his career, exhausted after an intense two-hour performance, and whom I knew to be ill on top of that, and who had a group of people waiting for him, proved to be incredibly humble, dignified and amazingly approachable. What was even more surprising was that, when I timidly introduced myself to him and tried to explain to him that I was a DJ, etc., he stopped me in my tracks and said, 'I know exactly who you are.' I couldn't believe it! But, it wasn't really that surprising, as Alain Bashung knew about a lot of things. Marc Besse's biography about him, published in 2009, tells of Bashung's insatiable curiosity, his constant thirst to experiment with new things, to explore new musical territories. Bashung despised monotony. He was also known in the business to be exceedingly demanding and permanently dissatisfied. Working with him was often a nightmare for his musicians. But, at the end of the day, Bashung delivered stupendous albums such as *L'Imprudence* and *Bleu Petrole*, comprehensive works that advanced freely, far from the usual trends or formulas.

So there you have it. There he was, Bashung, standing right in front of me – shy, fragile, but with plenty of rugged charisma. We spoke about his music for a bit. I told him how much his latest albums had influenced me. 'I know,' he answered very simply. He had read it somewhere and had been flattered. Now he was thanking me. The tables had turned! I finally got round to telling him one of the reasons why I had wanted to meet him, for my project, *Excess Luggage*. I explained that I was after the rights for Madame Rêve, but that his record company had said no, without giving a proper reason. He seemed annoyed; 'They never mentioned it to me … Tomorrow it will be sorted!'. On that note we said goodbye. The following day, F Communications received a fax from Bashung's record company apologising for any past refusals. Madame Rêve would feature on *Excess Luggage*. Madame Rêve epitomises the PBB Late Night Mix.

▶ Playlist
BEST OF BASHUNG

La Nuit Je Mens

Madame Rêve

Résidents de la République

Les Mots Bleus

Malaxe

L.U.V

Les Grands Voyageurs

J'envisage

La Ficelle

Faisons Envie

L'Imprudence

Noir de Monde

Je Me Dore

PBB (Pedro's Broadcasting Basement) is my internet radio station. My childhood dream came true almost overnight when a guy, who suddenly found himself at the head of Radio Nova, took me for a fool!

Nova had been losing money for years. Jean-François Bizot, the boss, had had enough of bailing out the station with money from his own bank account. So the time came when the group's shareholders started to threaten to pull out. It was then that someone was hired to transform the radio into a national network station and make it start earning its keep. So far so good, there's nothing wrong about that. Except that the guy in question began taking over, and Bizot, who was already very ill by then, turned a blind eye. The new guy fired several employees who had been at Nova for years, as well as several others who he felt didn't fit in with the new policies he wanted to put in place. He wanted obedient foot soldiers to follow his orders, not free-thinkers. Yet, the staff at Nova were essentially made up of music lovers who had zero interest in opinion polls or listening panels and would give you the brush-off if you tried talking to them about such stuff!

In 2002, foreseeing that the arrival of this new managing director might sever the radio from its musical roots, Jean-François asked me to head up the music programming. I accepted his offer. Unfortunately, I soon found myself having to deal directly with the 'technician' – that was the nickname I gave him. During our first meeting, all he talked to me about was audience ratings and surveys. I couldn't believe it! He no longer wanted tracks that had made Nova 'Nova', he wanted golden oldies: more Bob Marley, more Rita Mitsouko, and more Björk. Basically, more hits, more mainstream music that everyone could enjoy, from housewives to kids. Like everyone, I love Bob Marley and Björk, but I believe in everything in small doses. But for this guy, there was no question of that. He wanted hit tracks – No Woman No Cry, instead of a great old rocksteady track from the Wailers. Basically, his strategy was a million miles away from the Bizot-style that Nova had championed for the past 20 years. Yet, the 'technician' and I did manage to agree on a couple of points. That the music played on the radio should be available to the biggest audience possible was my plan, too. But, I also wanted to surprise our listeners, and not take the same well-trodden route as almost every other radio in France just to please a wider audience. I wanted Nova to stand out, and take an even more radical stance. In short, I thought we should adapt to these difficult times, just differently. And, above all, remain Radio Nova.

But we just didn't understand each other.

The first thing I did when I came out of that initial meeting was grab my phone; 'Jean-François, I can't work with him!' But there was nothing to be done. Jean-François simply wasn't in the right frame of mind to deal with that kind of thing anymore. So the 'technician' and I found ourselves working together on the following season's music programme. Then, one day in July, he invited me to lunch to smooth things over. But he also wanted to make things clear: under his leadership, Nova would become a polite, nice, clean radio station. I kept calm, 'You want James Brown on the radio? OK, but let's dig out a killer B-side. Don't worry, we'll do things properly ...'. Yet, deep down inside I was thinking, 'This radio station isn't going to be what you want it to be, mate.' But I was wrong.

The following Monday, I discovered that the playlist I had put together for the weekend hadn't been broadcast. The 'technician' had secretly broadcast his own playlist (just a 'test', as he later put it), taking advantage of the fact that I was away working that weekend, playing God knows where. One thing's for sure, the listeners must have had a heavy dose of golden oldies that weekend! I was so furious I stormed straight up to his office and started shouting, 'What the fuck is going on? You really took me for a ride at that lunch!' He replied, blablabla, golden oldies, audience ratings, and all that bullshit. Fuming, I resigned on the spot and created Pedro's Broadcasting Basement that very same week.

I created my web radio station, PBB, in the big old basement of my apartment, which also served as my studio. It ran 24-hours a day. At PBB, the rules of music programming and listener panels could get stuffed! The only formatting going on was bringing my record collection to life and playing all the styles of music that give me that special buzz: King Tubby, the Ramones, Underground Resistance, drum 'n' bass, gospel, Gainsbourg, acid house, 60s soul, electro from Berlin, John Coltrane, Fela Kuti ... a little bit of everything.

Back then, my apartment was a big loft in the old Yoplait factory in Ivry-sur-Seine. It reminded me of the derelict industrial areas of Detroit. Incidentally, it was my obsession with Motor City that pushed me to buy the loft in the first place. The Place de la Bastille may only have been a 10-minute drive away, but this area was essentially made up of ware-houses, deserted streets, wastelands and factories ... From the window in our living room, a series of 30 or so railway tracks stretched far out west. Further along, the two chimneys of a huge incinerator belted out thick plumes of white smoke, day in day out. At night, it took on a more sombre, forbidding appearance, but there was something about that huge beast that I loved. Something about its imposing outline, its brute shape, its constant activity that touched me. When friends came over to our house with their children, I would tell them that it was a cloud-making factory. The kids would look at me wide-eyed, 'Really?'. 'And I would reply, 'Yes, really!' That factory will always carry a special meaning for me as it inspired me to write the music for an album that I finished in early 2005 when my son was just a year old, *The Cloud Making Machine*. By far my most personal album.

Electroclash and minimal German techno, chiefly represented by the labels BPitch Control and Kompakt, were at their height. Furthermore, raw, brutal indie rock was winning out in the charts while techno was blending with housier sounds and slowing down the tempo – hence the name 'Tech house'. None of these trends particularly inspired me and, in any case, I had no real intention of falling into line with any of these styles. My period of introspection during the writing of *Electrochoc* added to my obsessive listening to Bashung, my love of film soundtracks and an ever-growing discomfort with being considered a techno artist – despite my best efforts to disassociate myself from this labelling. All of these factors conspired to push me away from the dance floor temporarily. I didn't want to release an *Unreasonable Behaviour* part 2, nor a sequel to Crispy Bacon, nor a rehashed Man With The Red Face. I wanted to give myself the artistic freedom to do my own thing, to take the public by surprise, to distance myself from the rest of the pack and revive the radical stance that Eric Morand and I had adopted after I won the Victoire de la Musique award. The expectation was that I would re-release my album with a big sticker stating 'Award Winner'. But, instead, we released only 1,000 copies of the EP *Dangerous Drive* and sold them direct from the F Comm office. 'You want to buy a copy? No problem, stop by the office!'

When I sat down to write the music for *The Cloud Making Machine*, I had for quite some time wanted to make the music for a film soundtrack and to delve deeper into more experimental music. I had always loved ambient music, a meditative style of electronic music that gets its inspiration from artists such as Erik Satie, Brian Eno, Tangerine Dream and Steve Reich. During the 70s, it was a trippy kind of music but it later became a significant genre in electronica and a laboratory for experimentation. Artists like KLF, Aphex Twin, Boards of Canada and Autechre took ambient music much further and to fascinating places.

This was a musical domain that I had never previously allowed myself to explore. Perhaps due to a certain modesty and perhaps also due to my insecurity about never having been a 'real' musician. As I have already mentioned, *Electrochoc* enabled me to free myself from some of my old fears. And, in many ways, it also forced me to step outside my comfort zone. As a result, after its release, I felt far more at ease and able to do what I liked. If I wanted to make a cinematographic album, then I would! To the people who tried to put me off by saying, 'Watch out, you risk leaving your die-hard techno fans behind,' I replied, 'So what? I'll lose the techno fundamentalists sooner or later anyway!'

I recorded *The Cloud Making Machine* with Sangoma Everett, Marc Chalosse and Philippe Nadaud, the musicians who had been touring with me for the past four years. The Norwegian pianist Bugge Wesseltoft and the Tunisian musician and singer Dhafer Youssef also participated in the making of this album. *The Cloud Making Machine* was mixed by Scan X, a major artist on F Comm, a brilliant 'scientist' and one of the first French techno artists ever to have performed live in concert. These collaborations resulted in an album filled with complex and contradictory moods. I still believe today that this album is the one that best reflects who I am.

And so came a time when I had to take the leap of faith and play the album to someone else. As always, Eric Morand was the first person to hear it. But this time was different; I knew it wasn't going to be a walk in the park...

We met in my studio and I played Eric seven tracks. He didn't say a word throughout, not even a grunt. He didn't even hint at a smile. Nothing. So it goes without saying that I wasn't feeling very sure of myself. The final track on the album came to an end and was followed by what seemed like a long, drawn-out silence. Finally, Eric turned to me with a serious look, 'How many do you think you're going to sell?' Me: 'Honestly? Probably no more than about 10 per cent of what I sold of *Unreasonable Behaviour*'. With a glimpse of a smile he added, 'As long as you know where we're going with this... let's do it! Oh, and by the way, I do really like it!'.

Making an album is first and foremost about exposing your true self. It's about putting your heart and soul into something, but the more you put in, the more the public's reaction affects you. When *The Cloud Making Machine* came out in 2005, it didn't strike a chord with people as much as I had thought it would. It was hard to swallow, as I thought this record was much stronger than any of the records I had put out up until then. As time has passed, I have become far less upset about how this album was received than I was when it was first released. Firstly, because it has aged well and, secondly, because it has enabled me to reach a wider audience who came from a very different musical background to techno. But, above all, this album represented an important step in my career, enabling me to distance myself for a time from techno. This album felt like the end of a long battle. For years, I had struggled to make people see that the roots of electronic music were found in all styles of music made since the 1950s. In 2004, I even organised a tour with Jeff Mills, Muzik: Expect the Unexpected, to defend this line of reasoning. We chose 10 cities (including Paris, Berlin, London and Lausanne) and in each of these we did a four-hour radio show followed by a party in a club, where the idea was to play anything except electronic music. Of course, this infuriated some people. But we could both feel the ground shift – people were listening and attitudes were slowly changing. As far as I was concerned, *The Cloud Making Machine* was a way to illustrate this way of thinking. The album coincided with the beginning of a new cycle; I was hungry for something different. I wanted to explore new horizons and initiate new collaborations, go places I hadn't been before. I just didn't expect it all to happen quite so quickly. Not in Paris, but in the south of France, where I moved with my family in September 2005.

After five years spent living opposite the 'cloud making machine' in Ivry sur Seine, my wife and I had had enough of the smoke, the noise of the trains right outside our window, and the view of the constant traffic on the ring road. But we had also had enough of Paris. The city had stagnated and seemed incapable of change. Thirty years on from the heyday of the Palace, two decades after the first raves in the suburbs, the Paris scene had become introspective, frightened of the outside world. And Paris' nightlife was in a pitiful state. Whereas in almost every other major European city new big clubs were opening every other week, Paris' fashion victims were dismally shunting back and forth between clubs that offered a bit of glamour but not much else, such as Le Baron or the Paris Paris. The reputation that Paris had enjoyed during 80s and 90s as one the centres of European nightlife was now just a distant memory. Paris had gone to sleep. Paris was as boring as hell.

So, when we stumbled across an old farmhouse about 30 km outside Aix-en-Provence, we didn't hesitate. We sold our loft in Ivry sur Seine, packed up 300 boxes of records, and moved to the countryside, to a house where we could invite all our friends to stay, have 20 people for lunch outside, and where I could make as much noise as I wanted in my studio in the garden without disturbing the neighbours.

A few months after we moved in, the contemporary dance choreographer, Angelin Preljocaj, contacted me. The building work was almost finished on his new rehearsal and performing space, The Pavillon Noir. This reinforced concrete cube measuring 3,000 m² would house four rehearsal studios and a 400-capacity theatre in the heart of Aix-en-Provence. Angelin was working on a performance that he was creating especially for the opening night, and wanted to collaborate with an electronic music artist. I jumped at the chance. I had been interested in

contemporary dance for a long time and was aware of the close ties it has had with electronic music since the 60s, with *Messe Pour Le Temps Présent* written by Pierre Henry and Michel Colombier for a ballet by the choreographer Maurice Béjart.

Forty years after the success of Psyche Rock, electronic music and contemporary dance were still well matched. Not surprising, really, as both the music and the dance are founded upon the exploration of new aesthetic horizons. Should you need convincing, just take a quick look at the work currently being produced by the Japanese choreographer Hiroaki Umeda, who uses innovative electronic sounds and groundbreaking video projections in his performances. Or just look at the work of Angelin Preljocaj over the past two decades.

With a sound knowledge of classical ballet, Angelin is someone who loves turning tradition on its head and researching new forms. Aside from being a fabulously bold choreographer, Angelin also enjoys collaborative work and, if possible, working with people from outside of his realm. For example, after a joint venture with the German composer Karlheinz Stockhausen, Angelin put together a very audacious performance entitled 'N' with the multimedia artist Ulf Langheinrich from the duo Granular-Synthesis.

So, Angelin and I met and immediately hit it off! And that is how I found myself working on a 25-minute piece of electronic music based upon Stravinsky's *Firebird*.

Marie-Claude Pietragalla, an ex-principal dancer of the Paris Opera Ballet who had run the Marseilles National Ballet and went on to start her own dance company in 2004, also got in touch with me around this time. She had heard *The Cloud Making Machine* and also heard about the work I had been doing with Angelin. Pietra, a charismatic and fiercely independent woman who also had a reputation for being uncompromising, asked me if I would be interested in writing the music for a piece that she was creating based upon the Marquis de Sade. During our meeting she explained exactly what she wanted from me and then handed me a copy of *Justine, or The Misfortunes of Virtue*. That evening I found myself deeply engrossed in the works of Sade ... thrilling stuff!

I worked on the music, carefully following the choreographic outline for Pietra's performance. I began by creating loose mood structures for each scene, which I would send to Pietra and we would discuss in detail. Then I moved onto the next stage, creating rhythms and sounds, and we continued like that until I had built a musical soundscape that both Pietra and I were happy with.

And then ...

… it was obvious that my collaboration with Pietra bothered Preljocaj! And so he got back in touch with me: 'We can do something even better!'. I was so happy, I said 'OK'. This time round, Angelin asked me to work on an entire ballet that was to be performed at the Pavillon Noir and at the Bolshoi in Moscow. There was no question of reworking an existing piece of classical music or a literary masterpiece. Angelin wanted me to create the music for a contemporary ballet from scratch, without a storyline, just taking the Apocalypse as the starting point. I was terrified.

I come from a place where a bare minimum is necessary to make people dance: a beat, a bass line, a 4-bar or 8-bar loop, etc. But in contemporary ballet, these conventions don't exist. Dancers can dance to a creaking sound, a single chord, white noise, any sound whatsoever. Dancers use discontinuities and incidences in a music score – however minute – as points of reference from which they work.

Without any sort of framework, I had no idea how to approach this project, which was suddenly looking more and more like a mountain to be climbed. Even though I begged Preljocaj for direction, something, however small, for me to get my teeth into so I could tell a story with the music, he was adamant, 'There is no structure!'. But because I was so desperate and kept badgering him he ended up by giving me a copy of the Apocalypse according to Saint John. Imagine this: me lying on a sunbed from dawn till dusk in the scorching midsummer heat reading Chapter 16 of the Bible: 'And I heard a great voice out of the temple saying to the seven angels, Go your ways, and pour out the vials of the wrath of God upon the earth.'!

It took time to get into it, but gradually I began to isolate certain elements of the Apocalypse, and from this I sketched a series of scenes: the beast, the seven bells, etc. Then I looked through my record collection and pulled out all the tracks that made reference to the Apocalypse: Aphrodite's Child's *666*, Pierre Henry's *Apocalypse de Jean* and used them as inspiration to create different mood structures. Not long after, I had dinner with Angelin who was still being very reticent, so I begged him to send me a list of 10 tracks that might inspire me when he got home. 'Don't think too hard about it. Take five minutes to do it and then send me the list!' He gave in and agreed to do it. Once I had the tracklist, I used it as a loose source of inspiration to compose my predominant themes stating that this track would accompany the beast, and that track the Seven Seals…

I regularly sent extracts of my 'work-in-progress' for Angelin to listen to. But, I soon learnt that Angelin was even more of a perfectionist than I am, which meant reworking each theme over and over and over again.

He pushed me hard and even got me to start from scratch if he wasn't satisfied. Once I had finished all the music, which, true to form, sometimes saw him changing elements of his choreography just minutes before a premiere, Preljocaj took my finished work and completely restructured it.

At the end of all this, *And Then One Thousand Years Of Peace* was a huge success. I came out of it mentally exhausted but enormously enriched and stimulated. By pushing me to the limit, Angelin had given me the opportunity to achieve more than I had ever accomplished before. It was 2007. I was enjoying having turned a huge corner in my career as an artist when I got tragic news that wiped the smile off my face.

Bizot was no more.

It was September 8. Jean-François Bizot was 63 years old. He had spent the last few years battling cancer and had written about his fight in a powerfully moving book *Un Moment de Faiblesse*. And then, that was that, my eccentric father figure was gone. My mad professor had done a runner. My nutty encyclopedia had upped and left us. And there we all were, stunned, left with our thoughts of what JFB had meant to us.

The story of Bizot's life is inextricably linked to the exploits of the independent music magazine *Actuel* and Radio Nova. *Actuel* had originally been a monthly magazine dedicated to free jazz, and Bizot took it over in May 1970. The aim was to make it the French answer to the free press movement that had appeared in the middle of the 60s in the US and the UK. (The free press movement was fiercely independent and uninhibited, giving priority to avant-garde subjects on urban subcultures, marginal art forms, drugs, free love, the environment, etc.) Then, Jean-François Bizot co-founded Radio Nova with Andrew Orr in May 1981, taking advantage of a situation where government control of the FM wavelength was being relaxed. Initially, Nova was dedicated to alternative rock, post-punk and electronic pop. But in 1985, the music programme changed radically to focus on 'world music', reflecting the mosaic of sounds coming out of Laos, Kingston or Oran that were currently popular in underground Paris. From then on, Radio Nova was out on its own. It defended a strongly held belief in the crossover of musical genres, taking an interest in everything, existing only to open up its listeners to the contours of shifting cultural spheres.

Jean-François was a great man in the true sense of the word. During the course of his extraordinary life, which he lived to the full, he hung out with legendary figures, the inventors of the avant-garde in the second half of the 20th century: Allen Ginsberg, Charles Bukowski, Fela Kuti, Brian Eno, Afrika Bambaataa, Robert Crumb, Abbie Hoffman, Timothy Leary, Joseph Kessel… He worked for the founder of *L'Express* magazine,

Jean-Jacques Servan-Schreiber, one of the last great press magnates in France. He launched *Actuel* together with Patrick Rambaud and Michel-Antoine Burnier, true disciples of the intellectually razor-sharp avant-garde. Thanks to Bizot, Radio Nova listeners discovered entire musical genres such as US hip-hop, afrobeat and raï. He invented the concept of 'world sound' and defended cultural and social diversity like no other. He provided opportunities for a whole generation of impassioned journalists and brilliant minds who would later become key players in the French media. People such as Bernard Zekri, Vincent Borel, Paul Moreira, Karl Zero, Ariel Wizman, Edouard Baer and Jamel Debbouze. He brought together under one roof the most cutting-edge DJs in Paris, DJ Gilb'R, Ivan Smagghe and Manu Le Malin, to name but a few. As a result, Jean-François enabled thousands of young people to discover key artistic trends and marginal concepts that, during the 80s and 90s (a period when culture was becoming more standardized at every level of the mainstream media), went against the tide.

In a previous chapter, I recounted the first time I ever met Bizot. But what I didn't mention was the extent to which Jean-François became a guiding light over the years, as well as a close friend and father figure. Regrettably, his funeral was limited to his immediate family. (Would Jean-François really have wanted it that way?) I consoled myself by remembering all the times he used to ring me, drunk, in the middle of the night to talk about the latest record by an artist that I had never heard of that he had come across in some place or another. Or the nights we spent setting the world to rights in his house in Saint Maur. That was an extraordinary place. It was a run-down chateau that he had turned into a sort of underground cavern, packed with books, records, paintings, photographs, souvenirs of his travels ... anything and everything! Every room was piled high with books, old magazines, tons of old faxes, records, CDs, cassettes he had brought back from Nigeria or Jamaica ... And in the middle of all this mess, Jean-François would dig out a record ('You have to listen to this!') or a novel ('You must read that!'), literally throwing them at me. This was his way of doing things, and what I loved so much about him.

Anyone who has ever spent time at the house in Saint Maur will tell you how mad and chaotic it was. It was a place of liberty, curiosity and exchange. People would hang out there (too many to name) and talk, discussing ideas all through the night, like the members of a secret society. Extraordinary encounters took place there that would never have happened anywhere else. Treasures were unearthed. Everyone was free to make themselves at home and do their own thing without Jean-François, or anyone else, ever questioning their behaviour. The basement was like a crypt, with a flotation tank watched over by a statue of the Virgin Mary. Next to this was a huge kitchen open to anyone and everyone at any time of day or night. To say that all sorts of weird and wonderful things went on in that kitchen is an understatement. Think about it! It was there that the first edition of *Actuel* magazine was put together hundreds of times over during sleepless nights when Jean-François would suddenly disappear to go out and do the rounds in the 'places where it's at'. It was there, too, that Jean-François could harangue his guests for hours on end with his hare-brained ideas. His invited audience included journalists, musicians, writers and madcap artists, all seduced by the 'work/leisure' mix or 'holiday/ reportage', which was the basis of JFB's vision of journalism (he was a passionate admirer of Albert London and Tom Wolfe). From the drawing room, or from the library with its 20-foot high walls, or from there in the kitchen, Jean-François intended to 'wake up sleepy France'. He was on a mission. This mighty giant of culture, who lived it up day and night for 63 years, was also a true gentleman. He may have been difficult to pin down, hard-nosed, intrusive and a seducer, he was also extremely kind-hearted. For example, one Sunday evening, when the Nova team were gathered together in the kitchen in his house for a 'crisis' meeting (the subject was how to reorganise the music programme), Bizot turned up three hours late. He had just got back from Madrid. Everyone was starving. With a big smile on his face, Bizot emptied out the contents of his rucksack onto the kitchen table. There was tons of chorizos and other cured meats. If we were going to be talking about the future of the radio through the night, then we might as well feast till dawn!

The announcement of Jean-François' sudden death was greeted with considerable emotion, to the extent that even those people who at one time or another had been at odds with his opinions (and there were quite a few) put their differences to one side. His death also marked the end of a period when media moguls were still trailblazers, visionaries and pioneers, capable of 'matching the contours of (their) dream', as Bernard Kouchner, a pioneer of *Actuel*, said. These words ring so true. Especially when you take into account the current deathly situation, where big business and investment bankers are helping themselves to huge slices of cultural media. To do what? Nothing for the most part, except to suck the life out of them. I suppose it's ok for some people for whom culture is a business, just like any other. And I suppose it's ok for some people whose vision is limited to the concept that 'profit shall be the decider'.

In his last few years, Jean-François Bizot had looked on these changes in French media with both discomfort and dislike. Discomfort because, in order to survive, Radio Nova had to make concessions – including accepting revenue from advertising, audience figures, and hiring a managing director to control the finances. And he disliked all of it – these practices, and the bureaucrats that represented exactly what JFB had always deeply despised and fought against. I can still remember him ranting about the bureaucrats in the press. He went to see them with new ideas that needed financing and they stared back at him with absolutely no idea of what this one man had accomplished in his life, simply judging him on his dishevelled appearance, before replying 'no' to his project. But Jean-François had no choice anymore. He was forced into communicating with these 'young upstarts' as he called them. Once JFB's money had run out, the radio was financially weak, and had no alternative but to embrace the laws of the business or die.

I wonder if Jean-François still recognised his radio station in the last few months of his life? All I know is, on the day that the guys from Underground Resistance and I decided to 'ambush' Nova, JFB was thrilled: 'Finally, anarchy!'. You could say that again ...

It was May 2003. I had walked out of Nova a year before. That night, the guys from Underground Resistance were playing at the Rex. I went to pick up Mad Mike, Juan Atkins, Suburban Nights and Buzz Goree from Charles de Gaulle airport. Once everyone was piled into the car we headed into the centre of Paris, where we soon found ourselves stuck in traffic. I switched on Radio Nova and it was playing golden oldies. Mike asked me if I still had my show on Nova. I told him the whole story that led to my walking out. And then I had an idea. 'Hey guys, what do you think about dropping by? We could take over the airwaves ... Are you up for it?' Mike gave me his warrior smile. I shouted to the driver, 'Take us to Bastille.'

I made a quick phone call to Aline Afanoukoé, who was live on air, to warn her that we were on our way. The guys from Underground Resistance and I stormed into the Nova building and headed straight up to the studios, locked ourselves in and hijacked the airwaves. I took the opportunity to explain to the listeners why I had left Nova after 12 years of dedicated service. Meanwhile, Aline was completely over-excited, 'Fuck, Mad Miiiike!!!! My brother! The house is yours boys!' What happened next? We stayed on air until 8pm; the UR crew took it in turns to play records that weren't exactly 'formatted' for the prime-time slot. And, of course, we talked about music. We also spoke about the importance of the media and the responsibility they have in supporting the artistic avant-garde. On the other side of the glass studio window, a dozen or so people had gathered, their mouths gaping in disbelief. Among them was Jean-François Bizot, with a huge grin on his face, loving every moment.

Just like me, he knew that for a little more than two hours his radio had become Nova once again.

And then that was that: a few months later Jean-François died and a hollow emptiness took hold. My wife and I both shared the same feeling of loss. As if we had lost a member of our family. We were in mourning. There were many phone calls, particularly to other Nova people – we reminisced about Jean-François' exploits. His priceless nocturnal escapades when in the same night he could go to a music hall in Nogent, go to dance in a Caribbean nightclub in the suburbs, go and drink in a Latino club, go and 'take stock', as he used to say, in a techno club in the centre of Paris, before 'finishing up' in some bizarre place in deepest darkest Paris. Bizot, who said 'no' to François Mitterrand. Bizot, who turned up in Lagos, one of the most dangerous cities in the world, on his own to go to Fela Kuti's 'Shrine' club (where white people were few and far between). JFB, squatting in the headquarters of the Jamaican Football Federation, determined that their footballers should wear shirts stamped with the Radio Nova logo during the 1998 World Cup … anything to keep hold of him a bit longer and keep his memory alive. But sometimes at night it would hit me. I'd wake up at three or four in the morning, thinking about him. That had been the time of night when he used to call, mumbling down the phone, 'Laurent, I've been thinking …' Then an hour or so later, just before he hung up, 'Hey, you know I love you, don't you? You know that?'

I missed him.

Jean-François' death marked the beginning of my loss of bearings career-wise. Electroclash was dying out and the domination of minimal techno was coming to an end, and then three emblematic clubs closed in quick succession. The first was the Pulp, which closed in May 2007. The council decided to buy back the property, and this just happened to coincide with the start of Nicholas Sarkozy's presidency. Over the past 10 years, the Pulp had been a breath of fresh air on the Paris nightlife scene, but they had come to the end of their lease agreement. The building was up for sale, and the club, which had single-handedly shaken Paris out of a slumber, closed. I felt the loss.

And I was inconsolable when the Yellow in Japan, in my opinion the best club in the world, ever, also closed the following summer. Again, the reason given was something about a property deal but, this time round, it wasn't only a club that I had adored for the past 12 years that was closing; it was becoming apparent that this was the end of an era.

Although I wasn't working until Friday, on the Thursday night I was already at the club. Fumiya Tanaka was playing all night. I had a confused discussion with the owners of the club. They were adamant; the club would close on Sunday at midday. I didn't say a word, but I planned in my head to stay behind the decks of the Yellow for as long as physically possible. On Friday night, I played a marathon set from midnight till midday on Saturday, when I handed over to François Kevorkian who, in turn, was supposed to play right through till 6am on Sunday morning. Then Joe Claussell, Danny Krivit and I were to join him to bring the club to a close.

Just a few words about François Kevorkian, as it is crucial to understand him to continue this story. So let me introduce the 'Mr Universe of Disco'. Kevorkian was in New York in the 70s, and lived through all the wild parties at Paradise Garage and Studio 54, the legendary clubs and birthplace of modern club culture. He was signed to the legendary disco label, Prelude, and hung out with the great DJ Larry Levan, while working with most of the biggest names in American disco. Few other artists have managed as well as François to consistently take the right turns in their career. As a result, he has always been perfectly placed at the heart of key movements in musical history. He has been involved in disco, house, techno, then later on drum 'n' bass and dubstep, always upholding his exemplary values. He has never copied anyone. On the contrary, he has always been a pioneer. As a DJ, producer, remixer or label boss (Wave), his attitude has always been incredibly gentlemanly, with great honesty and generosity. This, he says, he owes to his chosen city, New York, 'the mirror of who I am.'

Memoirs of a tireless music lover …

FRANÇOIS KEVORKIAN:

'I arrived in New York in September 1975 at the age of 21. Most of the music I loved came from New York – Miles Davis, Herbie Hancock, jazz, funk – so I thought it would be worth my while going to New York to see what was going on and to try and make it as a drummer. But I became quickly disillusioned. Every audition I went to was so competitive at least 150 other drummers had got there before me …

'At the time, New York was on the verge of financial collapse and the south side of Manhattan was in a serious state of neglect, but everyone hung out there because it was *the* place for music in the US. The disco boom was already up and running. It wasn't yet the sophisticated style of disco that would become so popular after the release of *Saturday Night Fever*. Up until 1976–77, disco was an underground phenomenon, reserved mainly for a black, gay crowd in the clubs in downtown Manhattan: David Mancuso's Loft, Crisco Disco, Flamingo and Galaxy

▶ Playlist

NYC DISCO CLASSICS

The Strikers
Body Music

War
City Country City

Double Exposure
Ten Per Cent

Roy Ayers
Running Away

Tom Browne
Funkin' For Jamaica

Loleatta Holloway
Hit And Run

Carl Bean
I Was Born This Way

Inner Life
Ain't No Mountain High Enough

Skyy
Skyy Zoo

Katmandu
The Break

Nick Straker Band
A Little Bit Of Jazz

Unlimited Touch
I Heard Music In The Street

Hamilton Bohannon
Let's Start To Dance

Chic
Chic Cheer

21. These clubs never advertised. They targeted a very specific audience. The alternative was the more commercial clubs situated uptown for the most part, in mob territory: The Sanctuary in the late 1960s and then, later, Studio 54.

'As competition among musicians was really intense, I decided to audition for a job as a DJ. I had already been a DJ in Strasbourg. But my job back then wasn't to make people dance, it was to keep them drinking at the bar! In New York, becoming a DJ was for me a way to earn enough money to pay for a roof over my head and have enough left over to eat. I watched how others did it. It didn't look that hard. As I had studied the piano and the guitar, as well as being a drummer, I understood how tracks were structured. I decided to give it a go and was offered one of my first DJ residencies at the Sesame Street Club. I played music that was popular at the time, such as Marvin Gaye and Salsoul Orchestra, things that were being played on the radio...

'There was a very strong connection between clubs and radio stations back then. Stations like WBNS, a black radio station in New York, were in tune with what was being played in the clubs. If a track was big in the clubs, you were guaranteed to hear it on the radio.

'In the summer of 1977, I played my first real DJ set while the Gallery, the other legendary club in New York alongside the Loft, was closing down. A club culture was building up around disco. And, the following year, disco exploded. Of all the clubs in New York, the Paradise Garage is the one that best summed up the New York vibe.

'The Paradise Garage was a garage situated on the first floor of a commercial building that Michael Brody and Mel Cheren rented out totally legally. It was one of the biggest clubs in Manhattan, holding up to 3,000 people. The club's policy was to serve the community before making profit, which was the polar opposite of the majority of clubs in New York at the time, where you always had the owner on your back or the boss to battle. The Paradise Garage was about people. It was a members-only club and, to become a member, you had to know the right people. Every weekend, that part of King Street was crawling. Hundreds of people crowded in front of the door at number 84, worrying about whether or not they were going to get in. Friday night was reserved for a straight crowd. Saturday was gay. The Saturday night members were allowed in on Friday but not the other way round. And once you were inside, you were free to do whatever you liked. Completely free. There was no one telling you what you could and could not do. The black community regarded the club as a refuge from the real world. Outside, they were still subject to discrimination but inside the club they could belong.

For all of these reasons, the Paradise Garage was a very special place. It had the best crowd. The best sound system. Not to mention the best DJ, Larry Levan.

'The Paradise Garage was his club. Larry had all the qualities you could hope for. He was talented, intuitive, generous and charismatic. He was one in a million. He had a very personal relationship with music and used music to create a special relationship with his public, to the point that every single person on the dance floor thought that the records Larry played were specially chosen with them in mind. Artists, producers and label reps regularly came down to the club to give Larry promos, months before their official release date. When Larry played a track, you could be sure that it would become a hit!

'At the beginning of the 80s, this honeymoon period came to an abrupt end with the arrival of AIDS. Every week I learned that a friend, or someone I had spent good times with, had died. Every week! It was a scourge. And it was made even worse by the fact that not only did the city not respond to this crisis in the community but, also, in most people's minds, AIDS was a "gay disease". The New York club scene was now defined by the "before" and "after" AIDS eras.

'It was around that time that I stopped DJ-ing to start producing music. I had been doing more and more studio work over the past few years, to the point that I was no longer really following all the music that was being released. I didn't want to end up playing tracks that were out of date. More and more people were asking me to work with them as a music producer, and I didn't want to pass up the chance.

'Some time after the release of Planet Rock by Afrika Bambaataa, everyone was rushing out to buy the new technology and new machines which soon replaced live musicians. Experienced session musicians gradually started disappearing from recording studios and their wealth of knowledge, harnessed by bands such as MFSB or Earth, Wind & Fire, was lost. The public soon got used to this new music made by people who were only able to program it, never play it, and drum machines became the norm.

'When I took up DJ-ing again, about 10 years later, the scene had completely changed. Before, a DJ was resident in a club. He never travelled, or hardly ever. He existed because of his talent. Suddenly, it was the complete opposite. DJs were travelling all over, and didn't exist because of their talent, but because they had a good PR person. The sense of sharing that was prevalent in the 70s club scene in New York no longer existed. Promoters were putting so much money on the table to make sure a DJ would turn up, that they wanted to make sure people saw him. That's

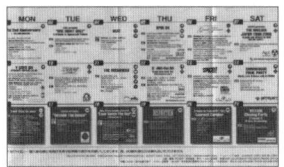

when individual DJs found themselves playing records perched up on a stage, in a sea of lights, with only two hours to capture the public's attention. From then on, you could no longer take your time to slowly build an atmosphere. You had to give it all at once! The public's attitude had changed, too. People seemed to know what they were going to like or not about a DJ, before the DJ had even played his first record ... Deep down, though, nothing much has changed for me. I still intend to have fun and touch people with inspirational music ... '

... Like at the closing party at Yellow, where Kevorkian worked his same old magic, sending everyone in the club deep into a mystical, meditative and profoundly emotional state.

Imagine the scene: Danny Krivit, Joe Claussell, François and I all glued to the decks, taking it in turn to play two records each, never once looking at the time. Six hours left. We were at fever pitch, dancing behind the decks, drifting in and out of reality. I can see us all choosing our all-time favourite tracks, consulting one another, being aware of each other's needs. I can see us united in one and the same cause – to nurture and preserve the incredibly special atmosphere there that night.

People in the crowd came up to touch us, to thank us, and we thanked them back. We played them some stunning music, paying extra special attention to the timing and to each mix as if striving for perfection. A quick look up. From one minute to the next, people in the crowd went from tears streaming down their faces to ecstasy. It was quite often overwhelming. It felt like we were in a state of grace. We allowed our emotions to take over, our minds to drift and tears to well up in our eyes. I don't know how many times I cried that night.

By midday on Sunday, Joe Claussell and Danny Krivit had abandoned ship. They were exhausted, but I had no intention of stopping. I had been awake for 48 hours but I wasn't flagging. I was buzzing. I was a ball of energy, sporting a t-shirt from the film *Tontons Flingueurs* (Monsieur Gangster). And that was that! I was there to 'shoot down' the crowd! Kevorkian was in a similar frame of mind. So with a knowing look, we carried on playing. Disorganized Corruption by the Lower East Side Pipes, I Exist Because Of You (Dixon mix) by Henrik Schwarz, Samurai by Jazztronik and Goodnight Tonight by Wings. Instead of trying to stop us, the people who worked at Yellow let us carry on, smiling and bringing us Umeshu drinks from time to time.

We played all through the night. At 7am on the Monday morning, Kevorkian played Miles Davis' Kind Of Blue and, at the end of the track, in an almost religious silence, he addressed the crowd in fluent Japanese. I didn't understand a word he was saying, but I didn't need to. I knew. With everyone in the club in tears, a Buddhist death chant played over the speakers, giving me goose bumps. I took François to one side, 'Hey, we can't finish off like that!'. He smiled and politely gestured to me to take to the decks. And we started playing music again, together as one, tireless, until … 3 o'clock that afternoon!

The emotional experience I underwent that weekend at Yellow was among the most powerful I have ever experienced in my career. I carried those feelings with me all the way back to France. I had said goodbye to my biggest love in Japan and was shifting between feelings of profound sadness and rushes of unadulterated joy. When I got back home, more bad news was waiting for me – the End, my spiritual home in London, was closing for good. That was another very emotional night for me. Once again, one of my most solid points of reference had disappeared. It was the end of a cycle. It was then that I decided I no longer wanted to play at the closure of clubs. Instead I elected to christen new clubs, like El Raw in Barcelona.

After this period of decline, I felt that a new era was beginning where it was time to build something new. But, what I didn't know then was that another kind of mourning was to come, just around the corner.

greed

We saw it coming. Evidently we were wary right from the start, trying to prevent what was happening, drafting new working models. But as we struggled to react quickly enough to the rapid changes, which from one month to the next, transformed the music business profoundly, our vessel began to list and water began to seep in. And then one day that was it. We had tried our best to ride the wave of the digital revolution but its force was too powerful. We had reached the point of no return.

In 2008, F Communications was celebrating its 14th anniversary. The label had experienced several transformations throughout its history. It will always remain inherently linked to the struggle for the recognition of techno and electronic music in France. With over 270 releases, F Comm had some very big successes. The label contributed to the discovery of some amazing artists who, over the years, have become reference points in the international world of dance music. In its final months, aside from my live CD *Public Outburst*, F Comm also released new albums from Vista Le Vie, Jori Hulkkonen, Mr Oizo, Aqua Bassino and Gong Gong. They were all great albums. Albums we loved. But they didn't sell as many as we hoped they would. When it came down to it, 'real' records were no longer selling at all …

In a short space of time, digital had taken over, in the recording studio through to distribution. In the beginning of the 2000s, peer-to-peer platforms (P2P) were built on the ashes of Napster, and new forms of digital file exchanges appeared, all with the central concept of being free of charge.

In 1999, if you wanted a record you had to go to a specialist record shop or to a large chain such as Fnac or Virgin Megastore to buy it. In Paris, fans of Chicago house or Detroit techno traipsed to Saul Russo's record shop, Bonus Beat on rue Keller. Fans of German techno only had to go one street further to TSF, and then there was Rough Trade for people looking for indie music. The people working in these specialist shops held the power. They were walking encyclopedias of music and were good at helping people navigate their way through the jungle of new releases as well as back catalogues. In the mid-90s, the record shop salesman in the Bastille dealt in 'big thrills' while the Fnac on Avenue Wagram also stocked an amazing selection of electronic music.

Behind the scenes, managing a record shop, however small, is a nightmare. I can vouch for this personally as I too opened a record shop, USA Import on rue des Tournelles, with two business partners. One of them oversaw this shop and two more in Lille and Belgium, while the other partner acted as manager. The latter, a very nice guy as it happened,

spent two years using the basement in the Paris shop as his personal darkroom, and the company cheque book to wine and dine his many lovers. Meanwhile, I was driving to England every month with a wad of cash in my pocket to buy all the latest releases and take them back to France with me. It goes without saying that I was never reimbursed all the money I spent on records. And so, one day, the shit hit the fan. We were too young, a bit naïve and, above all, far too amateurish to run a record shop. USA Import didn't make it to its second birthday. Nevertheless, those years were fun. It was great having all the DJs from Paris, as well as visiting techno legends such as Jeff Mills and Derrick May, hang out at the store. But those brief moments of happiness were not enough to distract us from the boring day-to-day shit that we had to deal with, as all record shops have to. This involved making regular trips to distribution warehouses to pick out the records we wanted to sell. Then we had to stock the shelves and listen to them. There was always a stock of records that remained unsold and had to be returned. And the profits? Never anything much. But, for the majority of record shops, profit wasn't their motivation. They were true music lovers, prepared to put up with complicated logistics and small profits. Most of them were in the game to share their love of music. They knew that, for music fans, spending hours going through their record bins meant that each record they bought was a personal investment, as much in time as in money.

Gil Scott Heron wrote an interesting piece in the booklet accompanying the release of his 2010 album *I'm New Here* on how to get the best listening experience: 'There is a proper procedure for taking advantage of any investment. Music, for example. Buying a CD is an investment. To get the maximum you must: Listen to it for the first time under optimal conditions. Not in your car or on a portable player through a headset. Take it home. Get rid of all distractions (even her or him). Turn off your cell phone. Turn off everything that rings or beeps or rattles or whistles. Make yourself comfortable. Play your CD. Listen all the way through. Think about what you got. Think about who would appreciate this investment. Decide if there is someone to share this with. Turn it on again. Enjoy yourself.' Ten or twenty years ago, this approach was familiar to music fans who spent their lives in record shops. Back home, they all shared the special feeling of finally owning THAT record, which held a certain magic that was just waiting to be tapped.

I have already spoken about my weekly two-hour pilgrimage from my house in the suburbs to the record shop on the Champs Elysées when I was a teenager. Once, when I was about fourteen, I paid 120 francs (the equivalent of 20 euros) for an import by the funk band SKYY. It was a huge amount of money back then. On my way home, I must have read the sleeve notes at least 30 times. I was counting down the minutes until I would be able to discover the music within. I must have listened to that record a good 100 times over ever since that day and the pleasure I get from listening to it remains the same. Over the years, I have developed an almost filial relationship with that album. Thirty years after buying it, I even sampled it for my track, No Music, No Life, in honour of a time that no longer exists, when hunting for music was a noble pursuit.

So, at the end of the 90s, there was a drastic change in the music industry as we knew it. Within a few months, the number of records being released soared. Distributors, records shops and DJs found themselves drowning in content. As a consequence, the music business experienced its first ever loss of impetus. There had never been so much music on the market, yet the number of customers remained the same. And while this was going on, the record buyer's spending budget was being eaten into with the arrival of mobile phones and the first internet subscriptions. That is when Napster first appeared, the peer-to-peer file sharing service, and thousands of tracks encoded in MP3 format were freely exchanged over the internet.

Two years after it was launched, Napster was forced to cease operations for copyright infringement following a decision by the US justice system. The music industry thought that this was the end of it. Little did they know. In the months that followed, dozens of copycat peer-to-peer file-sharing platforms appeared on the internet: BitTorrent, Limewire, KaZaA to name but a few. Every day millions of MP3 audio files were being exchanged over the internet for free.

Simultaneously, broadband was becoming widely available, sales of MP3 players were rocketing, and a new range of computers was beginning to appear on the market that simplified internet access. Anyone and everyone could now download music for free and store an entire record collection on a hard disk or an iPod. And all in one click!

The major record companies tried to get in on the game and chose to develop their own downloading platforms. They refused to make their releases available on other music websites, jealously guarding their back catalogues. However, internet users got fed up with not being able to find the music they were looking for on legal online music stores, and turned in their droves to file-sharing peer-to-peer websites. By 2003–04, the majority of majors finally decided to make their catalogues available on Apple's iTunes store, but, by then, internet music piracy was out of control. Out of their depth, the music business began screaming, 'Peer to peer is piracy!'

Gradually, record shops began to disappear. Vinyl became rare, too expensive to press. The CD sales market shrunk back drastically and eventually collapsed in 2007. By then, selling a record had become a nightmare. Why would anyone want to buy a CD when you could get someone to give you a digital copy for free? And why spend 20 euros on an album when you could buy a digital track on iTunes for 99 cents?

The majors were faced with the same dilemma as independent labels, the question of survival. How could a label survive when it had become impossible to win over a new breed of consumer who had grown up with the internet and for whom getting music for free was taken for granted? In around 2005, labels tried to educate the music-buying public as to why CDs cost so much – in short, illegal downloading was putting an already fragile economy in danger – but no one was interested. It was the clash of two different ideologies. On the one hand, the labels were trying to cling onto an out-dated business model, and on the other, internet users didn't see why they should have to pay for something when they could get it for free.

Like so many other independent labels, my record label, F Communications, was unable to fight back. We knew the day was fast approaching when we were going to have to wind down the label and put it to rest. And that day came. We had to shut up shop, only temporarily perhaps, but still we had to close.

Sometimes, I like to spend a couple of hours locked away in the little room in my courtyard where the bulk of my record collection is housed. I stopped counting years ago, but there must be several thousand records in there, all neatly arranged on row upon row of shelves. I love it in there. When my son was little, he used to come with me sometimes. We would stare at the wall-to-wall records and, at some point, I would invariably say, 'One day, all this will be yours.' And he would look at me in surprise and say, 'What? All that?!'

My record room is now bursting at the seams. I have resorted to making piles of records on the floor, which makes moving around rather awkward. Whenever I have spare time, I spend an hour or so putting records away, taking them out again, arranging them in order and re-arranging them. I pick out the odd one for PBB or choose an album that I haven't listened to in ages and take them into my sitting room to play on the turntable for the next few days. This record room is my Tower of Babel. It holds my musical memory. Beyond being my record collection, it also represents a world gone by, but I take great care to look after it and keep it alive. Locking myself away gives me the freedom to meditate on the not-too-distant past – when looking for, finding and owning a record was considered an honourable pursuit. A time when going into an independent record shop, or even HMV or Virgin Megastore, meant accepting advice from a sales assistant whose job was to sell records. Since then, these stores have all closed down and been replaced by online music stores. There's no advice available, no expertise, just lists of the latest releases. Faced with this unfathomable sea of music, it's every man for himself and one has to try not to drown. Or, at least, try not to lose heart…

Locking myself away in this small but incredibly meaningful room full of records is my way of reliving this world gone by. In which a collection of records was synonymous with an appetite for culture. One day, I wonder whether all those hard drives packed full of thousands of MP3 files will hold the same affection as my records?

Buenos Aires, spring 2007. I met up for a drink with Stuart MacMillan and Orde Meikle from the Scottish group, Slam. We have known each other for years, regularly meeting up with each other at the Arches in Glasgow where the two founders of the dance music label, Soma Records, have their DJ residency. We had a couple of drinks and the conversation got round to the main preoccupation burdening every DJ: the ever-increasing amount of music promos that we are receiving over the internet each day. 'And, there are two of us!', said Stuart. 'We share the task. You must be swamped!' Tell me about it!

I was drowning…

For, as MP3 gradually replaced vinyl and CD, the DJ's work tools were changing, too. In around 2001, the first Pioneer CD turntables (the CDJ) began to appear in clubs. Their functions were rigorously modelled on the legendary Technics SL-1200: a virtual rotating platter, pitch control, easy handling, great precision, etc. It was undeniably a very useful technological revolution. It marked the end of an era when DJs would lug around heavy record boxes and have permanent backache. This change in working practice, together with receiving music over the internet, meant that the majority of DJs embraced digital. The advantages were phenomenal. Just imagine: I'm in my studio. It's 5pm. I've just finished making a new track. I send it via the internet to several DJ friends so they can test it out that same night in Tokyo, Paris or Chicago. And all that free of charge and without the need for middlemen. In the past, this freedom of movement was the stuff of dreams. Suddenly, it had become the norm.

While the digital phenomenon was still coming together, I remember a handful of vinyl addicts predicting digital Apocalypse, 'Watch out man! MP3 will enslave you!' Back then, nobody took these warnings very seriously. But, by 2007, most DJs, including me, knew that was exactly what had happened...

The reasons why the volume of music promos increased were simple. In the past, if you wanted to send your track out to all the DJs, it would cost a fortune in postage. Then, overnight, distributing music digitally cost nothing. And, because of the technology, producing records had become a hobby that anyone could have a go at if they could afford a computer and a couple of plug-ins.

In the space of a few years, studios full of machines that had been instrumental in 1990s dance music production had vanished and been replaced by computer software that could imitate their sound. For me, these machines had a certain mysterious and welcoming presence. Even the most basic studio was kitted out with very expensive equipment. However, a simple computer jammed full of plug-ins soon sufficed. And, when you listen to the records made with this, no one would ever know that you didn't own a real Juno-106 or a Roland 909, just a simple 'add-on program' that contains over 3,000 different sounds.

Composing music became more like doing an intricate puzzle; a game that anyone could play. All you really had to do was to look on the internet, for example on the leading website Native Instruments, to find new plug-ins and build up an extensive sound bank. Half of them are available to download for free. Anyone could dive in and have fun composing a track. Whether it was good or not was a different matter. And whether a DJ would play it or not was another. In this new music democracy, novice producers had the freedom to send their music direct to their favourite DJs. And why shouldn't they? So MP3 files arrived each day in my inbox by the thousands. Even the record labels and PR companies no longer bothered to select what they sent to whom.

As a consequence, the couple of hours of daily listening sessions that made up part of a DJ's daily routine had turned into tedious whole days of trawling through new promos. Not only had listening to new music become a burden, but it had also had a huge impact on the way DJs tour.

Waiting for a flight at the airport now equated to being glued to my computer with my headphones on in order to keep on top of the huge number of MP3 promos I'd receive every day. Several thousand releases a week! I didn't have the luxury of time anymore. I had to quickly listen, rate the track, and send my feedback straight back to the PR company. A quick word about PR companies. There are now hundreds of them all over the world and their job is to get DJs to comment on their track and report back to the record label. And it's a battleground! As all these companies are trying to find the best system for DJs to be able to listen to music quickly and efficiently.

But I still spent hours each week on my laptop listening to tons of music, sorting tracks into those to keep for my DJ sets, PBB or my radio show, and binning the rest. The time I spent ate away at the time I had for other things, like my family life or making music in the studio. Several DJs I know hired assistants to help out with this task, but I couldn't see how a third party could know which tracks inspired me. So I had no other choice but to get on with it, even though sometimes it felt like a chore – to the point that, when I travelled, I no longer did anything else – from the airport lounge, to the plane, even to my hotel room, I downloaded, listened and reacted. When finally I get to the end … it's not finished! I still had to re-listen several times to each track I downloaded to memorise them before transferring them onto memory sticks. And the next day it's the same all over again. I did this every day. Not to mention the time I spent on Soundcloud, a sort of musician's Facebook where everyone can upload music, listen and download other people's tracks. It was unbelievably time-consuming. And what for? I calculated that, for every 100 tracks I received and listened to, probably only five or six of them caught my attention. Five or six tracks out of a whole day's listening … that's not much reward!

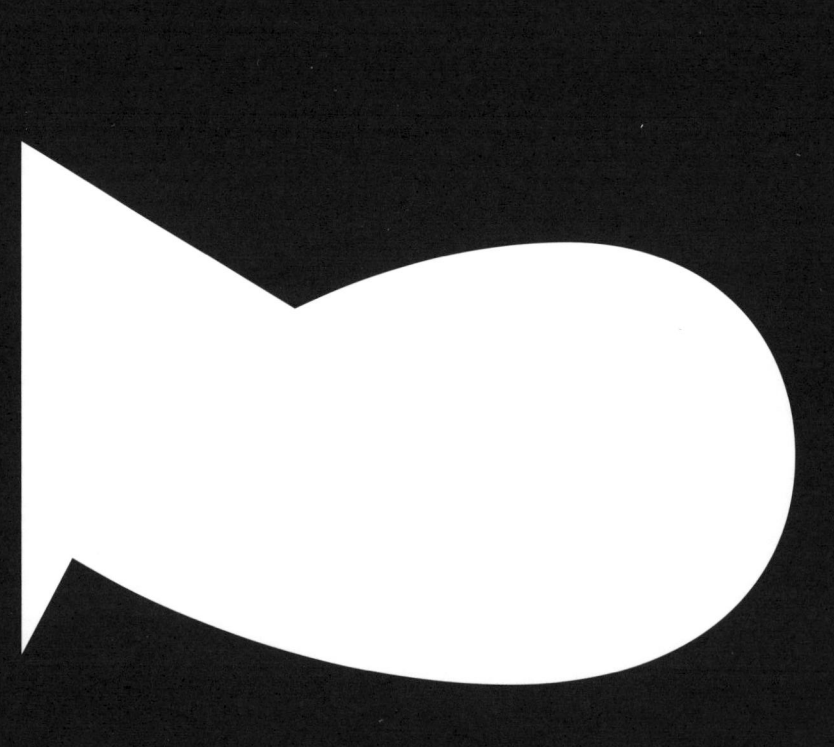

cycles d'oppositions

Late one afternoon at a festival in France in 2012, a young girl in her early 20s came up to me. She had just heard Crispy Bacon for the first time, and something was bothering her, 'Your track's cool, but when's it going to really kick off?' At first, I didn't understand her question, so I got her to repeat it. 'It's really long. Why doesn't it kick off sooner?' I stared at her in amazement.

The following day at another festival somewhere in Europe, as I was preparing my gear to go on, two guys were performing on stage. The techno they were playing was so crude that no DJ would have dared play it 10 years earlier; they would have been laughed off stage. As their set was coming to a close, one of them stage-dived into the frenzied crowd while the other guy, a bottle of champagne in hand, threw t-shirts into the crowd with the group's logo. When I took to the decks, a third of the room left and I struggled to keep the attention of those who remained.

Later that week, I came across the same thing in Rome, Barcelona and London. The dance floor was full of 18-year-old kids. I watched them dancing, drinking, chatting with their friends, using their phones to film, to tweet, to send text messages, to check Facebook and to identify tracks via Shazam. All at the same time. And then, I played a track, which apparently hit the spot and they came racing over to the DJ booth and started banging on the window, whooping with joy. Then, the next minute they were disinterested, as if overcome by a wave of apathy. This happened over and over again…

This change was taking place just as I was turning 40. I didn't give a monkey's about my age, but after the successive closures of Yellow, the End and F Communications, I found myself in a period of great uncertainty. I was afraid of the moment when, without realizing it, I would cross the line and no longer relate to the audience. Or worse! Wake up one day to the realisation that I was a 'has-been'. A worn-out old DJ, who people found endearing for nostalgic reasons, representing a time long ago when techno was exciting and living in the present. 'How to grow old gracefully?' was the question I couldn't stop asking myself.

I watched with great unease what was going on around me. Whereas, at the end of the 1980s, techno was very cutting-edge, this was no longer the case. The original techno was no longer in tune with modern thinking. Its aesthetic, its message and its politics were out-dated. Techno had gone all out into battle and won. It now had a legitimate place in the history of pop culture, in the same way as jazz, rock 'n' roll and hip-hop. It was now part of the musical landscape and was no more subversive or ground-breaking than punk.

At the end of the 90s, when techno was at its height, an unprecedented dumbing down of culture took place, and even minor artistic movements found themselves sucked in, chewed up, spat out and commercialised on a grand scale. The likelihood of a cutting-edge artistic underground forming in the shadows before going out to find a wider audience simply no longer existed. The internet meant that each cultural innovation was noticed instantly, sucked dry, then delivered to the masses in a diluted form that could be consumed by the greatest number. So, in these harsh commercial conditions, with no means to drive forward an ideal or be subversive, electronic music became a commodity to trade just like any other.

This state of affairs coincided with the emergence of a new generation who had grown up with the internet and for whom instant gratification was paramount. They wanted everything 'now'. The DJs and producers of my generation had come from a place where a DJ's set or even a single track were built over time, and many of them often found themselves at a loss as to how to give the millennial kids what they wanted. Many decided to throw in the towel; others didn't have any choice in the matter. I also was seriously considering putting an end to my DJ career, but New Year's Eve 2005, spent in London with François Kevorkian, persuaded me to rethink things.

The night didn't get off to a great start. I didn't know François K very well. When I arrived at the club in Kings Cross that afternoon for my sound check, I saw him with his beard, half-moon glasses and sandals driving the sound engineer mad with technical demands. Fascinated, I stood watching and began to wonder whether, in time, all artists become obstinate, obsessive about detail and exhausted by an incalculable number of nights spent DJ-ing. Of course, I was completely wrong about him. In reality, François K was calm, serious and very methodical. But, right then, I was worried about having to share the decks with a guy that I had labelled a 'turntable veteran'.

Six hours later, however, I was blown away. The guy in front of me was a tireless music lover, passionate about DJ-ing, and, above all, had the most incredible energy. Kevorkian was amazing to watch. He physically pulsated. Everything he played was exciting, in tune with the crowd and resolutely modern. At nearly 60, he was still an artist who was passionate about his music. It was a real wake-up call. It was there and then that it dawned on me that being a DJ has got nothing to do with your age, it's all about the passion inside of you. When music filters down to your core, as it does with François, you can continue DJ-ing to the end of time.

From that night on, François and I became close friends. Having spent time with him, talking for hours on end and playing records together, I came to see him as a sort of role model as much because of his diverse taste in music as for the passion that he has held on to. 'So what if these guys on the dance floor were young enough to be my kids, let's invent new ways to speak to them!' is a rather crude summary of where François' philosophy lies, but there is so much greatness in it, and it was one of the fine lessons I learnt from him that night we spent DJ-ing together in London.

That party triggered something inside me and changed my way of thinking overnight. I suddenly realised that I would never be out-dated or an old-timer or a has-been as long as I remained true. To move forward, I needed to understand the behaviour and expectations of this new generation of clubgoers. I wanted to know why this generation that produced dozens of really talented new artists also spawned dozens of others whose music was not to my taste but massively popular.

The truth is, there has always been a divide that separates the older generation from the younger one. The younger generation's culture and behaviour develops in reaction to that of their elders. To say that my generation doesn't understand the younger ones is so clichéd because it was the same in the 60s when the Flower Power generation challenged the British establishment, or the US government over the Vietnam War. And it was the same with my generation when we first got involved in dance music. No one from my parents' era could begin to imagine what we were experiencing. Raves and clubs were nothing like anything they had known growing up. If I try for a moment to put myself in their shoes, I don't know what I would have made of the arrival of punk, hip-hop or acid-house.

That is how it goes. Each generation must challenge its predecessor on their politics, culture, sexuality, etc. And from the outset, a rift appears between these two worlds, and a power struggle ensues. The outcome is always the same: the younger generation are scrutinised until they end up falling into line and their own innovations (aesthetic, musical, etc.) are swallowed up and regurgitated by the market. In turn, these young people become adults. As they 'officially' gain power, a new younger generation appears. And the same scenario is played out all over again…

Even though I am surrounded by a younger generation every weekend, we inhabit very different worlds. It makes sense that we don't appreciate the same music, or listen to it in the same way, or have the same idea of nightlife. But I know it's up to me to adapt and not them.

To 'adapt' is the key in my line of work. To reach out and touch those kids, I first have to understand what they want and what they are ready to hear.

▶ Playlist
FRANÇOIS KEVORKIAN (PRODUCER / SOUND ENGINEER)
Midnight Oil
Species Deceases

Loleatta Holloway
Strong Enough

U Roy
Rootsman

Kraftwerk
Electric Café

Erasure
Erasure

Depeche Mode
Violator

It goes without saying that their attachment to mass consumerism and their tendency to champion all that is fast and free of charge baffles me. But, aside from all this, their ability to adapt amazes me. People born in the 1990s and later have grown up in a world where immediacy rules. They crave control. They have an insatiable appetite for life. Their enthusiasm drives their ideas. Nevertheless, these qualities also have a down side. Like the culture in which they have grown up, their longing to be instantly gratified means that contemplating or surrendering to music is hard. How can you be swept away if you're tweeting, taking photos, filming, updating your Facebook status and dancing all at the same time?

Whenever I find myself playing to a young crowd, I always know I have to try much harder and tell my story differently. I look for a chink in their armour, which will enable me to hook them in and get them to follow me. Trying to win them over at any cost isn't the right strategy. Compromising in the hope of winning their loyalty is destined for failure. The fact is, the millennial generation doesn't regard music in the same way as I do, and older DJs have to accept this reality. Saying this, there are many areas of common ground that exist between the artists of my generation and later generations. Firstly, they are incredibly interested in the past. Even though Detroit ceased to produce anything very exciting in the 21st century, a younger crowd perfectly integrated Detroit's techno heritage into their music. The same goes for Chicago house, where there is now a street called 'Frankie Knuckles Lane'. And the underground is forever being redefined.

Several decades may separate the explosion of house music from younger generations, but they passionately find inspiration in the musical heritage of their elders. By embracing a musical legacy, they injected a new energy that's incredibly fresh, and reflective of a present mood. Kids know better than anyone how exciting it is to be in the here and now.

The here and now for techno in France in the middle of the second decade of the 21st century came from a group of young producers, all aged between 20 and 30 who, in one way or another, were all children of Daft Punk. Most of them were still young kids when *Homework* first came out in 1997. As teenagers, they got into music at a time when the barriers between musical genres were on the verge of collapse. They adopted and assimilated the musical legacy of the previous 30 years – rock, hip-hop, dub and electronic music – and made it their own without paying attention to different schools of thought. Curious, talented, fast-thinking and with an incredible capacity to feed off everything that surrounded them, they tore away the last remaining boundaries between musical genres, and delivered a style of electronic music that is upfront and spontaneous. These ambitious, dynamic, cultured artists go by the names of Gesaffelstein, Brodinski, Para One, Yuksek, Bambounou, French Fries, Rone, Marst, Madben, Spitzer, Vophoniq, Everydayz, Villa Nova, Souleance, Club Cheval, Maelstrom and Lowjack. And labels such as Infiné, Dawn Records, Clek Clek Boom, In Paradisum, Airflex Lab, Bromance or the Sound Pellegrino crew. And, of course, not forgetting all the artists that gravitate towards the flagship of French electro: Ed Banger, an influential label since 2003, with Pedro Winter at its helm.

Pedro, an outrider, is an ex-skate boarder who was mad about house music, rock and hip-hop. He proved to be a great unifying sprit and, incidentally, was Daft Punk's manager for 12 years. He first became their manager in 1996 and was with them from their beginnings at Soma, the label on which Guy-Manuel de Homem-Christo and Thomas Bangalter originally released Rollin' & Scratchin' when they first signed to Virgin UK (a first!), and then for the release of the staggeringly successful *Homework* in 1997 and *Discovery* four years later. After having brought together house and rock, then renovating pop music with a series of amazing singles (Around the World, etc.), Daft Punk and Pedro Winter decided to go their separate ways after the release of *Human After All* in 2005, and a series of storming concerts including Paris-Bercy in 2007, which was recorded live.

In the space of a decade spent at the head of Ed Banger, Pedro has released records by DJ Mehdi, Justice, SebastiAn, Mr Oizo, Feadz and Uffie, with unmitigated success, creating a fair share of jealousy en route. What's his secret? A savvy mix of fun and fusion, a large dose of intuition, and boundless enthusiasm. With plenty of style and conviction, Pedro has always put his heart and soul into everything he does. That is his way. With his intelligence, sure instinct and unnerving charm, this guy has had the entire music business eating out of his hand for the past 10 years. Even the prestigious *New York Times* published a full-page article about him in January 2012.

The position held by Ed Banger on the French electronic music scene confers a certain amount of responsibility on Pedro Winter himself. Firstly, to observe and understand each new generation. Faced with 'too much' everything – too much information, too much music, too many demands on their time – Pedro's job consists of helping these kids to tune into artists who can cultivate and inspire them. This is the exact opposite of what happened in the US, where at big festivals like ULTRA

▶ Playlist
ED BANGER
DJ Mehdi
Lucky Boy

Justice
Waters Of Nazareth

Breakbot
Baby I'm Yours

Cassius
I <3 U So

Mr Oizo
Lambs Anger

Squarepusher & Edrec
Cryptic Motion

Boston Bun
House Call

Busy P & DJ Mehdi
Let The Children Techno

Mr Flash
Radar Rider

in Miami the young are exposed to a style of music bastardised by producers who are in it for the money. In the US, the underground scene has been ground down for years, so these kids often don't have the choice but to put up with poor music.

Some unscrupulous producers began applying the same maximum return on investment policy that had up until then been reserved for rock bands to the dance music scene. The millennium revealed an insatiable appetite for money among certain international dance music artists. This minority of DJs and producers picked up exactly where dance music barons such as Norman Cook (Fatboy Slim) had left off – making maximum profits and six-figure salaries. Many of them had grown up familiar with the clichés surrounding hip-hop culture: bling bling, pool parties, girls in bikinis, private jets, first-class travel, Dom Pérignon, and all that shit. These were guys who had taken all this on board and wanted to do the same. But does this make people such as Bob Sinclair or Jean Roch bad guys? Definitely not. However, I can't help but wonder whether music takes a back seat for them.

Of course they do a good job, if commercial dance music produced for the masses is your thing. Their style of DJ-ing is all based on energy, 'working up a sweat' as they say, during a set that lasts a maximum of two hours, prepared weeks in advance, where the public is subjected to a run of ultra-formatted tracks and highly-calibrated digital projections. It swiftly became rare in the 2010s to find a DJ star performing without a personalised visual display which included a logo with his name projected from every angle. Because even DJs need logos, just like any other commercial brand. Which is how those DJs who fill arenas see themselves, as a brand. At least the message is clear: we deal in mass marketing. And what's the point of having a set of moral values and bothering about the quality of the music as long as business is good? And long may it last!

Reading a list of the highest paid DJs in 2012, I discovered that the Dutch DJ, Tiesto, champion of ultra-commercial trance, pocketed the neat sum of $22 million in one year. Two new American stars of the moment, Skrillex and Steve Aoki, both completely unheard of only a couple of years previously, earned $15 and $12 million respectively for performing 200 gigs that year. In view of the dubious quality of the music they play, it only seems right to me to question the reasons for their phenomenal success.

I think back to the early 90s, when the idea of one day achieving celebrity status, above and beyond the underground, was unthinkable. Suspicious even. A good 10 years later, kids were swapping their football boots for a pair of MKII turntables dreaming of becoming the next

Jeff Mills. Then, in 2001, the iPod was born. Suddenly, everyone was a DJ. From one day to the next, amateur DJs were popping up everywhere, in every cool bar, boutique or restaurant in Paris, Barcelona or London. Then the web became more accessible. And so the notion of 'underground' was gradually made obsolete by the internet. Shazam replaced trainspotters, and social networks became a 24/7 stage for people's lives. It was then that DJs became fashion accessories.

Part of the furniture.

When I first started out, the crowd was tough. People didn't joke with the quality of the music that we played. Once you set foot behind the decks, you were in the hot seat. And every DJ knew that the slightest faux pas or the slightest error in taste or how you judged the crowd and your sentence was handed down: Ejected!

In the 2010s, I saw stadiums packed with young people eager to hear pre-programmed artists who settle for playing nondescript music. And this begs the question, why are DJs such as these so popular? I'm sure part of it must be to do with the image they project, since the packaging outweighs the content, and even the music itself. The imperative is to make noise, only play tracks that privilege efficiency, put on a show and blow hot air to carve out a place for themselves. For examples, look to Hardwell, Sander Van Doorn, Benni Benassi and Dada Life.

To my mind, pop music is a creature of habit. It functions in 30-year cycles. Its workings feed off cultural or artistic movements from three decades earlier. If you look at the history of pop from the 60s on, you'll find that urban cultures are continuously recycled and regurgitated.

The cycle of 30 can be seen in the sensational re-emergence of rave sounds, or sounds from Chicago, in the middle of the 2010s. But, above all, in the way in which the DJs mentioned above think about celebrity, and music as a business. Thirty years ago, things were exactly the same. The rock scene was full of super-groups with very technical repertoires full of dull songs. They all had massive egos and money was their motivation. The next generation couldn't care less about being famous, all they cared about was being 'rock 'n' roll'. Their attitude was the complete opposite of the herds of permed-hair rockers who went before them: they kept a low profile and there was no 'look-at-me'. If anything, they preferred to remain faceless. The disciples of the underground techno scene adopted this same attitude in the early 90s.

A full 30-year cycle has passed since the ham-fisted antics of massively popular bands such as Guns N' Roses. It would seem that we are back at the beginning of a new cycle with 'maximum visibility' being the rule of thumb. This makes sense in a society where an artist's image comes before his talent. Whereas in the 80s no one could care less about what Mike Banks or Maurizio might look like, 30 years later anonymity was considered a bizarre concept (Daft Punk being a rare exception). In an era defined and driven by social media approval, few people care about having private lives, everyone and everything must be on show in order to exist. The social media are where stars of electro pop forge an international reputation, put their hectic daily lives on show, promote their records, develop loyalty among their fans, and sell their wares.

This image wouldn't be complete without mentioning the global superstar of dance music, David Guetta. Yet, his is a different case altogether. Firstly, because no other French artist before him has ever sold as many records in the US and UK and, secondly, because David singlehandedly changed the American Top 40. By introducing a 4/4 beat into American pop, he gave dance music the opportunity to break through and triumph. Twenty-five or so years after Marshall Jefferson released Move Your Body (1986) and Larry Heard released Can You Feel It? (1986), David Guetta managed to bring together electronic music and urban music (hip-hop and R&B), the two musical genres that had up until then refused to collaborate. Although it's ironic, as hip-hop and house music have exactly the same musical roots. It's simple. Take Planet Rock by Afrika Bambaataa (1982), an iconic early hip-hop track, and analyse it. What do you find? An electro beat, samples from Trans Europe Express (1977) and Numbers (1981) by Kraftwerk with hip-hop lyrics by Afrika Bambaataa and his crew. Despite this very clear example of how hip-hop and techno share the same roots, US hip-hop broke away from electro at the end of the 80s and never looked back – or rarely.

Subsequently the champions of hip-hop built their business empire as if dance music never existed. And then all that changed. In less than a decade, David Guetta profoundly transformed the urban music landscape in the US and gave birth to a new format: EDM (Electronic Dance Music), which is nothing more than a reconfiguration of commercial house…

Those of you who were at the launch party for *Electrochoc* in Paris in October 2003 might remember that on the decks with me that night were Manu Le Malin playing a special rocksteady set and David Guetta playing… hip-hop! At the time, his album *Just A Little More Love* was doing really well, and David was already the target of certain purists ready to shoot him down. That's how it goes in France – if you make it internationally, there are people just waiting to slap you down. Certain people didn't understand what he was doing at the launch party of our book, nor why he was playing Eric B. & Rakim or Public Enemy, and as for what I was doing still being friends with him ... The thing is, David and I had known each other for almost 30 years.

Before continuing, I'd like to make a few things clear. The first being, that I have the greatest respect for David. OK, the 'F*** Me, I'm Famous' parties aren't the kind where I'd go and play, and, OK, maybe the music he produces isn't exactly my thing; but I see in him an extraordinarily powerful commercial talent. I came to this conclusion one night when I went to see him playing at Pacha in Ibiza. I went with a friend and we sat at the bar to have a drink. Suddenly, his hit track Love Is Gone came over the sound system and a sea of hands shot into the air. Every single person in the club started singing along to the words. They all knew the track by heart. It was astounding. My friend and I both looked at each other in amazement, 'Do you know this track?' ... 'No, I've never heard it in my life!' All around us people were singing, 'What are we supposed to do / After all that we've been through ...'. At that moment, we both felt very out of place. The situation was so ludicrous we both laughed as a wave of mayhem took hold of Pacha. I think it was then that I realised the power of David Guetta's music.

Even though our career paths, our motivation, our artistic ambitions and our fans are very different, David and I have a culture and a history in common, which means that, above and beyond our friendship, we understand each other. We both started DJ-ing at a time when playing records was not very highly regarded. And we both come from a background of black music. We both defended our love of house music (or in David's case, hip-hop) at a time when other people dismissed it. In different ways, we both strived for the recognition of music in the clubs of Paris, and beyond. Thirty years on, despite our very different careers, we still talk music. We share certain values. We are both loyal to our roots. I would like to think that we have both remained artistically consistent and true to the music we believe in.

In the mid-1990s, David Guetta played hip-hop and house during his Unity parties at the Rex; subsequently he has contributed to the convergence of these two genres to create a new genre of pop. Just after the millennium, the biggest stars of hip-hop and R&B travelled to his parties at the Palace, the Bains-Douches or Ibiza; since then he has worked in the studio with them. And they were the ones desperate to work with him. David changed the face of urban music in the US. And this is how it happened...

Early 2000. David sold all the shares he had in his different club and restaurant venues to concentrate on working as a music producer. He had already released a first album and got to work on a second. The reaction was lukewarm. On the one hand he heard, 'Watch out, you're gonna end up with egg on your face!' And on the other, 'We don't want you here! Go back to running restaurants!' The thing is, behind his big smile and good manners, David is tough.

DAVID GUETTA:
'All those years spent working as a club promoter trained me in the school of hard knocks. At that stage in my life I couldn't devote my time to what I wanted to do, so the day I could, I worked at it much harder than anyone else. When success came knocking, I was already 32, so I didn't experience it in the same way as guys who have it at 20. At that age you think that you're a genius and that from now on life's going to be easy. When success came in 2002, my immediate reaction was the total opposite; I needed to work harder to consolidate my achievement. So when I went away on tour to DJ for three weeks at a time, I'd come home and immediately lock myself away in my studio. That's my temperament: I believe in taking the opportunities that life has to offer so I commit myself wholeheartedly to what I love doing.

'How do I explain my success? … First of all, I think that our job as DJs consists of discerning things slightly before other people. I'm also lucky in that I have always taken an interest in things before they become mainstream. This was already the case at the Unity parties at the Rex. Mixing urban music with house or mixing a gay and straight crowd was considered a weird idea at the time. But I saw it as a way for people of different ages and from different backgrounds to get together and share an experience. If I had to find a more concrete reason for my success, I would say that it was the result of a positive sequence of events …

'My first single, Just A Little More Love, came out in 2002 and was built around a house and a hip-hop loop. It quickly became a big club hit, but as we were in the middle of the Daft Punk boom, and disco-house (also known as filter house) was the happening thing, my track wasn't right for radio. They didn't want it. Then Don't Let Me Go came out and was playlisted on the radio throughout Europe. But it still didn't break in the US. In 2007, I released my third album *Pop Life*, with Love Is Gone as the first single. The track was played on radios all over the world, this time including the US. Not only were US radio networks playing the track, but also it remained at Number 1 in the US club charts for a whole year! Even the hip-hop clubs were playing it. That's what made the difference.

'It was then that Will.i.am got in touch with me, "Hey, will you do a track for me a bit like Love Is Gone?". And that's how I Gotta Feeling came about in 2009, the biggest hit the Black Eyed Peas have ever had.

Then I met Kelly Rowland from Destiny's Child, with whom I did When Love Takes Over and which came out on my fourth album *One Love*. I wanted to use this album to express a funk thing I have always harboured since I was about 12, and mix it up with the energy that I love in dance music.

'Not long after, I found myself playing at a festival in London organised by Radio One. It was there I met the rapper, Akon. He suggested we hook up and do a track together. That night we went into the studio together and recorded Sexy Bitch, a hip-hop track produced like a dance track. When it came out, and due to its success, US radio stations changed their format.

'Before Sexy Bitch, uptempo tracks weren't played on US radio networks. Urban music artists (hip-hop and R&B) existed in their own bubble. They concentrated all their efforts on the US market and were out of touch with what was going on in Europe. There may have been hundreds of thousands of young Americans going out every weekend to listen to dance music, but this music didn't exist in terms of record sales, and majors and urban music stars didn't pay it any attention. When Sexy Bitch consecrated EDM (Electronic Dance Music) as a new form of pop, most urban music artists followed suit.

'From then on, several producers (Timbaland, etc.) and artists (Rihanna, etc.) asked me to work with them. These opportunities enabled me to gauge the differences between the way we make music in Europe and the way most music is made in the States. We have a tendency to experiment, to try things out until we finally find the right balance and create something we are pleased with. Well, that's how I work anyway. In America, it's the opposite. When they go into the studio, they know exactly the result they're looking for. We're flexible with the gear we need to make music. Over there, they always bring out the big guns. So you can imagine when I went to meet Timbaland with just my laptop under my arm he didn't get it. He asked me, "Err ... what studio equipment do you need?" and I replied, "A mini-jack plug, please". You should have seen his face! Later, when I was chatting with Timbaland's crew, it was my turn to be stunned into silence. They were sure that house music came from Europe. When I told them that the first house music was made in Chicago, they couldn't believe it ...'

EDM went mainstream in the US, becoming a new form of pop music – born in the US, and then developed and transformed in Europe. House finally returned to its birthplace, America, and then made its way back to Europe again. EDM is the perfect example of a cycle of 30, and follows the same pattern as the artistic exchange between both sides of the Atlantic since the 1950s through to today. And it illustrates how pop culture has never ceased to reinvent itself by feeding off these continuous cultural exchanges, from one generation to the next.

Faced with the simultaneous arrival of a new crowd, a new generation of dance music artists, a new type of pop music, and new business strategies, DJs and producers of my generation each tried to respond to this shake-up in their own way: some simply dropped out or disappeared, others pursued their careers without changing their style of music or their way of doing things. Others jumped onto the EDM bandwagon. And a few exceptions, such as Richie Hawtin, managed the transition without surrendering the qualities and the values that made their name.

And me? I decided to risk it and stick to my values, to stay faithful to my musical roots, and to do what I loved. So, 4–8-hour DJ sets don't fit in with the new way of thinking? So what, that's the way I DJ! Being associated with a style of music is crucial to having a lasting career? I don't care, I can do without. Travelling in a private jet is important for your image? I couldn't give a shit! Being sponsored by a big brand and demanding astronomical fees is the norm, or having an agent whose only interest is six-figure fees? Out of the question! Before talking to me about money, I want somebody to talk to me about music. In any case, money has never been my motivation and I've always worked with people I like. You only have to look at the period following the original publication of *Electrochoc*, when I never worked so hard in my life. And as you can imagine, it's not working on a new live show or writing the music for a ballet that pays the rent. But so what? Is that a reason to stop doing what I really want to do? Of course not! But to be able to pursue all my different projects, to keep my weekly radio show on the Mouv' for example, I have to keep DJ-ing. Firstly, because I don't want to lose contact with the public, secondly, because my lifestyle depends on it, and thirdly, and most importantly, because it's my whole life. So I plan to keep it up and continue my way of doing things. It has paid off to do it this way up until now.

Let's just see how long it lasts.

This new way of thinking was my answer to 'how to grow old gracefully?', the question that had been bothering me since the release of *The Cloud Making Machine* up until that night spent DJ-ing in London with François Kevorkian. It was that night when I understood the importance of taking new turns in my career without fearing getting lost, that I had to continuously surprise the audience, challenge them even, to heighten their curiosity and share with them my love of music, past and present.

But I didn't want to go ahead just to stay in the game at all costs. I knew I risked quickly running out of steam. Or even worse, my passion would diminish. I realised then that it was imperative for me to take a step back. Too many changes had taken place over the previous few years for me to able to continue playing as a DJ as if nothing had happened. And I felt it, too. I too needed a change as symbolic and drastic in my career and in my private life. It was then that I decided to limit my DJ gigs to an average of two weekends per month in order to make time for my family as well as for other projects, and to give myself space to think about which way I wanted my career to go.

So there I was, putting my thoughts in order, as I paced up and down the garden. The weather was beautiful. Everything was calm, absolutely idyllic and I was bubbling away on the inside desperate for 'action!' It's the effect the south of France has on me. Living in a peaceful place where nothing saps my energy made me even more hyperactive. I wanted 'Action!'. OK, but what? I soon found the answer: release a new record and put together a new live show.

it's just muzik

13th March 2010. In a couple of minutes, 10 of us would be on stage. I could feel the nerves of each musician in the group. And me? Well, I was petrified. I stood hidden behind the curtain staring out at the audience. I spotted several of my friends who had come en masse for the occasion. I couldn't help thinking back to the film *Funny Bones*, where in the opening scene the protagonist is in his dressing room delaying the moment he has to go out on stage as he knows he is going to screw up. He turns to his agent, terrified, 'Tonight's the big night. I'm gonna do pirouettes and then I'm gonna die!' I understood how anxious he felt. The night before, my nerves had almost eaten me alive.

We had been working on this concert for months; months of me blowing hot and cold. I had days when I was exceedingly stressed out and – and I apologise – unbearable to be with. A few days before the concert, during rehearsal, I went absolutely ballistic. But this was it now. All the work I had done for all those years, all the gigs I had played before, formed a flexed arc that was about to shoot its arrow right now. A stage-hand came up to me to tell me it was time. I could make a run for it and get out of there. The thought did cross my mind. But there was no question of backing out now. An obsession came to an end that night. An obsession that had slowly developed within me, giving me nightmares, and made me say the same word every day over and over again to the point of exasperating all those around me:

'Pleyel'.

At the origin of Pleyel was *Tales Of A Kleptomaniac*, my fifth studio album, that I had pictured as a sort of homecoming. It was 2009. *The Cloud Making Machine* was a long way off. My aspirations had changed. Making people dance was my priority once again. With the singles Back To My Roots on the Berlin label Innervisions and Gnanmankoudji on PIAS, I took great pleasure in producing some uplifting and compelling techno. As both these tracks were well-received, I put my efforts into making more funky dance floor-oriented music. *Tales Of A Kleptomaniac* was an album into which I put everything I love without worrying what other people would think. I satisfied myself with imagining a certain place, and then I dived in headfirst, struggling for hours upon end to create the structures, sounds and moods to achieve what I wanted.

I have never had the patience to learn the ins and outs of a piece of studio equipment. My method consists of searching until the moment I feel, that's it, I've got it, that the track I'm working on naturally seems to be finished. Case closed. I stop when others I know can still spend days and days putting together the finishing touches. But I'm not meticulous in that way. I like to make a track in one fell swoop and get it out there.

Of course, this means that sometimes I kick myself later. I know all too well that some of my tracks in the past would have gained from having had more time spent on them. But I don't have that kind of patience. I have to fire out my music. This urgency reminds me of Derrick May's saying, 'You don't make a record for fun man!'. Not for fun, nor for money. In any case, who these days can claim to make big money from making techno records?

Once the album *Tales Of A Kleptomaniac* was finished, I signed to PIAS. It seemed like a natural choice, as we had known each other for so many years. Anyway, where could I go now that F Comm had closed? We included a second CD in the album with music I had composed over the past few years for Pietragalla and others (exhibitions, contemporary dance, a film). I saw it as a sort of extension of *The Cloud Making Machine* that anyone who bought the album could download free of charge. And then came a rather drunken dinner with the people from PIAS when I was asked a strange question, 'Would you be prepared to go and DJ for a fan?' I replied straight away, 'Of course!' That was when the idea came about for a competition on the internet: 'Laurent Garnier is DJ-ing at my place.'

A special website was created (www.laurentgarniermixechezmoi.com) to explain the rules of the competition. People had to send in a madcap idea for a concept for a party. It had to be free, it had to be limited to 200 people max, and it had to be held in an original setting and to be kept secret right up until the last minute. Then other internet users had to vote for the best idea. In return, I would DJ at the winner's party and, as an added bonus, PIAS would take care of the lights and the sound system.

Between November 25, 2009 and February 18, 2010, the date of the party, the website received over 5,000 hits a week. On the day of the party, Google recorded over a million searches using the terms 'laurent-garnier' and 'laurentgarinermixechezmoi'! All in all, we received more than 50 different party concepts. Twenty-five of those were shortlisted by voters over the internet, and I then chose the best three. The people at PIAS went to meet all three candidates and visit the venues. I finally decided on a winner, a certain Amélie.

A few weeks into the competition, this crazy girl from Brussels spent the whole night at a festival I was playing in front of the stage holding up a sign saying: 'Vote For Me'. I remember thinking, 'She's keen'. When I saw that she was one of the finalists with her 'pimps and whores' concept, I said yes straight away.

I turned up in Brussels to DJ in an apartment that had once been a whorehouse, for a party organised for 80 people in fancy dress. I went along with the theme and wore a huge pimp-like moustache, a pair of

▶ Playlist
GARNIER MIXE CHEZ MOI
Vitalic
Chicken Lady

Soulwax
E Talking (Remix)

Ghostface Killah
(Dnb Bootleg)

Afefe Iku
Mirror Dance

Johnny Cash
Techno Bootleg

Popof
Serenity

Omar
Feeling You (Henrik Schwarz Rmx)

Xenia Beliayeva
Analog Effekt

Rayban aviators, a gold chain and a garish suit. Eric Morand was dressed all in red and black like a pimp, whereas Kenny Gates, the boss of PIAS, accompanied by his girlfriend who was dressed as a hooker, made his entrance wearing a naked man jumpsuit, with a penis and all. Very classy! Once the introductions had been made, it was time to break the ice. It's not an understatement to say that the first half an hour was a bit strange. Amelie and her friends didn't quite know how to act around us. I suppose it was quite a normal reaction given that they had all been looking forward to this for weeks, and suddenly the night had arrived and there I was. I got the same feeling as when Mad Mike first came to play at the Rex, when expectations were so high that it took a while for the crowd to get into it. So, I decided to start my set a bit earlier then planned, firstly, to enable me to release my own anxiety and relax and, secondly, to establish a rapport between Amelie's friends and me.

That night I was riveted to the decks for a good six hours, dressed in numerous different wigs, boas and other ludicrous fashion accessories. As the guests slowly let go, taking it in turns to have their photo taken with me, the party moved up a gear, getting wilder and wilder as if tomorrow didn't exist. Imagine the picture: 80 people in a small, dark room with the signs on the wall stating, 'Say no to cigarettes. Say yes to pipes!'. (A 'pipe' in French is both a pipe and a blowjob.) It felt like I was DJ-ing at one of the most underground clubs on the planet. I was surrounded by drunken people, dressed in exotic wigs and feathers. They were mega vulgar and super classy at the same time, and partying like it was the last night on earth.

I had prepared myself to play in front of a small group of fans, yet I found myself DJ-ing in front of a mob of fanatics who were goading me on to give them all the energy I had and the best time ever. That night gave me a massive morale boost. But the idea of going back on the road as a DJ still didn't appeal to me. After that amazing night in Brussels I would have found it too hard to be beholden to a club night when the magic just didn't happen. It didn't take me long to decide: I was going to put together a live tour instead.

The concert I had given at the Olympia 11 years earlier felt like a lifetime ago. In hindsight, my approach to playing live was probably very naïve and has left me with some uncomfortable memories. I remember one particular time – a private concert organised at the Rex one Sunday night for about 200 friends, a couple of weeks before the release of *The Cloud Making Machine*. We had just finished touring and were all exhausted and anxious at the thought of performing in front of our families and friends. I was so nervous that when I got up on stage I couldn't even say hello. It didn't take long for the concert to fall apart. The percussionist Mino Cinelu, an excellent musician, but who without proper guidance can quickly spin out of control, went off on an improvisational tangent. Then it was as if all the other musicians were doing their own thing without listening to each other. A catastrophe. Not only was our performance rubbish, but to top it all, this disaster had taken place in front of friends who were far too polite to boo us. Yet, that night, that's all we deserved.

Another bad moment when I felt completely alone was in 2006 when I found myself on stage at the Olympia with the saxophonist and clarinettist, Michel Portal. We only had one rehearsal together and he didn't pay very much attention to the framework I gave him in which to improvise for Acid Eiffel and The Man With The Red Face. As with any good jazzman, he must have thought everything would be all right on the night. On the day of the concert we did a sound check and it sounded ok, but I wouldn't go so far as to say it was great. I suggested that it would be best if he stayed close to me on stage for the duration of the performance. When it came to performing live on stage, Michel Portal sat down … with his back to me! As Acid Eiffel began, he went off on one. The pianist who was with us, Jacky Terrasson, an old school friend who I hadn't seen for 30 years, tried as best he could to pick up the pieces, but it was too late. It was a disaster. The audience weren't stupid, there was no rapturous applause as we finished the second track. I disappeared backstage, devastated…

These two anecdotes go to show what a long and uncomfortable journey playing live has been, as well as a painful learning experience. I naïvely thought that telling a story on stage, as I do in my DJ sets or on the radio, would be enough, or that surrounding myself with musicians, who were also my friends, was a good idea. But I was wrong on both counts… In all honesty, to achieve what I so wanted to achieve in a live performance, not only did I have to have experienced musicians at my side, I also had to be able to lead them. Yet I had absolutely no idea how!

Added to this frustration was another element that I wasn't sure how to handle: the short amount of time a concert performance allows you. That was a big problem for me. Ever since I had started DJ-ing, I was used to doing five- or six-hour sets so I had plenty of time to build my set progressively and take the audience on a journey with me. And if there came a moment when the crowd switched off … hup!! a break in the track, lights out, and I'd kick-start the crowd with something different. And within minutes, I'd bounced right back. But you can't do that with a live concert. You have to grab the audience's attention within the first few minutes. And if you don't pull it off, either you have to just admit that you're wasting your time and carry on regardless or you juggle around the set list and try and salvage the situation. But, in any case, if you have no idea how to direct your musicians you're headed straight for a brick wall.

In truth, since my beginnings playing live, despite a handful of great moments, I rarely experienced any real satisfaction. And, as I have said before, no one in the business was there to help me out and support me. How many times did I hear, 'He's driving us mad with his saxophonist! Why's he so stuck on jazz?'. This lack of understanding from the public and the music critics was sometimes unsettling. This, combined with the difficulty I had performing on stage and communicating the musical ideas I had in my head, was incredibly frustrating. I almost threw in the towel on more than one occasion.

And then I met Bugge Wesseltoft, a 'nu jazz' pianist, composer, and producer from Norway. It was then that I started picturing how I could transform the way I play live, and things finally began to change. As well as being a supremely talented pianist, Bugge was also a formidable bandleader. I knew all his releases on his own Jazzland imprint before I started working with him. His music was a savvy blend of Scandinavian jazz that he took into new areas, whether introspective electronica (with the saxophonist Jan Garbarek), or more funky and tempestuous territories with his album *Nu Conception Of Jazz* (1996).

To test out whether we could really work together, we decided to perform live as a trio, along with Philippe Nadaud, for a tour lasting a few weeks. The concept was simple. I would play a couple of records and then follow on with one of my own tracks. As our ensemble was so small, Bugge could improvise over my music, as could Nadaud, and then we'd move on to my next track, and then to the next, etc.

I really worked out how to resolve the earlier problem of working live with musicians when working with this trio during those first few dates with Bugge. I think my own complex about 'not being a real musician' meant that I had far too much respect for the musical abilities of the members of my group to dare challenge them or tell them what to do. It made me feel awkward. I often thought, 'Who I am to tell these guys what to do when just hearing them play brings tears to my eyes?' Yet, they were expecting me to lead them. And this lack of direction ended up showing in the quality of the performance.

Watching how Bugge worked on stage was, in some ways, my musical education. And yet there was a second important lesson to learn, that you cannot have two captains in charge of a ship. I learned this lesson at my own expense. Democracy in a live band doesn't work. An example of this was one summer night in 2005 at the T in The Park festival in Scotland, where we were playing in the techno tent. I love Scotland. It's one of the only places I know where within the first few seconds, as soon the doors open, be it a club or a festival, people rush straight onto the empty dance floor with two pints in their hands, shouting at the DJ to bring it on! That is a typical beginning to any night in Glasgow or Edinburgh. So imagine the same crowd, but much bigger, with even more pints of beer in their system...

We had been on stage for 20 minutes. Seven thousand people were packed into the tent, rearing to go. My DJ instinct kicked in and I felt this was the right moment to let loose the canons. I turned to Bugge and shouted, 'Right now!' Bugge looked back at me coolly over his glasses and smiled. 'No.' I insisted, 'Please Bugge, now!' And again he replied, 'Not yet.' The result was, when we finally let rip, it was too late.

This illustrates the different approach of jazzmen and techno artists, musicians and DJs. Jazz musicians are performers. Their take on music is primarily intellectual. DJs are entertainers. Their job is to give the public what they want when they want it, and at the same time take them to new places. These are really two very contradictory approaches to music. Of course, they share certain things in common. But with Bugge, we couldn't always find this common ground where our respective talents could compliment each other.

At the end of this gig in Scotland, I was so furious at not having been able to take charge when it was needed, that I didn't sleep a wink. And Bugge? It didn't affect him in the slightest. Like Jeff Mills, he felt that if the crowd hadn't understood what he was trying to give them, it didn't matter; they simply weren't ready for it. Whereas I felt that if people didn't get it then I hadn't done my job properly. After this gig, I thought that, with or without Bugge, I was never going to manage to do what I wanted to.

Once back home in the south of France, all of this stuff was going round in my head, when the guy who had sold me the house told me about his brother who was a keyboard player, a certain Benjamin Rippert. 'However,' he explained, 'he's a bit different.' Different, in that he had phobias such as he never went out, refused to fly, etc. Within a few months, I knew this guy's whole family without ever having met him. Each time someone spoke about him they always said the same thing, 'Ben Rippert, he's a genius!' Knowing that Bugge would one day go back to Norway, I was actively looking for a new keyboard player to come on the road with me.

And then came the day in Spring 2006 when the drum 'n' bass DJ, Marky, asked me to do a remix for him. As his productions are always very lyrical, I thought this might be the perfect opportunity to contact the famous Ben. The following day, Ben made the huge effort to come to my studio with an old Rhodes Suitcase keyboard and an amp that weighed a ton. Once he had settled in, I played him the remix that I had just finished. As he listened, his facial expression changed … And then I understood, 'OK this guy has never listened to dance music before in his life! This is going to be fun!'. Then he got behind his keyboard and began to improvise … I couldn't believe it. He was amazing. When he had finished I said, 'Err, what are your plans for the next six years?' and he replied, 'Well, I'm not moving from here.' And so I went off on one, 'But wait! I'm on tour at the moment but I'm going to need someone soon for a new project… Won't you at least try, just once, just the two of us, in front of a very small audience?' And he replied, 'Yeah, but I never fly … so it would have to be in Marseilles.' I jumped up and said, 'OK, I'll find us a gig in Marseilles!'

I got Ben working on some of my tracks, but it wasn't easy. As he didn't know any of my work, he wrote down endless notes in a little book, glancing suspiciously over his shoulder from time to time to eye up my machines. A few weeks later, we were booked in Marseilles for a surprise 'DJ-live' gig.

The concert was a bit chaotic to say the least. With each new track I played, Ben would stare at me wide-eyed, a cigarette in his mouth, waiting for me to tell him the name of the track so that he could look it up in his notes and begin to play. But because it was so loud, Ben didn't get what I was saying, so he would launch into the melody from a completely different track. A right mess. But weirdly, it was actually a good night…

There was no question of it ending our association. After a lot of negotiating, and to-ing and fro-ing, Ben agreed to take a train for a second gig in Paris. But it nearly didn't happen. Ben was so anxious, that he somehow managed to break his leg a few days before we were due to go. I could have seen this as a sign, and our story would have ended there and then. But it was out of the question.

Ben performed with me live at the Trabendo on crutches.

Then came the summer of 2006. My tour with Bugge and Philippe Nadaud was coming to an end. One of the last concerts we did was at the Pont du Gard. It was only an hour away from where Ben lived, so I asked him to come and play on First Reaction, one of the last tracks of the set. When the time came, Ben sat down behind his Rhodes and improvised like he was possessed. Caught unawares, Bugge tried to outdo him. Not being one to back down, Ben upped the stakes once again. Bugge, ready to burst ... took the track to new heights. Once the concert was over, Bugge came up to me with a smile on his face and said, 'I think you've found your guy.'

A dozen or so dates and several boxes of sedatives later, Ben agreed to work with me on a new live tour that would include my ever-loyal Philippe Nadaud, and two old friends of Ben's, Laurent 'Tutu' Thuaud, a sound engineer, and Philippe Anicaux, a trumpeter. It was then that I really learnt how to drive my musicians. We quickly found a good dynamic, to the point where I could see my music evolving each night. I have to thank Ben Rippert for helping me to free myself of my inhibitions. He kept telling me, 'You don't need to tell me when it's time to let rip, I can tell by the way you move your shoulders!'

Yet in spite of this big step forward, I still felt like a prisoner. I was surrounded by excellent musicians but spent most of my time on stage managing the machines. As a result, I found it hard to take a step back and listen to what we were actually playing. Now that I had tasted the thrill of being a conductor, I wanted to take it a step further, but in order to do this, I would have to free up my time on stage. So it was then that I called in Scan X for back-up. Complex procedures and extreme focus are right up his street. From then on, I could finally concentrate all my efforts on stage on doing what I wanted to do, that is, re-invent my tracks each night and enjoy a similar freedom that only DJ-ing gives you. We must have performed at least 20 different versions of Gnanmankoudji and Back To My Roots. I felt so liberated. I no longer thought twice about dashing across the stage to Nadaud or Rippert to hum them a melody that they'd play straight back, and the others would follow. Of course, it didn't always work out exactly as planned. But once in a while we hit the jackpot. We used several of these musical phrases that we invented live on stage for months after. The same went for themes we came up with during sound checks and then used later on, developing them each night as our tour progressed. For months, the band and I had a blast. The more we let go, the more we managed to captivate our audience. It was great! It was then that my agent Christian Paulet, who had been at the heart of the Rex Club for 20 years, called me to discuss an idea.

I remember his tone of voice, very calm as usual, telling me, 'So, right, listen up, errr, we've been offered the Salle Pleyel ...'. Caught off-guard, I think I mumbled back something like, 'OK. Can I see the venue first ...?' To be honest, Pleyel didn't mean that much to me back then. I had never even stepped foot inside.

Pleyel is Paris' equivalent to Carnegie Hall. Legendary pianists Vladimir Horowitz, Samson François and Arthur Rubinstein have all performed there. And artists such as Louis Armstrong, Keith Jarrett, Ray Charles and Michel Petrucciani have all given concerts there. In a word, you don't approach performing at Pleyel lightly. Not only because of this venue's prestigious past, but also because it has one of the best acoustics in Europe. And finally, because performing at Pleyel means playing in front of a seated audience.

For all of the above reasons, 'doing' Pleyel, meant doing something memorable and unique it its symbolism (the arrival of techno in a Mecca of the classical world). It required creating something new and special. There was no question of just turning up at Pleyel with the same show that we had been on the road with for the Kleptomaniac tour. No way. This had to be memorable. For the audience and for us.

Within a very short space of time, we found ourselves putting together a huge production. We had to create visuals (we didn't have any), reconfigure the stage, re-examine our repertoire from beginning to end, rewrite certain arrangements, and beef up the band with new musicians capable of integrating quickly into this new vessel. I sent out my invitations. The UK poet and slammer Anthony Joseph was the first to accept. Then the expert turntablist Crazy B from the group Birdy Nam Nam, the percussionist Xavier Desandre, and two brass musicians were also added to the band. For the rest, well, we ate, slept and dreamt Pleyel for six months, working like crazy to get the show right.

During the week leading up to the concert, the 10 musicians in the band got together in a rehearsal room in Paris we had rented for the occasion for three long days. There were moments of doubt, doors were slammed, followed by reconciliation. The rest of the time we worked, worked and worked more to find the right balance and build the show so that, from time to time, I could be alone on stage just with Scan X to play … techno. I mean, *I played techno* at Pleyel. In a venue that had seen whole generations of classical musicians perform on its stage, the place where Charles Trenet performed his last ever concert, where Miles Davis recorded an outstanding record, a legendary venue in Europe, and where we were to perform Crispy Bacon.

That night, at Pleyel, the audience was a real mixture of people from such different musical backgrounds that I am sure that they had never rubbed shoulders before. On the one hand, there were my fans who had come to dance. On the other, there was a slightly older generation that included Pleyel season-ticket holders, there with their children or their grand-children probably thinking that this would be one of the rare occasions that they could share a musical moment together as a family. In any case, everyone was there to experience a techno concert … sitting down. Regarding the seating, once the concert was well under way, I addressed the audience between two tracks, 'I know that many of you out there have never been to a concert before where you are seated, and that others have never been to a concert where you are standing.' The fact that it was a seated venue was a real challenge, and we had tried to take this into consideration when building the set list. I kicked off with darker, contemplative tracks like Downfall, a moody and emotionally intense track. Starting like this was a way of setting the tone and saying that this wasn't going to be a rave, it was a concert. Ben then came and sat at the grand piano and we continued together exploring the ambient passages I had written for the contemporary choreographer, Pietragalla. Later on, the rest of the band joined us on stage for the track 63, with its heady brass section, or Dealing With The Man, a high point in the evening where I left the stage deeply moved, incapable of speech. After, we slowly built up Gnanmankoudji and at the end I asked the audience to all stand up ('It's not everyday you can do this here, so enjoy it!') and they went wild.

It's funny. I'm not really sure whether I did a concert at Pleyel or not… I know I have watched the DVD several times over, but it still feels like a dream. Yet, I know I did it. It has left a long-lasting impression on me. I know that there will be other concerts in the future, that some will be great, too, that I'll become obsessed again about the idea of playing in some place or another… Yet I have to say, I don't think I will ever experience what happened that night at Pleyel again. Because what happened that Saturday March 13, 2010 was a coming together of what I had been trying to achieve for years, and for that reason there will always be a 'before' and 'after' Pleyel. Before, I had been looking to do that concert but was unable to find the right language to make it possible. Exactly that. Now that I have done it, I have the ability and confidence to go and play in any venue, knowing that I can recreate that magic again.

The day after Pleyel, the sense of euphoria had faded and was replaced by the chronic baby blues, a real comedown and something that I hadn't really expected. I was afraid. I truly believed that I might never reach that state of liberty, grace and fusion with my musicians ever again. I thought about stopping doing concerts altogether. I was in a dark place and thought, 'I've experienced that. So what's the point of relentlessly pursuing that thrill again? And what if it never happens again?' The thought was terrifying… And then I pulled myself together and slapped myself out of this self-indulgent gloom to realise what I had achieved:

we set Pleyel on fire! We had succeeded in introducing electronic music to people who knew nothing about it! Isn't that the point? To share our music, to strive constantly for new horizons. Otherwise, we'll get tired of it. And I have no intention of doing that…

food for thought

September 4, 2010. In exactly one week, I was going to play at the Bolshoi for a performance with the Preljocaj Ballet. Before this great honour was bestowed on us, the band and I were invited to perform a live concert in the centre of Moscow, as part of the on-going festival to celebrate The Year of France in Russia. The morning of the concert, we did our sound check in the middle of a big square in Moscow surrounded by busy rush-hour traffic. It was still early in the morning and cold. The noise of the traffic made the whole thing quite surreal. A few feet away, the huge ex-KGB building stood over us as we struggled to find the right sound for Nadaud's saxophone. I was thinking how weird this situation was to be in when suddenly the traffic came to a stop, as if someone had pressed the 'pause' button. I asked, 'What's going on?' but got no reply. But I didn't need one. In the distance, I saw hundreds of soldiers marching towards us rank and file. They came and posted themselves right in front of the stage with expressionless faces, impeccable uniforms and iron discipline. 'Err, what's going on?' Finally someone answered, 'The army will be in charge of security.' Aaaah…

A few hours later, a sea of faces, mainly families, stood facing our military escort. They had come to celebrate City Day and to listen to the Russian DJ, Bobina, a concert by Scan X, and then us. When Stephane 'Scan X' began, there was still a whole hour before we were supposed to be on stage. The KGB building fascinated me and I filmed it with my mobile phone from backstage. I kept thinking, 'A lot of people must have disappeared inside there.' Then I turned my camera back to the stage and filmed the crowd dancing and enjoying themselves, 'And there's this lot having a great time.' The contrast was like Moscow itself, dazzling!

A good hour later and we were playing The Man With The Red Face to an over-excited crowd, who seemed to be overtaken by a collective hysteria that nothing or no one could control. And the military? They remained still, as if nothing was happening. At the end of the concert, people in the crowd were screaming and shouting while a small group of very formal, grey-faced city officials got up on stage to present us with flowers and give a speech.

Following the lead of Chile, Argentina and China, Russia has opened its doors to electronic music over the past decade. Several super-clubs have opened in both Moscow and St Petersburg attracting crowds of wealthy youngsters. Ten years ago, these young people were never seen in Europe. Nowadays these young Russians flock to Ibiza, London or Barcelona, destinations that up until recently were reserved for European clubbers outside of the former Iron Curtain. They can sometimes be wild, excessive and diehard. But that is nothing compared to what they are

KAZANTIP REPUBLIC

capable of in their heartland. KaZantip, a sort of wild, liberal Burning Man festival, takes place every year on a private beach in Ukraine.

KaZantip is crazy! For one, it's not strictly a festival. It's a Republic. A Republic that has its own government, constitution, currency, visas, national anthem, flag, religion (belief in miracles), laws, citizens and uniform (Bermuda shorts and an orange t-shirt). Here, forget any rules of etiquette or bureaucracy that may exist elsewhere in Europe. At KaZantip you live the dream of Nikita Marshunok, president for life and 'psychic guide' of the Independent Orange Republic.

To start out, Marshunok was a keen windsurfer who became a millionaire through some business deal or other. He decided to do something he had always wanted to do and bought a 3 km^2 piece of land in southeast Ukraine, on the Black Sea, in an area that was very popular with windsurfers and then gradually became known for open-air parties. Ten years later and the site officially proclaimed itself the Republic of whatever goes.

KaZantip doesn't conform to any known criteria. There is no advertising. There are no flyers. No posters. In the early years, there was no information available on how to get there. It was everyone for himself. The Republic moved every year, so thousands of festival-goers would wander around the Ukraine coast until they happened upon it. Nowadays, KaZantip is in a permanent location. Its structures are built out of concrete. To get into the festival each 'citiZen' must follow a compulsory entry procedure. They must have a special photo passport, obtain a visa and they must read a copy of the constitution written by Marshunok himself. The official constitution states that, 'Be the one you wanna be and live your life your way.' Further on you are invited to learn the mantras of the Republic by heart: 'This land is ours, so fuck the haters!' or 'For the life with no pants, for summer around the world!'

At KaZantip, the star of the show is the party itself, not the artists. The staff and the musicians are treated in exactly the same way as the 'citiZens' – the proof being that there is no predetermined line-up. It is decided on a whim, depending on the president's mood. He regularly hands out yellow suitcases with black spots stamped with a large letter Z, the official KaZantip emblem. These suitcases are a reference to an old Russian fairy tale where a man made children happy by handing out sweets from a yellow suitcase. At KaZantip, these suitcases are handed out to young DJs that the president chooses to sponsor. They are the most sought-after prize of the whole festival. Whoever has one can go to any stage and take to the decks.

At this open-air mad house, nudity is encouraged and everything and anything is acceptable within the limits established by the constitution. You can have sex on the beach if that's what floats your boat, or get completely off your head, not sleep for a week, or perhaps behave like a chimpanzee. But, beware he who is predatory or invades another's personal space without consent or who makes the mistake of peeing on the beach! Security will come down hard on you, fine you and throw you out, after a few strong words. This almost happened to Fred, our tour manager, in 2012.

I came to KaZantip with my LBS ('Live Booth Sessions') project with Scan X and Benjamin Rippert. After Pleyel and 18 months spent touring, during which I really enjoyed re-writing my tracks each night live on stage, I was worried about going back to touring as a DJ; the format now felt too restrictive. Instead, I set about bringing together my DJ-ing skills and a live concert. There were my machines and Scan X's as well as Ben's three keyboards all plugged into a mixer and then, in turn, into my DJ mixer. I could play this mixer like a third turntable. This clever, flexible layout enabled me to play tracks as a DJ or my own tracks, chopped up into segments (rhythmic loops, beats, etc.), onto which Ben's Rhodes keyboard or Scan X's machines could play on top. From that moment, any combination of sounds was possible. I could remix a track live, take the introduction of one of my tracks and completely change it, etc. In short, with LBS we were in new terrain. If it was the right moment, we let rip. If the mood was deeper, no problem. If we wanted to play a deep funky bass, drum 'n' bass, Detroit techno or dubstep, all we had to do was say it! In the two years we spent on the road with LBS, we never once played the same set twice. Quite a ground-breaking achievement.

At KaZantip, LBS had been booked to play in a sort of bar-cum-restaurant-cum-club on the beach, similar to the kind of places you come across in Ibiza. When we arrived, the festival was coming to a close. All the other stages were being dismantled after the big closing night party, which had taken place the previous weekend. Most of the bars, restaurants and shops were shut. With most of the festival-goers gone, KaZantip looked a bit like a ghost town. The only people left were the staff, close friends and a handful of clubbers who, for one reason or another, hadn't been able to – or didn't want to – leave. Even though all the people there looked quite smart, they also looked like the kind of people who had made it through an extreme experience and had since regrouped into a sort of community of extreme clubbing survivors.

That night LBS played for six hours non-stop. Six hours which must have driven our tour manager to go off and pee under the stars… but he was caught red-handed by the security guards. Even though Fred repeatedly told them that he was working with us, and that maybe there was a way to sort this out, they didn't want to know. They were on the verge of throwing him out when he had a brainwave and threatened, 'If you throw me out we'll stop the music right now!' It ended with a friendly little slap round the back of the head. Meanwhile, Ben, Scan X and I were looking after the 'citiZens'. And, I don't know, but we must have done a good job that night because the president came to see us in person to present us with the Kings of the Dancefloor medal in the middle of our set. Not bad, eh?

If KaZantip remains an isolated phenomenon, probably unique in its genre, it nevertheless illustrates the newfound freedom in Russian and Ukrainian nightlife. Like the majority of countries in South America, Hong Kong or Thailand, nightlife is far less controlled than in most countries in the West. The restrictions are basic – or sometimes non-existent – and so the atmosphere seems much more edgy, and far less easy to predict.

Playing in those kinds of places sometimes feels quite raw and as if I am right back in touch with that same thrill that made me fall in love with DJ-ing in the first place – when I search for that tipping point, when people on the dance floor switch over into a collective trance and lose control. Discovering new places like India, Kuala Lumpur, Chile and Argentina, coming face to face with a new public and being confronted with unknown codes of behaviour, is a bit like going on a first date. Seduction is at the centre of the process, as well as a certain amount of apprehension.

I remember a night in Rio de Janeiro for which I had prepared a special selection of baile funk records, a rough, heady, alluring genre of music. To play a bit of this Brazilian funk in its birthplace was a way for me to tell the public, 'I'm interested in you and I love the music you make.' Except what I didn't know was that for the Brazilian crowd, baile funk is the music of the favelas. I naïvely thought I was creating a connection with the people in the club, but in fact it was the total opposite. They all refused to be associated with this music and deserted the dance floor in their droves.

The experiences I have had in these new territories over the past 10 years have made me realise that a dance floor is never a neutral space but a place for breaking free and for civil disobedience. A place like no other, where the spirit of that time and the challenges facing each new generation come together. So whether in a basement, a club, a community hall or out on the street, in the middle of a wasteland or in a car park, in a field or in a warehouse, or even in a lobby, the dance floor is above all a place dedicated to happiness, letting go, sharing, but also a certain amount of narcissism and sex, of course. It's the place where people come to dance and be together, united against what is going on outside and in the real world, against what oppresses and threatens their being. In this sense, the dance floor is a political space. It is a meeting point, where different ways to say no and to not accept the status quo are both invented and expressed.

The restrictions that hit nightlife in the vast majority of European countries during the noughties (the smoking ban, noise-level restrictions, sometimes ridiculously early closing times) have gone a long way towards destroying these fundamental freedoms and robbed nightlife of its essence. As a consequence, for a good decade in Paris, people satisfied themselves with just going out. Going from one desperately trendy place to another, where nothing was really happening, except a gathering of deathly boring beautiful people. And some of the music played can only be qualified as dreadful.

At the time, I shuddered to think what clubbers in New York, London or Berlin must have thought when they came to Paris and decided to check out the ultra-trendy Parisian nightlife hangouts. Of course, the French capital still held onto a few enclaves such as the Rex, the Social Club and the Nouveau Casino, where you could listen to good music. But these clubs were few and far between in a city that numbers two million inhabitants. Where was Paris' equivalent to Berghain, Fabric or Womb? Where was the club that would put Paris back on the world's best nightlife map, where the city had once shined? We would have to wait a little longer, and in the meantime, put up with a few more years of this dreadful Parisian fondness for VIP clubs with shit music. A sad state of affairs found nowhere else in Europe. And certainly not in London!

But London isn't Paris. London invented the underground music scene. It is etched in the UK capital's memory. And has never left it since. From Brixton to Dalston, from the confines of the East End to Notting Hill Gate, the spirit of partying has always been alive. All over the city, every month, new artistic trends surface, new venues appear, new careers are launched, fashions come and go in an endless merry-go-round that sees each new generation stand up and confront the generation before with incredible energy. It's in their culture. In their DNA. It's the business of a cultural tradition that sees new avant-garde ideas not judged or rejected as in France, but embraced and supported, from London to Sheffield, Manchester to Liverpool.

Since the start of the new millennium, dubstep has been the new soundtrack to UK club nights. When it first appeared, thanks to the

Tempa.

distributor Ammunition, or young artists like Horsepower Productions, the style laid down a slow beat, with prominent sub basses, manipulated frequencies and a taste for dark, bare-boned, sometimes almost non-existent melodies. Then, as is often the case in the UK, the style fragmented into a myriad of different genres and sub-genres and ended up becoming just another umbrella label under which new UK electronic music trends such as grime and bass music were placed. But between these two musical reference points, dubstep has significantly changed the UK's musical landscape over the space of a decade. First there were the parties (FWD>>, DMZ, etc.), pirate radios (Rinse FM, etc.), labels (Tempa, Hyperdub, Wicky Lindows, Hench, Deepheads, etc.), the fast-rising artists (Burial, Inja, Jazzsteppa, Foreign Beggars, etc.), DJ stars (Skream, Benga, etc.), which in turn went on to inspire a myriad of new, audacious UK and international artists (Flying Lotus, Martyn, Matta, Caspa, The Gaslamp Killer, etc). So, whereas house and techno were descending into a creative coma, dubstep injected some welcome excitement into the electronic music landscape.

Following its arrival in the early noughties, dubstep went on to leave its mark on all spheres of urban musical life in London. Then its influence spread to Belgium, Italy and France, where it found fertile ground to take seed. It then spread to Germany, and Berlin in particular, where dubstep has carved itself a permanent place in the city's musical heritage. If the truth be known, Berlin is, after London, *the* dubstep stronghold in Europe. In fact, for nearly two decades now, Berlin has been the international capital of underground culture. Berlin is a laboratory, an unequalled city for accelerating trends and a major crossroads for cultural exchange. In fact, when you talk about passion, creative genius, urban frenzy and the artistic avant-garde, no other city in the world compares to modern-day Berlin.

After the Berlin Wall came down, people feared Berlin might lose its edge, but the exact opposite happened. Soon after, the city became a strange place, incredibly exciting, where everything existed in... double! There were two city centres, two city halls, two main stations, two airports, two national stadiums, two television control towers and innumerable police stations, fire stations, hospitals and schools that, all of a sudden, were obsolete and deserted, the doors left wide open and the electricity and water supplies left intact. Walking around the German capital at that time meant venturing into vast, abandoned neighbourhoods. Silent urban pockets that went on for miles, that anyone could lay claim to, to do whatever he/she wanted; open a club, a restaurant, an artist's studio, a gallery, absolutely anything! In the early 90s, the freedom in Berlin was almost limitless. And what was strange and exciting was that no one knew exactly what the city was going to become, be they the inhabitants or the politicians. Berlin may have been gloomy, poor, run down, and abandoned, but in some parts of the city it was very alive, vibrant and bursting with potential. The cost of living was next to nothing. Everything was there, ready. All you had to do was help yourself and invent. Thousands of creative people came to Berlin and made it their home during those years. They settled down in urban wastelands, in old factories, sometimes taking over whole buildings and going about their business without checking with anyone first. If the police came to evict them? No problem, they upped and left and set up shop a few blocks further away. Honestly, at that time, where else would you want to live?

I got to know Berlin back then. The first time I went there I was blown away by the buzz in the city and struck by its similarity to the abandoned industrial areas of Detroit. Yet, the similarities stopped there. Because in Motor City, the vast majority of artists wanted to get out fast, whereas artists in Berlin were united behind the same grand project: to optimise the formidable range of opportunities that their city had to offer. Musicians, DJs, artists, filmmakers, writers, designers and promoters offered a future for Berlin during that decade. These people, whether Berlin-born and bred or having adopted the city as their home, had the imagination to reinvent Berlin as an international crossroads of the arts and nightlife. Furthermore, they made their city a symbol of resistance against 'all-about-making-money' and the standardisation of tastes and cultures. This last point is crucial if you want to understand what Berlin is all about. The German capital has a fundamentally rebellious nature. More than any other major city, Berlin knows every single way to say no. And this has been the case for at least seven decades, when the first steps towards what we would call club culture were taken in its basements.

The story is incredible, to such an extent that in Germany it has become a legend. It illustrates the tenacity and recklessness that has reigned for a good century in Berlin (cabarets, etc.), and the dancing, nightlife, and a 'political' sense of diehard partying far from curious eyes.

Listen to this….

It was August 1941. Two decades earlier, Berlin was famous throughout the world for being a cosmopolitan city as well as a city of pleasure. The city had an international reputation for being the world capital for liberated sex and partying. Epicureans of all types came from across Europe to discover the cabarets, erotic venues, pickup joints, gay and lesbian clubs and numerous brothels to satisfy their sexual appetites. The Foreign Minister, Gustav Stresemann, ran the Weimar Republic

▶ Playlist
SWING KIDS
Duke Ellington
Take The A Train

Sydney Bechet
Original Dixieland One Step

Glenn Miller
In The Mood

Louis Armstrong & His Hot Five
Heebie Jeebies

Count Basie & His Orchestra
Jumpin' At The Woodside

Cab Calloway & His Orchestra
Zah Zuh Zah

Bennie Goodman
Sing, Sing, Sing

and introduced Germany to an open regime of socialism and consumerism. The result was a great sense of freedom and peace in Berlin, as well as a certain tolerance where each person was allowed to organise their business according to their personal tastes (whether sexual, festive, etc.). But, 20 years later, there was no longer any question of freedom or late-night excesses; Berlin and the rest of Germany were under the rule of the Third Reich.

During that time, young people in their teens would still gather regularly in secret in the basements of the buildings in Berlin. In Hamburg, Munich and the capital Berlin, there must have been about a thousand of them and they were known as the 'Swingjungen', or 'swing kids'. They were mad about British and American culture and were fans of British clothes and American jazz, music that the Nazi regime considered as 'Entartete Kunst' (Degenerate Art). Being a jazz fan in Hitler's time, or worse, owning Dixieland records, could get you into serious trouble. But these kids, from middle-class and upper-middle-class backgrounds, were defiant. They were rebels. They resisted in their own way. There was no question of them joining the Hitler Youth. Marching in shorts, Nazi propaganda, 'useful work' policies, the collective effort, a blind allegiance to national socialism … could all get stuffed! What the Swingjungen wanted most was to have fun. These pleasure-seekers went all the way and spent nights on end taking amphetamines and dancing to the sounds of a jazz band or jazz records played on a gramophone. In private apartments or abandoned basements in the suburbs, the swing kids were looking to escape reality. Through the music, dancing, sweat and adrenaline that their secret gatherings induced, they invented their own freedom. It may have been fragile, or naïve, but who cared, as all that mattered to them was to live life to the full.

Word soon got round. The Nazi leaders judged the Swing Kids parties for what they were: the expression of a rebellion. In the summer of 1941, the Youth Guidance Office released a statement branding these kids as the enemies of 'the greatest adventure of all times'. Not long after, the police began to raid parties on orders from Heinrich Himmler. Hundreds of kids guilty of loving jazz and rejecting the Nazi doctrine were thrown into youth concentration camps to be 're-educated'. But these mass arrests didn't bury the movement. Those who managed to escape arrest became even more radical, publishing flyers condemning Hitler's Germany, and they continued to organise underground parties, as if exhilarated by the danger.

In January 1942, after Himmler demanded more radical measures be taken against them, the leaders of the movement were hauled off to forced labour camps. Meanwhile in Paris, the 'Zazous' were feeling the weight of STO (Service du Travail Obligatoire, or Compulsory Work Service) for having expressed a taste for British and American culture and spending weekends on end dancing to jazz, Duke Ellington and Cab Calloway. When Pierre Laval ordered the first mass arrests in Paris, the swing kids from Hamburg and Berlin had already largely been wiped out.

In Berlin, people still recall the tragic fate of the swing kids. Their story has been handed down so that people remember the deeply defiant nature of the city. Saying that, these events have forged its character. The city still carries the scars of the violence of World War II, and the absurdities of the Cold War are still visible in the neighbourhoods of East Berlin. But Berlin is still passionate about the present. And about the future. Poor but sexy. Proud but humble. Enigmatic but welcoming. Berlin has reinvented itself as an unrivalled Mecca for culture. There are 65 museums, 146 libraries and 65 theatres, and for those interested in the underground scene, Berlin is unbelievably rich, and really comes into its own at night… it is a hotbed of pleasure.

Berlin has been changing the face of nightlife for the past 25 years, where the legislation that regulates clubbing in the UK or in France plays no part. Boiling, corrosive, unpredictable. As free, radical and diverse as the aesthetic images that make up modern-day Berlin. Somewhere between resourcefulness, diversity and absolute craziness, the future of club culture is being created here right before our eyes. Prohibited signs don't exist. Or hardly. You can go about your business. No one gives a damn. No one is looking or judging. Anything goes. In this vortex where your senses and your stamina are tested to the limit, you can have a lot of fun, but some do get lost along the way. They go and live there with the sole aim to party and are drawn into Berlin's spell. Those people get swallowed up. Like Tokyo nightlife, you pay the price for an extended honeymoon stay in Berlin. Where once this no man's land where everything is permissible, a sort of weird *Escape From New York* filled with harmless freaks and attractive '24-hour party people' seemed appealing, suddenly those people wake up and find Berlin grey and hostile. The city will get under your skin, crush you and spit you out…

Like this city in a constant state of flux, huge numbers of venues reflect both the contradictions and extremes of Berlin – whether the huge super-clubs, Weekend and Watergate, or cosier venues like Tresor, Kater Holzig or Wilde Renate. It would be unthinkable to write about Berlin's current nightlife scene without dwelling on the club where I have spent most of my time, the Berghain-Panorama Bar. Ever since it opened in December 2004 as the worthy successor of the defunct E-Werk, the Berghain-Panorama Bar has become the emblem of Berlin's very special brand of nightlife culture. It's simple – as far as I know, no other club in Europe has ever pushed the ethos 'zero taboos' so far.

It is a parallel universe, heaven (or hell, depending), a liberal beast, the ultimate experience for the senses, sweat and sex, a debauched urban Babylon, a temple of techno excellence, a Mecca for international DJs and the celebration of life in its most liberal of forms; the Berghain-Panorama Bar is undoubtedly one of the best clubs in the world. Maybe even *the* best club in the world.

The club is open every weekend, round the clock. It is located on wasteland in the former Friedrichshain power plant that was built during the Cold War near East Berlin's train station. The surrounding area is predominantly quiet and residential. Every weekend, hundreds of clubbers queue for hours in front of this imposing concrete and steel edifice. Most of them are regulars, others have been lured in by the club's reputation. But not everyone is necessarily prepared to experience what is waiting for them inside – that is, of course, if the bouncer decides to let them in. It is known for being one of hardest clubs to get into in Europe…

Once inside, there are four whole floors to explore. On the ground floor, the huge concrete expanse sets the tone with a chill-out space and a cloakroom. It can hold a good 1,000 people. On the same level is 'the laboratory', which attracts a predominantly gay clientele looking for sensory thrills. There are darkrooms for those who wish. Further along, in one wing there is the Kantine, where the record label Deutsche Grammophon organises contemporary music concerts during the week. On the first floor is the main room, so to speak, of the Berghain Club. The ceilings are 60 feet high, the room has a capacity for several thousand people, and it has one of the most powerful sound systems I have ever heard. Finally, on the top floor, is the legendary Panorama Bar, which has a much warmer sound system. The ceilings are lower and the capacity smaller, making it more humane. Perched up on the top floor, the Panorama Bar almost seems cosy in comparison. Every weekend, it generates the most unbelievable energy. The music is in the hands of a group of extremely talented resident DJs. There's no star system here. The Berghain couldn't care less about big-name DJs. Booking DJs that are used to filling stadiums is the antithesis of the club's philosophy. Here, they book DJs who are able to maintain the very special atmosphere. So, being invited to play at the Panorama Bar makes you feel a bit like a member of a secret club. It's also good to contribute to the magic of a place where time doesn't matter. Unsurprisingly, that is exactly what happens whenever I am asked to go

BERGHAIN

▶ Playlist

BERGHAIN

Terrence Dixon
Minimalism (Ben Klock Remix)

Modeselektor & Sound Pellegrino
Negativity

Heiko Laux
Splinter

Der Ausgang
Merijn

Phase
Perplexed

Robert Hood
Drive

Terence Fixmer
Psychik

and play there; the notion of time evaporates and becomes insignificant, for myself and the crowd, who hang out at the club and sometimes we're all there for a whole weekend without realising it! This has got nothing to do with the state some people are in; the Berghain is entirely responsible. It's special. Everyone there feels it. A tour manager that came with us once remembers that night very clearly. At about 6am, our LBS set was coming to an end. He was insistent on going straight back to the hotel to sleep once all our gear was packed up. I suggested one last drink at the Panorama Bar. He replied, 'Just one then!' 'Yes, yes, just the one', I said. The next time he looked at his watch … it was 3pm!

I wonder whether this wild side of Berlin will last much longer? A couple of years ago I never would have asked myself this question. But Berlin has reason to worry. The survival of the underground is in danger. Low-cost clubbing, squats, nightlife excesses, all of this is not to the council's taste – to the extent that the council has started a crackdown campaign. They no longer want all things alternative. They want to develop Berlin's economy through luxury branding. This open desire for gentrification can already be seen in traditionally bohemian neighbourhoods now inhabited by a wealthier class of people. 'Yuppie' bars, restaurants, art galleries and international brands have started appearing. Once 'renovated', these areas are victims of soaring house prices. The artists who once contributed to breathing life back into areas such as Mitte or the banks of the Spree have been forced to move out, in some cases, literally.

Berlin is experiencing the same fate as other inner-city areas that were once poor and then became fashionable with the urban bourgeoisie (Soho in Manhattan, Williamsburg in Brooklyn, Shoreditch in London, Abbesses in Paris). Except, this time the difference is that it is a political ambition to clean up the city. The first symbolic example of this strategy was the closing of Tacheles, the renowned squat on Oranienburger Strasse, after months of battling with property developers who wanted to build high-end apartment blocks. Then it was the club scene that became the target. And no one had seen that coming …

The big bad wolf in this story is the German performing rights collecting society Gema – Germany's equivalent to Sacem. Like Sacem, Gema is privately run. And, exactly like Sacem, nobody knows precisely how the money they collect each year from public venues that play music, including clubs, festivals and even restaurants and shops, is redistributed. And Gema shows no more interest in electronic music than Sacem. What's it all about? Collecting money. A lot of money.

In 2012 Gema announced to the clubs that they were going to increase their licence fees. The official reason was to allow them to better allocate budgets to future music events. Basically, they were planning to review the criteria for which the licence that every club in Germany is subject to is calculated. The size of the venue, its capacity, opening time, entry fee, type of event, etc. On top of this, Gema intended to apply a rate of 50 per cent to all events that went on for more than five hours … in other words, every single club night in Berlin. For the clubs' finances, this new measure spelt disaster. To understand why, you just have to look at in detail. The weekly magazine *Der Spiegel* calculated that, for an average-sized club measuring 400m^2, with an entry fee of 8 euros, that puts on two nights per week from 10pm to 5am, the annual rate would rise from 14,500 to 95,000 euros! The Berghain currently pays Gema an annual rate of between 30,000 and 40,000 euros. With these new rates, their fees would increase by 1,000 per cent, and as for Watergate, their fees would increase by … 2,000 per cent!

Berlin clubs naturally resisted the idea of increasing ticket prices, believing that it would undermine the spirit of Berlin nightlife, that has always prided itself on being reasonably inexpensive. Initially the clubs couldn't negotiate with Gema because the organisation stated they were not open to negotiation. But would the owners shut down their clubs? No, no one would dream of it! Hey, this is Berlin after all! History has proven that resistance is in this city's DNA. The council was well aware of what it would lose if the club scene collapsed, as clubbing represents an important source of income for the city. Berlin isn't rich.

However if the worst-case scenario was to happen, and Gema put their new policy into place, it is hard to imagine that the Berlin underground would die. You can be sure that the underground would strike back. Within a few weeks, clandestine clubs and illegal parties would pop up all over East Berlin. Berlin remains full of deserted industrial zones, isolated warehouses and empty buildings. The underground would take refuge there, exactly as it did when the Berlin Wall came down. And there is no doubt that illegal raves would happen once again and Berlin would reinvigorate itself with the energy on which its greatness was built.

Thankfully however, an agreement was reached in late 2013 which saw 'moderate' fees increased by Gema, instigated over a long period of time. Initial increases in entrance fees were almost unnoticeable, even if the plan is for some clubs to raise prices by up to 64%. Berlin found a way to keep its underground going.

our future

In the middle of the 90s, it was the ambition of people who were mad about dance music, but who were neither DJs nor producers, to organise parties. For some, this was limited to small gatherings, mostly of their friends, and friends of friends. For others, from the outset, this meant arranging larger events: finding a warehouse, a disused building, or even an old car park, and putting on a rave. For an even more select group, the plan was to create an annual event. Not necessarily something huge, but big enough to be representative of the main electronic music genres.

Naturally, many never got past the planning stage, the organisers being either intimidated or discouraged by the risks involved and the huge amount of energy that organising a large-scale event requires. However, many others went ahead. Usually the organisers played at being promoters at a couple of small events, to learn the ropes and earn a bit of money. As they got more and more involved in their local music scene, a minority discovered a talent for events management. Decades later, some of them are still there – but not organising raves anymore, rather, they're putting on festivals.

Before continuing, it's important to note that the raves I went to in the 80s and 90s in Europe are completely different from those of the 21st century. Of course, you could still find free parties in the heart of the Balkans, or teknivals in Brittany in the middle of the 2010s, that resemble the kind of events I attended in my youth. But those types of raves often appeal only to a small radical underground.

Generally, the spirit of raves is no longer found in suburban warehouses, as was the case once, but now resides at electronic music festivals that were launched at a time when people were still fighting for the recognition of techno as a legitimate scene. Some of these festivals established themselves as key events in European underground culture. In the middle of the second decade of a new century, that original spirit of raves could still be found at Sonar in Barcelona, I Love Techno in Belgium or at the Amsterdam Dance Event. These huge gatherings, where you'd find almost the entire global electronic scene, evoke the good-natured coming together of an event such as Universe. In 1994, Brittany became home to a great festival called Astropolis, and it was a more visceral, underground kind of event. Despite being organised with unquestioned professionalism, Astropolis retained the spirit and essence of once-illicit techno gatherings.

At Astro you must expect the unexpected. It is the only festival in the world where I have DJ-ed in the pouring rain in front of 4,000 nutters who danced and screamed for 12 hours non-stop. This extraordinary festival's success and longevity are the result of three key elements: an exceptional crowd ready for anything whatever the weather, a beautiful setting (the gardens of Keroual Manor near Brest), and a tight-knit team of music-mad organisers who know how to make you feel at home. Their approach, their notion of friendship and their insanity (sometimes quite ferocious), which was the key to raves in the 90s, are always very much in play. They have made Astropolis a unique annual event, and remind us of the extent to which it is the spirit, the essence and the energy of the organisers, that drives an event. Which brings us back to the same old point: if the DJ isn't made to feel welcome and at ease, and isn't excited about the place where he is to play, then he isn't able to communicate any magic to the crowd. In the same way, if organisers aren't passionate about what they do, their festival will simply be one event among many. And, in this respect, if there is one person who is passionate about music who should be mentioned here, it's Steffen Charles, the founder of the Time Warp festival in Mannheim.

From its launch, Time Warp became *the* world techno gathering. All the cutting-edge DJs, old and young, are always especially excited about going to play at Time Warp, to the extent that, come autumn, we'd all say on meeting, 'Hey man! See you at Time Warp!' With the debut event in 1994, which remains for me an outstanding example of mayhem, Steffen developed a very privileged relationship with the artists who perform at the festival. A music-mad real gentleman, he is tireless, and very talented at bringing people together. In my view, this guy is a great master for whom all artistic and creative ideas are valid. You just have to suggest a new project to him, especially something that hasn't been done before, to see his eyes light up.

In 2007, during the week leading up to Time Warp, Steffen organised the Jetzt Musik festival, which gave a cultural platform to innovative new trends. Every year, the Jetzt Musik festival aims to encourage us to think about our era through a series of seminars, workshops and debates chaired by leading artists and university researchers. At the end of seven days of intense musical and intellectual stimulation, the Time Warp party kicked off. For 19 hours, 40 or so extremely enthusiastic artists perform in front of 18,000 people inside three huge halls, or in smaller rooms such as the Dome – which became a second home to me as soon as I'd worked there. Every time, without fail, at around two or three in the morning, the dance floor becomes a giant playground for 900 clubbers, and that's when anything can happen. At dawn, when the first rays of sunlight pour through the glass dome, the crowd experiences a second energy burst, and so builds a collective hysteria…

At the end of my set, once the room shuts down (always after several minutes of hearing, 'Encore'), comes the time when I can really enjoy the last few hours of the festival. What happens then is totally unique, as far as I know: all the artists gather together on the main stage for a sort of grand finale where everyone goes on a massive bender. We all love that moment when, at around 10am, the DJ booth on the main stage is packed full of people partying – and always right in the middle, thrilled to be surrounded by his friends and the artists he admires, is Steffen Charles.

Despite Time Warp's colossal success for over two decades, and despite the fact that all the big names in electronic music vied to play there (absolutely everyone performed there at one time or another), Steffen never made any compromises to commercialism. He manages his events with remarkable integrity: financially independent, with full artistic relevance and always a sense of sharing. Such values were also magnificently adhered to by the Nuits Sonores festival in Lyon. With people like this, not only is the spirit of techno certain to be upheld for a long time to come but it is also capable of inventing a future for itself.

The original team behind the Nuits managed to create a festival with meaning, and they put their all into it. In fact, they put their whole life into it. They had all been active on Lyon's electronic music scene for quite some time when the cancellation of a rave planned at the Halle Tony Garnier in 1994, swiftly followed by the closure of a house club on the slopes of La Croix-Rousse, spurred them into action. But exhausting themselves by trying to organise an illegal party wasn't – or at least was no longer – their thing. For this group of young people, fighting back meant taking pen to paper and creating a project that would legitimise the culture of electronic music in a city that was the symbol of anti-techno repression in France.

Once they had drawn up a plan, Vincent Carry, DJ Agoria, the girls from Arty Farty and their gang got motoring. Really motoring. Driven on by the fact that the new mayor had made a promise during his election campaign to make 'more space' for youth culture, they took him at his word and laid siege to his offices. They spent hours in meetings with his staff, and in the end got the go ahead, along with some salutary advice from the new mayor of Lyon, who told them, 'Go ahead, but don't fuck about too much, OK?'

When, in May 2012, the Nuits Sonores festival celebrated its 10th anniversary, its organisers could reflect upon a decade of momentous work, during which many had thought their aims to be impossible to achieve. But the festival de-ghettoised electronic music in the Rhône-Alpes region, gained access to symbolic buildings and spaces within the city (the banks of the Rhône, the Marché gare, the old Brosette factory site or the Hotel-Dieu, a 17th-century hospital and birthplace of legions of little Lyonnais), and established Lyon as an epicentre of digital culture in Europe. I take my hat off to them.

My love affair with the Nuits Sonores dates back to the first time I played there in 2005. It was an official rave at the Sucrière, an emblematic building in Lyon that was to be pulled down soon after. It was about 8am. I was coming to the end of my three-hour set. Daylight was streaming in through the windows. The dance floor was still packed and the crowd seemed intent on continuing to dance with an almost brutal intensity. They weren't ready to stop. They wanted more. I felt like I had been transported somewhere else and it was as if each person there was bathed in a vibrant, sensual energy. It was at that moment that the organisers of the Nuits Sonores appeared on stage, their arms loaded with bottles of champagne. Corks popped. We all started spraying the crowd. And we carried on for a good hour or so in a state of total euphoria. I have made a big print from a photo that was taken that morning, and it hangs in my studio, serving as a reminder of the kind of state of grace achieved that morning.

It was one of those nights that justifies this job, rewards all the hard work, the determination I give it – and that makes me want to carry on. Since that night at Nuits Sonores, I have been back every year, in every possible configuration: playing live and then with LBS, doing a back-to-back set with Agoria, playing an afternoon DJ set for children, and performing a cinemix at the Insitut Lumière. Playing this festival every year is always a special time for me. Special because, like Time Warp, taking part means being involved in an annual event that thrives on curiosity and excellence, that chooses family over business; and these, believe me, are values not shared by all festivals.

There was a time when the majority of music festivals were considered as a sort of extension of a village fete. People came to have a laugh, get drunk with their friends, roll around in the mud, pee under the stars, pick someone up if the opportunity presented itself, and then listen to music. Once the festival was over, you'd go home sated, satisfied and ready to start all over again the next time. That attitude changed and evolved, however, as a new generation of music events started to appear. These sorts of events do not just stick a tent in a field and put a series of bands on stage in succession. On the contrary. They clearly advertise themselves as an alternative to old-school festivals. They are organised in original places, their line-up not only offering a vast array of contemporary music, but also an insight into visual and digital arts.

Such is the case with the pioneering Sonar festival or, again, the Nuits Sonores, but there's also the excellent N.A.M.E festival that was first put on in the north of France in 2005 by a collective known as Art Point M. It is also the case with the amazing Worldwide festival in Sète, co-founded by Gilles Peterson. Worldwide takes place on Sète's beaches, at its open-air theatre, and has a dance floor on the seawall lapped by the waves. Beautiful! It's also the case with Bestival on the Isle of Wight, founded in 2004 by the UK DJ, Rob Da Bank, where the crème de la crème of international electronic music artists and DJs vie to perform in a laid-back, family-friendly, slightly crazy environment. Due to their success and innovative ideas, such events forced more traditional festivals to react in order to stay in the game. Yet, while people may have expected traditional festivals to question their choice of artists, or become more humane, that didn't happen. Rather, most of them preferred to spend their money on becoming even more mammoth in scale, and more aggressive than ever.

The boom in popularity of new music events came at a time when the record industry was losing power and influence. So, of course, the music business as well as the press and brands soon began wooing the festivals in order to attempt to regain valuable lost revenue. The equation is simple: since the music industry crisis, an entire economy has been trying to re-coup its losses by monetizing live events. The time when a festival was predominantly for upcoming musicians hoping to be talent-spotted and signed to a record label belongs to the past. Increasingly, live events became vital to the financial survival of the vast majority of artists. As a result, the fees demanded from venues increased, and the fees that artists' agents demanded from festivals went through the roof.

Since the beginning of the music industry crisis at the turn of the century, fees increased two-, four-, ten-, fifty-fold … complete madness! Of course, a large fee is not necessarily unreasonable if it reflects the artist's notoriety, rarity of stage appearance, the complexity of the set-up on stage, etc. However, it can become tricky when the promoter asks the artist to justify their fee. After all, if you're paying, you have a right to know exactly what you're paying for. And this is precisely where things come unstuck. Because often the performers can't justify their monetary demands.

In fact, nobody can.

When the music industry was all-powerful, things were clear. An artist's fee was calculated on a scale that was more or less understandable – i.e. their record sales. But in the 21st century it's all about the buzz. People talk about an artist being all over the internet, how many friends they have on Facebook, how many followers on Twitter, how many clicks they get on Spotify or Deezer, whether they are being hyped by a certain media, etc. Basically, it's all hot air! But as festivals pulled in larger and larger crowds, the less scrupulous players in the music business looked for cash where they thought they'd find it.

As ticket prices increased, and more and more festivals sprung up, you might think that the public would have gradually turned away from these sorts of events. But it proved to be the exact opposite. People might have thought that, because the music business was so much tougher to succeed in, there would be fewer musicians and fewer festivals to choose from. Again, the opposite proved true. By the middle of the 2010s, there had never been so many festivals in Europe to choose from. And, as a result, the competition between festivals for customers became fierce.

The situation in Europe mimics what happened in the UK at the end of the 90s, when everyone suddenly wanted a piece of dance music. After a bumpy start, house and techno were considered 'cool' and became a veritable Eldorado. So, every month, a new super-club opened somewhere, and it all went to certain DJ's heads. Of course, the scene eventually collapsed. One decade later, and it appeared that festivals had become the new places to be.

I see one specific reason for this. Festivals represent a return to the communal experience, providing an antidote to the dehumanising of relationships created by the dominance of technology in Western society. In a period cleansed of spirituality, and in which the omnipresence of the 'virtual' has distorted what is 'real' to the extent of degrading its worth, the festival is a return to a profound collective experience. It is a place of true physical experience shared by many – everyone hears and feels the same a bass line; they cheer, look up at the same sky (or lighting effects) and feel their feet in the mud or on concrete. But they're always together, with heightened senses, following the same course for a few hours or a few days. In my mind, it is all of this that explains the success that festivals enjoyed. They became key events in 21st-century cultural life, and consequently an observation platform for spotting trends in the music business.

One such trend is enough to send shivers down your spine: the standardisation of music played. Or worse, the pick 'n' mix style of programming that consists of throwing together anyone and everyone, so that on the same day on the same stage you might find Pink and Radiohead, or a Eurodance act followed by an underground techno DJ.

In the summer of 2012, at a festival in Serbia, and then in Belgium a few weeks later, I was profoundly struck by this odd phenomenon.

While setting up my gear with the guys from LBS, I was forced to listen to a band on stage playing the worst kind of ultra-commercial crap. How can promoters, who less than three years previously had put together a great line-up, subject the public to such a mishmash, I wondered. And why? What was even weirder was that, when our set began, a large section of the crowd didn't seem to notice the difference between what we were playing and the fairground music they'd just heard.

Such an episode illustrates something that bothers me. Does this mean that the more audiences are exposed to mixing anything and everything together, they will end up believing that all music is equal, I wonder? That those with the least musical knowledge will end up thinking that Pink and Radiohead must be the same thing because they are playing on the same stage?

One major artist who purposefully chose to turn his back on this whole circus is James Murphy. Co-founder of the New York record label DFA, captain of the disco-punk vessel LCD Soundsystem, James Murphy is a musical purist. He is also a great guy who has known hard times in the past and never compromised when success came knocking at his door, which helped propel him to the level of being an electroclash icon. After several great singles (Daft Punk is Playing at My House, Tribulations, etc.) and three brilliant albums that defined the contours of a hybrid style of pop music somewhere between rock, new wave and disco, James Murphy, an ex-punk who had by chance fallen for electro, decided to kill off his creation at the end of a masterful concert he gave at Madison Square Garden on April 2, 2011.

Subsequently, this tall, somewhat shy and unlikely idol popped up at several electronic music festivals including Sonar, and Nuits Sonores in May 2012, where he performed the most extraordinarily elegant DJ set. That night, James Murphy delivered with exemplary generosity on the policy that he had managed to put into place with the now-defunct LCD Soundsystem, i.e. opening the public's ears by giving them something different to dance to.

JAMES MURPHY:
'My real job is as a sound engineer. I did it for years, in every possible configuration, on the road, stuffed in a clapped-out van with a sad group of punks, in awful venues, or in recording studios that were barely functional. The challenge of being behind a mixing desk has always been the same – producing a sound that will make a deep impression on people.

'One night I found myself in the studio with the Irish DJ, David Holmes. Later on, we went to a party where someone offered me an ecstasy pill, so I took it. It was that night that I realised that I fundamentally loved dancing. It really opened my eyes. At the time I had stopped working on the punk circuit. I couldn't see the point anymore. But the label DFA that I co-founded with Tim Goldsworthy already existed, with its policy of back to basics: good records, simple artwork, and a hand-crafted attitude to music and the music business.

'It was during that time that I started DJ-ing more and more. The first time I was 29. I finally felt ready to share my tastes with others without worrying what they might think. After all, the majority of DJs I listened to at the end of the 90s seemed to be buying boring records to play with other deadly boring records. It made me mad. I thought, "One day I'll die, and these guys are wasting seven good minutes of my time playing abominably dull music!" So it was then I started playing stuff I liked: ESG, Can, Liquid Liquid, Bauhaus, Donna Summer, etc. Then, all of a sudden, for the first time in my life, people thought I was cool. But I soon realised that much younger kids were also playing the music I liked. It came as quite a shock. I thought, I'm dead! (laughs)

'I was always angry back then. One day, I met up with Ad-Rock from the Beastie Boys to play basketball in West Village. He was on his way back from a garage sale and gave me a boombox that he'd bought for a few dollars. That was where the beat in Losing My Edge came from. I recorded that track in one hit at my studio after playing around with it on my way home. I played the track to the staff at DFA. They all looked at me weirdly and told me, "That's awful!" Only one person actually liked it. Losing My Edge was sort of ironically funny and was a way for me to hide how down I felt at the time. Then Losing My Edge came out and everything went very fast and I was asked to perform live. The problem was, I didn't have a band, just a boom box! (laughs)

'Ten years after the first ever LCD Soundsystem concert in London, I decided to end it. It's a policy I've always stuck to: three albums and then stop, because the fourth record is often one too many. When you get to that point, you're not really being creative, you're acting on reflexes. Of course, you might produce music that's slightly different from before, but probably nothing substantially different. When you get to a fourth album, you have to make music professionally. And then what can you expect? Another single played on the radio? Playing a bigger stage at a bigger festival? A bit more money? So what? I like a bit of a challenge but not like that. Anyway, the idea of being at the head of an enterprise freaks me out.

'Everyone around me understood the reasons behind my decision. In hindsight, ending LCD Soundsystem was the right thing to do, even if from one day to the next I found myself without work. That's why I went back to DJ-ing for the next couple of years. It was a way not to lose touch, to stay in contact with the public and above all to carry on enjoying myself.

'I think my position as a DJ is very clear. I'll never be the kind of guy to play all new tracks, the kind of guy to bang it out all night long or be really "deep". I think of myself as a guy who isn't afraid. The 10 years I spent with LCD Soundsystem taught me how to communicate with the public, whatever. Some festivals that book me only see me as "James from LCD" so I sometimes find myself playing in places to crowds that I would probably never have come into contact with. I've always dealt with it by asking myself the same question, "What can I get out of this moment?" The answer is always the same: communicate with the people dancing, even if that means unsettling them a bit in order to play them music differently.'

James Murphy – a great performer – has rapidly gained recognition for being an instinctive, cultivated and refined DJ. LCD Soundsystem's impeccable discography largely foretold this. Both the man and the artist are incredibly modest. James Murphy presents himself as vector of the music that he listened to while growing up and the music of today. His DJ set at the Nuits Sonores was exemplary. Not only, during that magical night, did he manage to create an intimate club atmosphere in a 3,000-capacity warehouse, but he also managed to express better than anyone that there has never existed so much good music to nourish people, to make them vibrate, feel inspired and rethink reality.

And let me repeat that. With each passing day there has never been so much good music around, to the extent that any DJ could entirely refresh his selection every week. Yet, although the possibilities of reaching out to new audiences is constantly on the increase thanks to new technologies, the majority of big events, with a few exceptions, continued to book the same artists or serve up an incoherent mishmash of a line-up as the 2010s progressed.

However, despite the omnipresence of ultra-commercial artists at festivals, a new generation of music producers emerged, too: Brant Brauer Frick, Noze, Daphne and dozens of others, who are free from past conventions, took house and techno into hybrid territories that had never been explored before. European record labels like Noir Musique, Mobilee, Exploited, Pampa or Freerange revisited the language of American house music and made it their own. In Germany, artists like D.B., Dixon, Fritz Kalkbrenner or Henrik Schwartz stylishly blended techno and pop music, while others such as Nosaj Thing, Cadik, Cab Driver or Magic Panda built a future for electronica. In the UK, record labels like Red Seal, Shogun Audio, Samurai, Earnest Endeavours, Girls Music, Black Butter, Brainfeeder or Brownswood redefined the frontiers of urban music, and found new horizons for drum 'n' bass, dubstep and hip-hop.

Even techno looked forward to a glittering future. Record labels such as Dirty Bird, 50 Weapons, Dystopian, Ilian Tape, Hypercolour and Hotflush provide a solid basis for artists to grow from. The same goes for tougher techno, with artists like Ben Klok, Rod, Clouds, Marcel Dettman, Proxy, Duke Dumont, Nina Kraviz and Crackboy reviving techno with tougher, more biting sounds. Meanwhile, the very talented Ian O'Donovan, David Granha, Oniris and Satoshi Fumi proved that Detroit techno is no longer only made within the boundaries of 8 Mile Road, but also in countries as far and wide as Ireland, Portugal and Japan. Then there is all the music being made in Chile, China, Russia, Argentina, South Africa or Brazil. All the places where electronic music seeded itself are developing their own original music, which is sometimes astounding in its freedom and its desire to break away.

Among these artists and the musical genres that are evolving and developing from the new epicentres of electronic music in the world, I see the opportunity for dance music to bring to a close this first cycle of its history and begin another. This new stage in its history will unquestionably happen through sharing, cultural diversity and the renewal of a musical language that is over 30 years old. By forcing house and techno to be incorporated into the present, a generation of DJs and music producers are building a form of music that reiterates the ups and downs of the here and now. By pursuing their art, far from the beaten track, these artists offer their era a vehicle to express the present and envisage the future.

epilogue **dance to the music**

In the spring of 2012, Pedro Winter called me and asked, 'Hey, what's that track on your video?' I had just finished posting a short film on YouTube retracing the adventures of LBS the previous year, and used a techno track I had made for the soundtrack. Pedro loved the track. As well as his legendary spontaneity, what I love about him is his ability to speak simply. He had lost one of his best friends, DJ Mehdi, just a few months before. And very naturally, he said to me, 'You know, Mehdi would have loved me to sign this track.'

Me: '…'.

Him: 'Really, I really want this track for Ed Banger.' It was all sorted very quickly. Especially as we had both wanted to work together for ages. But nothing had ever come of it before; because of our busy schedules we had never found the time. Pedro is a very busy man (isn't that his nickname, Busy P?), so up until then, the right opportunity to do something together had never really presented itself. But the idea had been around for ages. Ever since one night at the Nuits Sonores, when Pedro, who had been at the vodka, got down on one knee and said, 'Laurent, I love you! One day, we'll have to do something together!' I laughed and replied, 'I never dared ask!' Hugs all round. Declarations of love. And so, two years on and Jacques In The Box quickly became one of my classic tracks.

I have often wondered if my most popular tracks are the ones that best reflect who I am. Crispy Bacon, for example. It has been such an important and symbolic track in my career, but does that make it a self-portrait? The same goes for The Man With The Red Face. It was consistently voted the all-time techno anthem in Belgium by a radio audience year after year, well into the second decade following its first release on F Comm, but does it really sum up who I am? When I really think about it, Last Dance At Yellow or Downfall are among the tracks that best represent me. And I would add Jacques In The Box, too, as it's a track I particularly love. Firstly, because it relates to a time with LBS when we wanted to create 'the happiness track', a dance track that was fun, immediate, that we would enjoy playing live and that would communicate happiness. And also because it's the only track that we have ever recorded together in the studio – following its release in 2012, Ben had to take time out for health reasons. Scan X and I carried on as a duo for several months but finally wound up LBS at the end of a final goodbye gig in Lyon, on December 21, 2012.

Jacques In The Box also marked my return to a techno sound I love, but from which I had distanced myself to concentrate on other projects:

composing the music for the documentary film *Play* by Manuel Herrero; composing the music for an exhibition by the artist Gerard Allary and then the photographer Gerard Rancinan. Beginning the developmental stage of a feature-length film based upon *Electrochoc*, and my weekly radio show It Is What It is, broadcast on the Mouv' in France, Couleur 3 in Switzerland and Pure FM in Belgium. Added to this was, of course, a long list of live tours and DJ tours.

I look back on that period as a mad rush, driven by my hunger for adventure, new experiences and change. It was a marathon that I tackled head on, but it was also a time when I did my best to enjoy family life. In some ways, Jacques In The Box sums up this slightly hectic period, during which I spread myself thin, leaving techno aside for a while, but knowing that I would go back to it one day. Which I did when I threw myself headfirst into it with LBS, making music that's direct, made for dancing, for putting your hands up in the air, for being happy. And, the icing on the cake was that it was Pedro Winter who signed it.

Initially, our collaboration came as rather a surprise. Because people were expecting me to release a record on a more traditional techno record label such as Cocoon, Poker Flat or Innervisions. Not on an electro label that was worshipped by Paris' fashion crowd. Our collaboration got people talking. Some of the things people were saying were quite funny, others were completely ridiculous such as, 'Laurent is getting old, so he needs Pedro who's young to stay in the game.' Or, 'Ed Banger is working with Garnier to gain credibility.' Really? Even though our reasons for wanting to work together were the opposite of any kind of strategy, certain paranoiacs were convinced that Jacques In The Box was a conspiracy! We found it funny. We let people talk and after a while the bad-mouthing ended. Especially as this track went on to do well, reaching out to strictly techno fans as well as fans of the Ed Banger label, who weren't necessarily techno fans. It also happened to coincide with Paris renewing its ties with its nightlife.

In the months that followed the release of Jacques In The Box, nightlife in Paris was on the up once again. Not long before, the capital was asleep, then great parties began regularly taking place on a riverboat, in an old print works in Montreuil and in the Bois de Vincennes. And I don't mean a handful of clubbers looking to have a bit of fun on a barge on the Seine. I'm talking about thousands of kids, crazy about underground house and techno, breathing new life into Paris' nightlife! It's unbelievable.

In the space of two years, Paris went from being a lifeless city to one full of energy. For, not only were the old-school bastions such as the

Rex and the Social Club still going strong; not only was the Machine at the Moulin Rouge packed out every weekend with a very cutting-edge line-up; not only was the Gaite Lyrique showcasing avant-garde urban culture; and not only were new record shops popping up all over the city; but on top of all this, the promoters of Cocobeach amazed everyone by regularly attracting a crowd of 4,000 people to their colourful outdoor parties. And twice a month, the guys from Concrete organised 19 hours of non-stop music on a riverboat moored at Quai de la Rapée, and so started a trend for all-day-long parties (opening at 7am on Sunday morning). They also attempted to break down the barriers between musical trends by organising the excellent Weather festival in Montreuil and regularly running events in Bordeaux, Nancy and Berlin.

This renaissance in the Paris nightlife scene was largely due to a new generation who had grown up with Ed Banger. They ended up taking the techno route, drawn to a fresh new techno (and house) sound made by artists in Berlin, Amsterdam, Oslo or Tokyo. Festive, fun, pretty girls, cool people in their 30s, hardened clubbers and young skaters, these parties were responsible for electrifying Paris, ridiculing VIP clubs, contradicting the politicians who cling to the idea of a genteel Paris, and above all reminding us that, as Bob Dylan wrote in *Chronicles*, 'There is no need to worry about the future. It is infinitely close.'

It was with all these positive things in mind that I began a very special day in October 2012, when I was to celebrate 25 years as a DJ. For the occasion, Patrice Blanc-Francard, director of the Mouv', entrusted me with the music programme for 24 hours. For many reasons, this learned lover of the arts reminded me of Jean-François Bizot. They both understood how music had the power to change people's way of thinking and therefore change society. During their careers, they were determined to share their passion with the greatest number of people and educate the public with an admirable sense of dignity and excellence. Like Claude Nobs, the incredible boss of the Montreux Jazz Festival (who died on January 10, 2013), these pioneers strived to change their times by showcasing artists capable of encapsulating the spirit of the age. For their courage and integrity I count these three men among my heroes. For their love of mixing up musical genres and of innovation, they have become my role models.

I have already spoken about Jean-François Bizot, who was delighted when the guys from UR and I 'hijacked' Nova on air, but I remember one night in July 2007 at the Montreux Jazz Festival when I had been asked to choose the line-up for the closing night party. It was amazing to see the childlike grin on Claude Nobs' face when, dressed up like a disco dancer, he performed a DJ set as the warm-up act for the Underground

Resistance concert at the Miles Davis Hall. I was reminded of that by Patrice Blanc-Francard's cheeky smile when he discovered the extremely eclectic music programme I concocted for the Mouv', that was giving the Radio France music programmers the sweats. That day, Patrice gave me the chance to programme a different style of radio. And I thank him for that. I also thank Jean-François Bizot for all the reasons I have already mentioned. And I thank Claude Nobs for inviting me so many times to perform at his festival that was, for 46 years, one of the best festivals in the whole world.

At 9pm that October day, at the end of my stint in the studios of the Mouv', I hurried to the Rex to get my gear ready. For the past few hours, I had been hearing all sorts of rumours about the show. It was mad. I heard that people were coming from really far to be there for my 25th celebration. The organisers at the Rex were feeling slightly overwhelmed and were worried that the queue outside would stretch for miles so they sent out a rather hysterical email stating, 'Don't turn up! Or if you do, turn up late!'. I did everything I could to remain calm, plugging in my machines, trying to contain all the memories I had of the Rex. Fuck, 25 years! It seemed almost surreal.

But if I let some of the memories surface, I would remember ... everything. The first time I stepped foot inside the Rex when I was doing my military service, the Jungle parties in 1988 organised by a bunch of crazy English people, the first ever Wake Up, the mad party we did for my 30th birthday, the emotional after-party after the Olympia, the amazing nights during the Rexperience festival, the Dog's Bollocks parties, the back-to-back with Jeff Mills as part of our Musik tour, and more recently, the urban music night with Akenathon from the group IAM ... So, yes, if you put all of that together it makes 25 years of history.

Fuck, 25 years...

Then David Brun-Lambert came up to me just as I had almost finished getting ready. We had begun work on the follow-up to *Electrochoc* a few weeks earlier, and we spent a while chatting in the DJ booth, both excited about working together again but also a bit anxious about the enormity of the task that lay ahead. Then came the moment when we both fell silent and stared at the empty dance floor of the Rex club ...

As that gig came to an end, sometime around 9am the following morning, I was trying to delay the moment when I would play the last track, and the question that David had asked me a few weeks earlier popped into my head. 'Who am I, now?' The answer was clear. The answer was there, in front of me, among the hundreds of people cheering and dancing.

It hit me. And I thought: That is who I am.

I am that person with a thirst for music. That jack-of-all-trades who loves storytelling, and who the crowd trusts. I am that person who has asked himself quite a lot of questions about the relevance of what he does and what he has to offer, and who has managed to achieve a kind of peace. Who carries on. Who continues looking for moments of grace that allow him to touch people.

At subsequent gigs, some to promote the release of new recordings, others because I love the club, the promoter and the dancers, I have been brought back to the thought that thankfully, I *am* still that person.

I have always been that person. What has kept me moving forward has never really changed. My desires have remained the same. Exactly the same – to open people's minds and to give. To give, constantly, unconditionally. Night after night. For that is my job. That is what I do.

I try and inspire people on the dance floor, those who follow me now, and those who will follow me in the future. I try to communicate emotion, relieve them of their worries, and enable them to live again for a few hours, or all night long. I am that person who for them manages, on occasion, to create a certain magic. I am the guarantee that the party will go on.

And the party will go on.

index

roll of honour

The publishers gratefully acknowledge
the contribution of everyone listed below,
whose generous support has helped bring
this project to fruition.

Adam Harris | Adam Jenkins | Adam Kaye | Ahac Meden | Akos | Alan Crawford | Alan Kennan | Alejandro Anabel Lara del Pino | Aleksandar Stankovic | Alex Blake | Alex Forrest-Hay | Alex Moulton | Alex Oxley | Alex.McLean/G | Alexander De Tey | Alexander Drewniak | Alexandre Tenreiro | Alexi Delano | Alistair McLauchlan | Alistair Sawyerr | Amanjit Bains | Amey family | Amie Roberts | Amrish Nayan Haji Shah | Anderson Bartlett | André Alçada Padez | Andrew Watson | Andrew Weaver | Andrius Keblas | Andy Bubbles | Andy Calder | Andy Daniell | Andy Foster | Andy Kay | Andy Kewley | Andy Newbound | Andy Pietrasik | Andy Poole | Andy Wilson | Anna Niczyporuk | Annie Horng | Antonella & Andrew | Antti Hasanen | Arjan Mind Desire Mind Action Nomember | Arnaud Schoenmakers | Arnheim | Ashley Jaworski | Atila Cintosun | Aurélien Antoine | Ayoze(vala) Hdez Robayna | Azal Al Sayadi | Azpecialguest | Barnt | Bassik Grooove | Beckford | Ben Clifford | Ben Lloyd Hurst | Ben Lowes | Ben Sebborn | Ben Whitaker | Benjamin Sumbler | Bijan Dharas | Billy Scullion | Bitch Moo Salmon | Bjorn Schipper | Bobby Richardson | Boris | Brad Lambert | Brandon Ireland | Braxtron | Brian Nolan | Brian Variengien | Bruno Pereira | Bryan Atkinson | Cain Farrugia | Calum R Donald | Caomhán Ó Luain | Carlierke – Clerkie | Cathelijne | Cezar Nica | Ch@rlie | Cheeky Chops aka Mazzy Star Dog | Chloe Arkenbout | Chloe Rambo | Chris Ashton | Chris Atherton | Chris Burgon-Miller | Chris Corcoran | Chris Howell-Jones | Chris Manning | Chris Worthy | Christian Lacarte | Christian Lüdi | Christian Yavin Rinow | Christian Zingales | Christopher Williams | Claire McFarlane | Claire Phillips | Claude Kiwi | Clemens Drost | Clement | Colin Nicol | Connor Scott | Conor Walshe | Craig Brindley | Cramer Rice | Curt Stringfellow | Dainius | Dale 'Bogdownavitch' Fernandes | Damian Broadbent | Damien Schneider | Dan Butler | Dan Edwards | Dan Gilbert | Dan Pollard | Dan Whitton | Daniel Askew | Daniel Gargan | Daniel Kaarill | Dash Badcock | Dave 'Slam' Clarke | Dave Chapman | Dave Letorey | David & Agneta Leitch | David A. Clarke | David Carr | David Evans | David Horrocks | David John McEnaney | David Lawrence | David Leitch | David Murray | David Packer, David Schumacher, De L'arbre Daniel, Dean-O-Matic, Demi, Dennis Sandoo Jr., Derek Parsons | Dermot McCarthy | Dietmar Lustig | DJ Green | DJ Manny | DJ Rich | DJ Three | DJ Waxman | Djonny Longen | Dobie | Dom Conway | Domocon | Dushi | Dustin L. Kalman | Dylan First | Ean Radcliffe | Ed Norris | Eddy | Edward Lyle | Edwin Versteeg | Ekoyn da Bassbreaker | Eleanor Moore | Enric Calabuig | Eric Shaw | Ernst van Giezen | Estelle Mageean | Evandi | Exitnode | Fabian Herold | Federico Spadavecchia | Feelaz | Fiona Ambrose | Francesca | Frank De Wulf | Frank McWeeny | Frankie Fagan | Frankie Mami | Fraser Fearn | Freddy Fresh | Frédéric Pascal | Fredrik Hoffman | Full Phat | Gabriele Palma | Gail Britten | Gary Botello | Gary Hunt | Gary Woodhouse | Gavin Cochrane | Gavin Daruvalla | Gavin Fraser | Gavin Kennan | Gavin Thomson | Geoff Muncey | George Alatas | Gergely Török | Gerry Murphy | Gert Meier | Gert van Holland | Gestalt Effect | Gianluca Pedrolini | Graham Learner | Graham Sahara | Granny Franks | Greg Lord | Greg Mind Desire Mind Action Nomember | Greg Wilkinson | Gregor Flüggen | Gregory Aoustin | Guido Durante | Guy Rotem | Hans Rymenams | Happy 40th Robert

Draper | Harris Koutsioubas | Harry Lawson | Heine Andre Aasen | Howard Canavan | Hugo Cassidy | Hugo Kallienke Koefoed | Ian Bailey | Ian Davies | Ian Fraser | Ian Robinson | Ian Tew | Ian Void | Ihab Ataa Elnaccash | Ilias Panagiotopoulos | Ivo Kruyt | Jack Colt | Jack Sedgwick | Jacopo Verworner | Jade Keithman Damo | James Irvine | James Lawless | James Masters | James Mills | Jamie Garside | Janet Lea | Jaroslav Kaisler | Jason 'Techno' Quinn | Jason Murphy | Jason Paul Johannes | Jasper Mind Desire Mind Action Nomember | Jasper Smit | Javier Lema | Jay Robinson | Jean-Albert Brière | Jeff Rautiola | Jeremiah C. Green | Jeremy and Diana Costa | Jeremy Bispo | Jérôme De Boysère | Jesse Sins | Jim Harling | Jim Rivers | Jim Shanks | Jimmy Sandford | Jiri Pross | Joe Riedl | Joe Skinner | Joel Åberg | Joel Bosshardt | Johan Soetewey | John Athiropoulos | John Clark | John Craig | John Houle | John Ramonas | John Selway | John. J. Stewart | Jon Bennett | Jon Harris | Jonathan Allen | Jonathan Emmins | Jonathan Mills | Jonathan Pardon | Joost Zegers | Jordan Haworth | Jorge Watts | Josh Hughes | Julien 'Cb...' S | Julien Delange | Julien, La Tribu des Pingouins | Jürgen Dhooms | Justin Barish | Justine Murphy | Känninen Roisto | Karen Desmet | Karen Slinger | Keith Matthews | Kelvin James SM | Ken Jukes | Kenny MacAskill | Kered | Kerry Anne Lynn | Kevin Eveleigh | Kévin Guillotte | Kevin Thomson | Kim Booth | Kirstie Gee | Koen Van Impe | Koot365 | Kostas Magoufis | Kotryna Sokolovaite | Kowalski Ann & Gijsens Bart | Kristen Steiner | Lee 'silky' Houghton | Lee Mcinnes | Lee Smyth | Lee Welsh | Lee Wren Booth | Leigh 'Lebo' Whittley | Leigh C Thorne | Lenny Patelli | Leon Alexander Hulm | Leon Blakely | Leon Neville | Leone Manfredini | Lex Veenendaal | Liam Browne | Liam Gleeson | Liam O'Hare | Linus | Lorenzo Brescia | Lorgeray J. | Lothar Mind Desire Mind Action Nomember | Louis Poncet | Luc Molkens | Lucie Hubbard | Luke Finlay | Luke Thornley | Luke Warnes | Luqmanhakim Salleh | Lydia Laws | Macky Marvel | Mal O'Connell | Manoj Rajagopal | Marcel and Jen | Marcus Corrieri | Marcus Emptage | Marian Allex Lohnicky | Marianne Thidling | Marijke & Christophe | Mark Adams | Mark Bateman | Mark Clowes | Mark Fanciulli | Mark Forshaw | Mark Moore | Mark Rietdijk | Mark Rocca | Mark Spegy Henderson | Mark Stemman | Martijn Wubbolts | Martin Milleding | Marty Mills | Martyn | Martzolff | Massimiliano Gra(ss)i | Mat Irvine | Mathew Reilly | Matt 'SanchoPanza' Brown | Matt Acornley | Matt Carswell | Matt Haler | Matt Holbrook | Matt Radford | Matt Tangent | Matthew Dallat | Matthew Francey | Matthew Garcia | Matthew Sogorski | Matthew Tyson | Maxime Beaurepaire | May Tox aka Rafael de Matos | MC SuperGreen & Janer the Caner | Melina Klein | Mete Tavukcuoglu | Mfdj | Michael 'Bear' Liall | Michael 'Hirsi' Hirsch | Michael Grunden | Michael Merhaut | Michael Pieplenbosch | Michael PJ White | Michael Wells | Michal Netolicky | Michiel van Dijl | Mick Melly | Micon Schorsij | Miguel Ferreira | Miguel Henriques | Mike Boorman | Mike Dyer | Mike Mengham | Milo van Buijtene | Mimi Nestorovska | Miquel Testar | Monique Biermans | Morten Larsen | Mrspring | Murray Mckee | Natalie Stevenson | Natasha Marie Wilson | Natasha Tilly Owen | Nathan Hill | Neil Mcmeechan | Nenad Taskovic Nestore Ferrara | Neven Popov | Niall O' Brien | Nicholas Arvelo | Nick Cave | Nick Collins | Nick Dawe | Nick Fairfax | Nick Jacobs | Nick King | Nick Whittingham | Nico | Nicola Pastore | Nik Phiniefs | Nikhil Dhumma | Niko De Haes | Nikos Karas | Nitzan | Nuno Beira | Nuno Dos Santos | Oliver Way | Ollie Davies | Ori Morag | Oscar van Wijngaarden | Ozgur Arici | Paolichi | Patricio Ferrer Murguia | Patrick Salvi | Paul 'Dylan-Niambh' Hamill | Paul Cuthbert | Paul Docherty | Paul Filep | Paul Kelly | Paul Reid | Paul Ward | Paulo Henrique Canto | Petar Lončarević | Pete Blaker (Malfunktion) | Pete Ross | Peter Collins | Peter Deschamps | Peter McKeown | Peter Walker | Peter Wohelski | Pez Monster | Phil Robinson |

Philip Henry Turner | Philip Prout | Proud Mother in-Law | Quintin Christian JoziLovechild | Rachel Collins | Raf Van Hoof | Ramón Lith | Raymond Robert Costello | Riaz Mcginley | Rich S from The End, Richard 'Gaspipe' van Nellestijn, Richard Anthony Leigh, Richard Chapman, Richard van Hoek | Richie McNeill | Rick D | Rob Adema | Rob Whittaker | Robbert | Robert 'Robob' van Woezik | Robert Deutsch | Robin and Kerry Coleman | Robin Ghosh | Robin Kampschoer | Robin Meure | Roger Jones | Rory Dowling | Ruby Gaile | Rupinder Singh | Russ Gray | Ruud Brouwer | Ryan Whiston | Sally Kefi | Sam Ellery | Sam Red | Sam Tremethick | Samuel Pemberton | Sander van der Heijden | Sander Zegveld | Savvas Fellas | Scattle | Scott Lewis | Sean Brady | Sean Harris | Sean Nortz | Seppo Tahvanainen | Sergio & Olivia | Shane Fennelly | Silke & Christian Stebler | Simon Evans | Simon Metselaar | Simon Pascoe | Simon Stokoe | Sophie Lee | Stacey A Hickman | Starr Guzman | Stefan Flynn | Stephen & Rebecca Marsh | Stephen banks | Stephen Braybrook | Stephen C. Hunt | Stephen Cunnew | Stephen J. Bice | Stephen McCarroll | Stephen Tew | Steve Hunt | Steven Harley Storah | Steven Mackenzie | Steven Mo Morris | Steven Tolson | Steven Verdeyen | Stuart Barton | SuperBfred | Tanja Janßen | The Rooney's | The Warburtons | Theo 'The Good Doctor' Nicolaides | Thomas Adam | Thomas Aky | Thomas Schreiber | Tiago Senos | Tim Mead | Tim Shepherd | Timo den Hartog | Timur Sardarov | Tom Armstrong | Tom Bailey | Tom Blacksoul | Tom Grace | Tom Kihl | Tom Wheeler | Tony Lee | Trevor Bacon | Twisted Vibe | Ultan Quin | Ushkat | Victor de la Serna | Vincent Bosina | Vincent Vega Louis Stevens | Vito Di Rosa | VJ Matthew Lee | Vladi & Ju | Von Coppinger | W. F. Robertson | Wankelmut | Wave2 | Wayne 'Svek Moran' Edwards | Wes Holland | Wesley Verbraecken | Wibo Lammerts | Will Lau | Yamo | Yann Seyroles | Yorick van Wageningen | Zack Orr | Zee Ahmed | Zue Yang

acknowledgements

This book could not have happened without the help of many friends and artists, whose contributions, support and advice have been essential.

Extra special thanks goes out to :

Olivia de Dieuleveult | Mike Banks | Vincent Carry | Steffen Charles | Delia Garnier | Carl Cox | David Guetta | Dave Haslam | François Kevorkian | Manu Le Malin | Jeff Mills | Eric Morand | James Murphy | Christian Paulet | Gilles Peterson | Mike Pickering | Gideon Rathenow | Sonar Crew (Ricard, Enric, Georgia) | Sven Väth | Pedro Winter | Yamina Arras | Alexis Bernier | Fred Bernard | DJ Bone | Philippe Corti | Fred Djaaleb | Jeffrey Eugenides | Gregoire Galian | DJ Gilb'R | Arnaud Godefroy | Buzz Goree | Suzana Gostimirović | Eric Grosjean | Laurent Hô | Eric Napora | Jack de Marseille | Angel Molina | Alex Prat | Celine Renard | Eric Rug | DJ Sasha | Scan X | Paul Sherry | Ivan Smagghe | Marc Bénaïche (Mondomix) | Chaya Hazan | Elsa Prat-Carrabin | Maximilien | Wyndham Wallace | Matthew Hamilton | Bella Ivins and Rachael Renié